Praise for W

"In *What Do You Say?* Stixrud and Johnson function as guardian angels who show up at precisely the right time with precisely the right advice. Deploying an ideal mashup of research, relatable scenarios, and instructive dialogues, they guide you to be a calm, loving consultant to your child while helping you counteract the impulse to push, pull, or control. Your kid grows capable and resilient from their strong interpersonal connection with you, the competency they develop, and the autonomy you're giving them. This book is a must read game changer for all parents. It's already changing my life!"

—Julie Lythcott-Haims, *New York Times* bestselling author of *Your Turn* and *How to Raise an Adult*

"*What Do You Say?* challenges parents to see the ways we can accidentally impede our kids' autonomy and development. Full of examples, this book guides us in how to communicate with our children in ways that not only build skills, resilience, and motivation but that deepen the parent-child connection. Stixrud and Johnson, wise and funny, help us navigate conversations about homework, bedtime, screen time, and more, all while helping parents find a 'non-anxious presence' in the process."

—Tina Payne Bryson, LCSW, PhD, *New York Times* bestselling coauthor of *The Whole-Brain Child* and *No-Drama Discipline*, and author of *The Bottom Line for Baby*

"*What Do You Say?* is my most-trusted resource when it comes to navigating complicated dynamics with our kids, including (perhaps especially) differently wired kids who struggle with more intensity, emotional dysregulation, and executive function challenges. I most love that it promotes treating our kids with respect and dignity while supporting their unique developmental path."

—Debbie Reber, founder of Tilt Parenting, author of *Differently Wired*

"What parent doesn't worry about how to talk to their child about tough conversations like anxiety and depression? And then how do you keep those chats open and helpful? Well, stop worrying. *What Do You Say?* holds those answers. Stixrud and Johnson have written another must read—this one an essential guide to help you talk through those critical conversations with sound advice that is also reassuring and empowering. I wish I was able to give this book more than five stars—it's that good and necessary." —Dr. Michele Borba, author of *Thrivers* and *Unselfie*

"Stixrud and Johnson have written a wonderful sequel to *The Self-Driven Child*. This second book, *What Do You Say?*, is filled with wisdom and practical advice. And it's a pleasure to read. Throughout the book, the authors help parents reflect on what they might say versus what they should say. And they don't shy away from any of the toughest topics. As a developmental-behavioral pediatrician, I endorse their call for parent-child collaboration. This much-needed book shows parents how to avoid conflict and practice empathic problem-solving. I will be enthusiastically recommending *What Do You Say?* to all families in my practice." —Dan Shapiro, MD, author of *Parent Child Journey* and *Parent Child Excursions*

"*What Do You Say?* is the instruction manual every parent has been waiting for. Offering clear guidance on how to best communicate and connect with your child, parents will be prepared to be the source and secure base that children need as they develop. Through many relatable examples and sample dialogues, parents are guided on how to achieve the right balance when it comes to expectations, rebounding from common errors we all make as parents, and creating a calmer home environment, priming their child for a happy, successful future. Filled with practical suggestions such as building in one-on-one time with your child and being mindful to your own well-being, the reader will walk away with countless ideas on what to do as a parent. When the relationship between parent and child is strong, challenges are navigated more easily, difficult conversations can happen with relative ease, and the child's self-esteem is protected. This book nurtures this most sacred relationship and is an absolute must read for all parents."

—Bonnie Zucker, PhD, author of *Anxiety-Free Kids* and
A Perfectionist's Guide to Not Being Perfect

"This brilliant book 'says it all' about how to motivate your kids to approach life and learning. If only parents could download it into their heads! Excellent research transposed into easily accessible conversations between parents and kids, great advice and perfect pitch. Stixrud and Johnson have great insight and empathy for each side of the parent child relationship, and their examples are enlightening and empowering. Reading *What Do You Say?* will bring down the negative drama and raise the happy quotient in any family!"

—Catherine Steiner-Adair, EdD, author of
The Big Disconnect and *The Golden Cage*

"A must read for any parent who finally wants to stop arguing, bickering, and negotiating with their kids, but who also wants their children to succeed and do well in life. Stixrud and Johnson provide clear, actionable guidance on how to motivate kids to do well school, to conquer their fears and anxieties, and ultimately to pursue activities that bring joy and happiness. The advice in this book has already helped me become a kinder, more effective mom."

—Michaeleen Doucleff, *New York Times* bestselling author of
Hunt, Gather, Parent

ABOUT THE AUTHORS

William Stixrud, PhD, is a clinical neuropsychologist and a faculty member at Children's National Medical Center and George Washington University Medical School. He lectures and writes widely on the adolescent brain, meditation, and the effects of stress, sleep deprivation, and technology overload on the brain. He is on the board of the David Lynch Foundation.

Ned Johnson is the founder of PrepMatters and the coauthor of *Conquering the SAT: How Parents Can Help Teens Overcome the Pressure and Succeed*. A sought-after speaker and teen coach for study skills, parent-teen dynamics, and anxiety management, his work has been featured on NPR, *PBS NewsHour*, *U.S. News & World Report*, *Time*, *The Washington Post*, and *The Wall Street Journal*.

What Do You Say?

How to Talk with Kids

to Build Motivation, Stress Tolerance,

and a Happy Home

WILLIAM STIXRUD, PhD,
and NED JOHNSON

PENGUIN BOOKS

PENGUIN BOOKS
An imprint of Penguin Random House LLC
penguinrandomhouse.com

First published in the United States of America by Viking,
an imprint of Penguin Random House LLC, 2021
Published in Penguin Books 2022

ISBN 9781984880383 (paperback)

THE LIBRARY OF CONGRESS HAS CATALOGED THE HARDCOVER EDITION AS FOLLOWS:
Names: Stixrud, William R., author. | Johnson, Ned, 1970– author.
Title: What do you say? : how to talk with kids to build motivation, stress
tolerance, and a happy home / William Stixrud and Ned Johnson.
Description: [New York] : Viking, an imprint of Penguin Random House LLC, 2021. |
Includes bibliographical references and index. |
Identifiers: LCCN 2021012465 (print) | LCCN 2021012466 (ebook) |
ISBN 9781984880369 (hardcover) | ISBN 9781984880376 (ebook)
Subjects: LCSH: Achievement motivation in children. | Parent and child |
Stress management for children. | Self-reliance in children.
Classification: LCC BF723.M56 S77 2018 (print) |
LCC BF723.M56 (ebook) | DDC 155.4/138—dc23
LC record available at https://lccn.loc.gov/2021012465
LC ebook record available at https://lccn.loc.gov/2021012466

Printed in the United States of America
1st Printing

BOOK DESIGN BY LUCIA BERNARD

To my children and grandchildren, who have helped me—and continue to help me—learn how to communicate with kids.

—Bill

To Vanessa, who said "Yes" to me all those years ago, starting this wonderful life we've built together.

To Matthew and Katie: I love you, no matter what. You make my life rich in all the ways that matter.

—Ned

CONTENTS

What Do You Say?

Introduction

Why Effective Communication with Kids Is So Important Now

B ill got a call from the parent of Sarah, a seventh grader with a reading disability whom he'd recently tested. He expected the call to be a pleasant one; after all, Sarah's latest scores now showed her reading at grade level, a feat that had seemed beyond her reach just six months earlier. But the conversation quickly turned to something else entirely.

"We have a rule that the kids have to finish their homework before they can have screen time for the night," Sarah's mom told Bill. "Sarah's friends were all playing a game together online, but she hadn't finished her homework yet. She knows the rules, but she absolutely lost it when I told her I wouldn't let her log on until she was done. The rest of the night and the next morning she wouldn't speak to me—acted like I wasn't even there."

Sarah's mom understood that she couldn't make Sarah do her homework or make her *want* to do her homework. What frustrated her was that sometimes—like when enforcing a reasonable, longtime family rule turned into an all-out battle—her best attempts to communicate with her daughter went nowhere, or made things even worse.

"I hate being the bad guy," Sarah's mom said, "but she knows the rules. She gets why homework comes first. I just can't figure out what I said that made this blow up."

If you're a parent, you've had a moment—maybe many of them—when you've thought, *How did that conversation with my kid go so badly? What did I say, or how could I have said something differently to get my kid to open up more?* Maybe the conflict started with a simple request to eat their dinner or make their bed in the morning. Maybe it started with their plea to go to a concert on a school night. However seemingly benign or innocent the beginning, the encounter ended with an "I hate you" that still echoes in your mind hours later. Or maybe the impasse was triggered by something as simple as "How was school?" No matter how welcome and open-ended the question, you're met with grunts and one-word answers.

You're a reasonable parent. Your underlying interests are all about wanting your kids to be safe, to be healthy, and to be able to engage with things other than screens—not just now, but for the rest of their lives. So why, then, are you still fighting with your kids? Just as important, why do you think they're fighting with you?

Communication in general is *hard*. Communication between kids and parents is even harder. At some point after the sixth grade, the same kid who would not stop asking "why?" at age four suddenly stops talking freely and willingly to you. The conversation you wish you could have easily with your child suddenly feels as complicated as trying to extract your car keys from a gutter grate.

If parent-child relations seem more complicated than when you were growing up, you're not wrong. We wrote a good part of this book during the COVID-19 pandemic, when the relationship between parents and kids reached new levels of physical closeness and boundary blurring, and stress reached new heights. Dependence on screens—a lifeline for education, social connection, and entertainment—nevertheless caused consternation about tech addiction and more than a few arguments, as parents pleaded with their kids to just shut it off for a while. Parents also became de facto teachers, whether the dynamic with their kid was suitable for the role or not. And behavior problems increased as kids had few outlets for their frustrations, or for anything else. During one video talk we gave, a mom explained how she was fighting with her first-grade daughter every day to stay focused on her distance learning. She then explained that her little girl had just drawn a picture of "a meteor hitting Mommy." The mom wanted to know, "How much do I need to worry about this?"

Even before COVID-19, we worried about mental health in kids. Suicide is the second-leading cause of death for ten- to twenty-four-year-olds, and the rates have increased every year since 2007.[1] More than 60 percent of college students recently reported experiencing overwhelming anxiety, and 40 percent said they were so depressed it was difficult to function.[2]

We wrote our first book, *The Self-Driven Child*, in part as a response to these alarming statistics. Though we come at issues facing kids from different angles (Bill as a neuropsychologist, Ned as a test prep guru), we see a similar problem: kids increasingly feel a lack of control over their lives. From a brain science perspective, there is little that is more stressful than feeling you do not have agency. Think about it: some of the most stressful moments we experience are when we're stuck in traffic, when we're waiting on someone else to make a decision that affects us, when our kid is sick but it's not clear why, or when we're in any number of unpleasant scenarios and *there's nothing we can do about it.*

Many of our kids feel like this all the time. They're constantly told where to stand and what they need to learn, they're told when they can go out or not, or they're put in situations where someone else is making a decision that will impact their future. We wrote our first book to explain why we need to change our approach with kids—to help adults understand and meet their children's need to gain a sense of control over their own lives. Now we're here to elaborate on *how* to implement this approach.

The parents who attend our talks often ask questions that are less about our philosophy and more about the nuances of putting it into action: "How do I get my kid to understand that he shouldn't spend so much time doing [fill in the blank]?" (And by the way, that blank is most often filled in with "video games" or "social media.") Or they ask us, "How do I talk to my kid in a way that encourages him to do what's in his own best interest?" "How do I talk to my kid in a way that avoids constant battles?"

Any approach to parenting is easier said than done, right? It's one thing to intellectually understand the wisdom of a certain style or approach; it's quite another to be able to summon the right words in the heat of the moment. How can you be assertive and understanding at the same time, especially when the stakes are so high? How can you be accessible to your child and still maintain healthy boundaries? How can you take a step back when they are driving you completely crazy, and possibly driving themselves off a cliff? We are continually asked what the alternatives are to begging, scolding, lecturing, ordering, and threatening. We love it when parents ask these questions, as doing so shows their interest in changing themselves—and the way they do things—rather than changing their child.

Focusing on effective communication with our kids is a powerful way to grow our relationship with them (and often with our spouse, students, and coworkers as well) and to support their development.

Between the two of us, we have been talking with kids for more than sixty years, finding language that they understand, that influences and motivates them, and that helps them understand themselves. And throughout that time, we've also been helping parents use that language at home. We're eager to share the kinds of conversations that work.

The sections of *The Self-Driven Child* we hear back from readers about the most are dialogues we re-created between us and our clients, dialogues that illustrate some of the principles of effective communication. And we heard that some of the book's sample language for parents, like "I love you too much to fight with you about your homework," transformed their relationships with their children. Since the publication of *The Self-Driven Child*, we have been asked repeatedly to write "a manual" with even more specifics to help parents put the principles of that book into practice, and the volume you hold in your hand is designed to be just that guide. What you won't find in this book is guidance on how to talk to kids about race, or about death, or about any other number of issues that are better left to subject area experts. We have great respect for the work these experts do, and we defer to them while sticking to our own area of expertise—which comes from the realm of the science of performance, and the many ways we have been able to apply what we know about neuroscience to the everyday struggles facing our clients and their parents. The dialogues in this book come from discussions with our clients and our own children, as well as focus groups that we conducted with parents.

As the book's subtitle promises, we'll cover ways to talk with kids about motivation, stress tolerance, and happiness. We are not here to promise you will figure out exactly how to motivate your kid; rather, you will understand how motivation works, and what kinds of things we say all the time that actually deflate motivation when we want the exact opposite outcome. We are not here to say your children should never be stressed; rather, we want to help them build up stress tolerance, so that they go into coping mode during stressful situations instead of flipping out. We are not here to insist your home will always be happy or conflict-free; rather, you will understand that your connection with your child is the most important thing of all, and that when it's strong, almost everything is surmountable.

Chapter 1

Communicating Empathy: A Recipe for Closeness and Connection

So often we're asked about the specifics of what parents should say to guide their kids while still giving them room to make their own decisions. Indeed, that's what this book's about—communicating in a way that fosters a healthy sense of control. Our goal in this chapter is to adopt the role of Cyrano de Bergerac, sharing what words might work, and to weave that advice together with a little Robert Sapolsky, explaining the brain science behind why.

In our first book, we emphasized the importance of autonomy—of kids having a sense of control over their own lives. Autonomy has a starring role in this book, too, although we focus on how to promote it through conversation. This first chapter, though, steps back to lay the groundwork for future independence, because before we can promote their autonomy, we have to be connected to our kids, and they to us. *A strong connection with a parent is the closest thing to a silver bullet for preventing mental health problems in kids.* A healthy bond with a parent is a predictor of emotional health and resilience, and it can lessen the impact of even significant adversity on a child's health and, eventually, on their life span.[1] A close relationship with parents allows kids to feel safe, accepted, and respected—which ultimately helps them develop a sense of control and the self-drive that goes with it.

Building closeness begins in the first months of an infant's life when parents and other caregivers respond to the baby's needs. Through repeated interactions, infants and toddlers learn that a caregiver can be trusted to feed them, change their diaper, help them fall asleep, and comfort them when they're upset. With a secure attachment, toddlers then use their parents as a safe base from which to explore their world—and to which to retreat if things are too stressful. A secure bond with a caregiver (usually a parent) is the most important outcome of the first eighteen months of life, as children who feel securely bonded to their caregivers have stronger emotional regulation, are more likely to develop healthy self-motivation, achieve at higher levels, and are happier and more confident than those who don't.[2]

Kids don't stop needing connection with their parents as they get older. In many ways, they need it more. Still, the *ways* in which we connect change over time. Ten-year-olds can feed themselves; sixteen-year-olds don't need to be picked up when they cry. But they still need closeness, and they *always* benefit from warmth and responsiveness. Although teens are biologically driven to spend more time with peers—and to push their parents away to some extent as they forge their own identities—when they feel close to their parents, they are much less likely to develop anxiety or mood disorders, abuse drugs or alcohol, or engage in delinquent behavior. They are also more likely to listen to their parents rather than exclusively to their peers. They are more likely to integrate their parents' values as their own. This is key because no one can *make* a child do anything. Parents can't *make* them work hard, or care about others, or nurture a spiritual life, or vote Democrat or Republican, or even vote at all. But if kids are close to their parents, and the parents value hard work, caring about others, spirituality, and civic engagement, their children are much more likely to as well.

When Ned's son, Matthew, was a sophomore in high school, they were taking a walk one afternoon when Matthew asked an important question. He was planning to attend a school dance that evening, and then a party at a friend's house afterward. He was concerned there would be drinking at the party. He asked Ned, "What should I do if kids are drinking alcohol?"

Ned suppressed an urge to pump a fist in the air and holler, *Yes! Parenting win! My kid is talking to me about this!* Instead, he suggested they do some mental role-playing of different scenarios, and what Matthew might do in each.

Matthew's coming to Ned was a very vulnerable move. Matthew trusted his parents, because his parents had long trusted him. Ned could have said, "What? Drinking! You're not going to that party!" Had Ned and his wife, Vanessa, constantly been on Matthew or failed to treat him respectfully in general, Matthew never would have risked sharing his concerns. Instead, they had a great conversation about the pros and cons of staying at the party versus leaving. As they talked, the issues became more nuanced. Matthew confessed he was really bothered by a cautionary tale he'd heard about a student who'd attended a party where people were drinking. One kid was so incapacitated that the police and paramedics were called. While most of the partygoers fled, a student stayed to take care of the incapacitated kid, and as a result was fined $500 for being at a party where there was underage drinking. The moral of this story, as Matthew seemed to understand from classmates, was "don't be guilty by association." Ned told Matthew he saw it differently. What if this kid who stayed actually saved the other's life? He was fined $500, which was unfortunate, but wasn't that more than worth it to save a life?

The point is, when our kids feel close to us, these nuanced conversations—about values, ethics, and consequences—are possible. And there are more and more of them as kids grow up.

Fostering and Maintaining Connection

A close attachment requires the development of a one-on-one bond with a parent, and the power of "private" time never diminishes. The way we get to really know someone is to *spend time alone with them.* If you have dinner with a married couple or a group of friends, you can feel close to your companions, but true intimacy requires being one-on-one. This is as true for parent-child relationships as it is for any relationship, and we've seen dramatic turnarounds in discouraged kids when parents started to spend one-on-one time with them—instead of just family time. This is clearly easier to do if you have one child than if you have five, but even when you are dealing with just one or two kids it can be hard to carve out the time to be alone with them.

A friend of ours, Raina, worried that she was losing her connection with her middle school daughter. Though the busy family prioritized time together, it was just that: time that all of them were together. Then one day Raina and her daughter had two hours to kill in between errands. They went on a long walk, and Raina said it was like the floodgates opened. "She told me everything—not just about what was going on in her life, but about what was in her brain. She went from talking about a cafeteria drama to how she would decorate her dorm room one day, to whether dogs could cry, to what she wanted for dinner." All that was in her head had been there when she was surly that morning. But having her mom's undivided attention let the stream of consciousness flow.

Bill feels lucky that he learned about the power of one-on-one time when his kids were very young. He had weekly dates with each of his two kids from when they were three until they left for college. *There are 168 hours in a week*, he always thought to himself, *so surely I can devote two of them to one-on-one time with the most precious things in my life.* When the kids were little, they'd draw or play a game with Bill, and as they got older, private time often involved Bill pitching or hitting grounders to them, going for ice cream, riding with the kids while they practiced driving, or running an errand together that they were both interested in. Bill would usually ask the kids what they wanted to do for private time, and if they weren't sure, he'd offer choices. He promised not to take any phone calls, and every week he'd write the time for the next week's private time in the family calendar. He also consciously made eye contact with his kids during private time (and throughout the week as well). Research has documented the extremely powerful effects when two people look into each other's eyes for a few minutes.[3] There's also important research showing that what people really feel, while they may try to hide it, is given away by the smallest of expressions around the eyes. While we don't need to "stare" at our kids, making eye contact when we talk is a powerful way to connect with them.[4]

Especially in an era of smartphones and multitasking, when our attention is really divided, something as seemingly simple as focusing your full attention on someone else is powerful. One high schooler told us he liked talking to his mom, but not his dad, because "When I talk to my dad he doesn't seem as interested. He looks around, goes on his phone, doesn't really look *at me*." Your full attention shows them they are worth your time. Luckily, Ned learned this lesson before kids came along. Early in his career, when Ned would come home from work, he and Vanessa would have dinner together and Ned would have half his attention focused on the newspaper. It's understandable, really—he was mentally fried and the paper was a bit of a mindless temptation. But Vanessa's perspective is understandable, too—she felt like what she had to say wasn't as worthy of Ned's attention as the paper was, and she told him that. It was hard for her to say, and hard for Ned to hear. But he heeded the oft-given advice to treat people like they have a sign on their forehead that says MAKE ME FEEL IMPORTANT. Now, decades later, their two teenagers keep honored seats at the table—the paper still isn't welcome. (And neither are smartphones!)

Individual time matters, and *proximity matters*. Show your kids you care by sitting alongside them—even when they're playing dress-up . . . or, more likely, video games.[5] Several experts have suggested that one of the best ways parents can help regulate their children's use of video games, in fact, is to understand the games and even play with them. At a talk we gave some years ago, a father, nearly in tears, described his supreme frustration with his elementary-school-aged son effectively shutting himself away for hours at a time playing "some STUPID video game." Ned asked what game his son played. "I have no idea," said the dad. "Something that's a complete waste of time." As we'll talk more about in Chapter 8, we can more effectively guide our kids' use of technology if we watch them play or see how they use their social media.

Proximity also means showing up and being present at events that are meaningful to our kids—like their games, performances, birthdays, and parent-teacher meetings. Obviously, you won't be able to attend everything that's important to them. But you can say, "You have two games a week for the next few months, and as much as I'd love to, I can't go to all of them. Which are most important to you? I want to be sure I am there when it matters most to you." The *being present* part means actually paying attention to your kids at these events and not to your phone or other adults. There are few more powerful ways to show kids that they are loved and important to us than to take time out of our day to share something that's important to them.

Look, we get it—you're not going to love everything your kid does. But *finding an area of shared interest* is incredibly helpful for connection. A friend of ours loves outdoor sports and competition of any sort. He wanted nothing more than for his kids to share his love for any one of a variety of sports—he wasn't picky!—and had dreams of coaching them one day in whichever one they chose. But his daughters love theater, music, and crafting and have no interest whatsoever in anything competitive or overly physical, or in anything that takes place outside. So they've found some middle ground. They have movie rituals together, and they all became passionate about the Percy Jackson book series. This dad also acknowledges to them that while he doesn't love theater the way they do, he loves being with them and hearing them sing. He also makes sure to use his daughters as resources in areas where they're skilled, which communicates respect and fosters connection. For instance, since the girls are so into music, he asks them to make him exercise playlists based on their favorite songs.

Family rituals also offer a way to connect with our kids and let them know that they are important members of our family. Rituals don't have to be elaborate. One of Bill's family rituals when he was growing up was getting drive-in burgers on Christmas Eve on the way to his grandparents' house. Rituals can involve religious practices, making pizza every Sunday, or something like going to the library together once a week. One mom reported that when she drops her kids off at school, each kid gives her a fist bump and says "Team Jackson," before hopping out of the car. It's a way to give them confidence before they go out to face their day, to stay unified, and to remind them that they are part of something larger than themselves.

Individual time, proximity, shared interests, and family rituals— these elements together foster a pretty simple foundation for closeness. We worry, though, that more and more parents are missing out on this closeness with their kids, and that the kids are missing out in the process. Twenty years ago, researcher Suniya Luthar was shocked to discover that kids from affluent families and high-achieving schools are actually at significantly higher risk than kids from disadvantaged families for anxiety and mood disorders, for chemical use and abuse, for self-injury, and for certain kinds of delinquent behaviors[6]—a finding that remains true today. The two main factors that appear to explain this finding are excessive pressure to excel and a lack of closeness to parents.[7] Many affluent parents are surprised by the latter finding, particularly those who spend a lot of time driving their kids to practices, rehearsals, tutoring, and therapy—and are intimately familiar with their kids' school assignments and grades. That's proximity, sure, but without the other three: individual time, shared interests, and family rituals that make kids feel like they belong to something larger than themselves. As a result, the kids from these families don't feel as *emotionally* close to— or as connected with—their parents.[8] Ned recently asked one of his clients, the daughter of extremely wealthy parents, who she feels closest to in her life. She answered, "My nanny." Ned asked who she feels next closest to and she answered, "My driver." Ouch.

We all have to do the slow, intentional, and transformative work required for connection if we want our time as parents to yield bonded, healthy relationships with our adult children. While parents with lots of resources—financial reserves and privileged contacts—may feel that those opportunities and networks give them a leg up or give them a way to outsource this work, that's not the case. Resources can create a false sense of security for parents ("we've got everything they need!") and unintentionally foster competitiveness, daunting standards, and kids feeling overwhelmed, while lowering the sense of connection.

Empathy and Validation: A Playbook for Better Connection

One evening, Ned's daughter, Katie, came downstairs, simply fuming after losing a video game. Despite great care and what she thought were heroic precautions, she'd fallen into lava, ending her game and losing the online treasures she'd spent hours acquiring. Her well-meaning brother jumped into problem-solving mode, asking questions and offering suggestions that, to Katie, all boiled down to "could've, should've" advice. Vanessa, knowing next to nothing about the game, simply paraphrased what Katie had told her and then validated Katie's frustration. "So you fell into lava and lost everything you had collected. Jeez, that sounds SO frustrating." Feeling heard not only helped Katie cool off and put things into perspective, but also to pivot to possible solutions.

Demonstrating empathy is one of the most important things you can do to be close to your child. One of our children's deepest needs is to feel heard, and by listening carefully and expressing empathy for their feelings, we help to fill this need.[9] We also strengthen our bond with our child every time we indicate that we understand their experience. There's extensive behavioral research to support this,[10] and biological research that validates the connection between empathy and bonding, specifically research on empathy and the bonding hormone oxytocin. If someone has a higher level of oxytocin in their bloodstream, they are more empathetic. And it turns out the reverse is also true: if they feel empathy, even if it's just from watching a touching video, their oxytocin levels rise, making them feel more connected to—and generous toward—others.[11]

Showing empathy and validating our kids' feelings and experience may not seem hard, but it is. If our kids are not doing well, parents often feel the need to be disapproving—otherwise, they reason, the kid will think they're okay with the behavior. Also, when our kids are upset, their distress induces what is called a "righting reflex"[12] in parents—or the desire to fix whatever the problem is for the child by using logic. But logic doesn't calm emotions—empathy and validation do. In our interviews, many middle and high school students told us they felt closest to the person who listened with understanding and didn't judge them—and more often than not, this wasn't a parent. Instead, they reported that they felt closest to a sibling or a cousin or another adult, like an uncle or a teacher. There's nothing wrong with that, but it does beg the question: Why not us? It may well be that we need to do a better job of communicating empathy.

"It would be better if parents acted like they related to their kids," said one student. "We all make mistakes. We're learning. Relate to your child so they can feel better about the stuff they're going through."

Fortunately, there's a pretty clear playbook on *how* to do this. Dealing with kids' emotions in a productive way involves a four-step process, and the first two steps happen before you say a single word.

1. Stay calm and think of your kids' strong emotions as a great opportunity to connect.

2. Understand and accept rather than judge; be curious rather than accusatory.

3. Reflect and validate their feelings.

4. Explore—ask follow-up questions.

Let's go through each step.

Step 1: Stay Calm and Think of Your Kids' Strong Emotions as a Great Opportunity to Connect

Consider the bonds that develop when people share stressful experiences. It's not like we expect you to jump for joy when your kid's having a meltdown, is grumpy, or is having a hard time in his life. But when you stay calm and reframe big feelings as an opportunity, it's easier to exercise patience and compassion. Also, if we can stay calm as they vent or cry or yell, we can lower their emotional charge, which will enable us to communicate prefrontal cortex to prefrontal cortex (rather than stress response circuits to stress response circuits). The prefrontal cortex is the part of the brain (often thought of as the "pilot") that can think logically and clearly, and put things in perspective. No meaningful communication happens when one person is hot. Meet their intensity with your presence, and don't get upset yourself.

Step 2: Understand and Accept Rather Than Judge; Be Curious Rather Than Accusatory

When your kid's upset, you inevitably have subtitles running through your head telling you to use the opportunity as a teaching moment. It's hard, but turn these subtitles off. The thinkers who have long guided our perspective on this are Ross Greene, an eminent child psychologist, who says, "Children do well when they can"; and Barry Kaufman, a psychotherapist and writer, who makes the same point: "People are always doing the best they can."[13] Take the generous position that even though your child is in distress, this distress represents their best effort right now—and that's okay. Every misstep doesn't have to be a teaching moment. From this position of grace, you can get curious rather than accusatory and then peel back the layers to investigate what might be going on with them.

For decades, Bill has made a living by testing kids with learning, attention, social/emotional, and behavioral problems. So he has met with countless parents who were angry at or frustrated by their child, only to find out through the testing process that certain skills—like following directions or inhibiting impulsive behavior—were much harder for their child than they are for most kids. The parents then felt terrible for having criticized or punished their child for something that was not really their fault. Once they understood *why* the child didn't follow directions, had trouble following through, or acted without thinking, the parent moved from judgment, criticism, and attempts to force, to understanding, acceptance, and support. We don't think you need a testing process to adopt this approach. If all parents take the position that their kids are doing the best they can given where they are right now, imagine the emotional wear and tear it would save.

Bill recently met with a client, Molly, whom he had diagnosed with an autism spectrum disorder a few months prior. The diagnosis initially was very helpful to Molly and elevated her mood, as it gave her a way of understanding herself as someone who is socially awkward but extremely talented in other ways. But Molly hit a rough patch over the summer and became anxious and depressed. In talking with Bill, she mentioned that school was really stressful and that the social part of school was terrible. She explained that her parents were in denial about how bad she feels, and she added that if she calls her mother from school and tells her she is depressed, her mother says, "You need to push through it," but little else.[14]

"My parents don't listen," Molly said. She then explained what it feels like when she is depressed—the self-loathing, the loathing for everyone else, and the feeling that she can never live up to her own standards. No wonder she wanted to call her mother! Molly went on to say that when she is feeling unhappy and isolated, her parents challenge her tendency to conclude that she will always be alone, and they point out that she does not show interest in another kid unless the kid shows interest in her.

Bill then asked Molly who understands her the best. She mentioned her friend Marcus. Marcus, she said, listens the best and "understands me and doesn't judge me," whereas other kids judge her for being different. Molly then started to cry and said, "It's okay if my parents have constructive criticism, but it doesn't help if they tell me what I should be doing when I'm really depressed."

We get why Molly's parents (who are wonderful parents and love her deeply) responded the way they did. They knew that most of the thoughts that lead to high anxiety or depression are based on disordered thinking, such as blowing things out of proportion or being overly negative. Her parents wanted to help Molly reorder her thought processes and see the positive, and to provide constructive suggestions. But the problem with this is that the first thing Molly needed when she was really upset was a safe place to vent.

Step 3: Reflect and Validate Their Feelings

Reflective listening developed out of the work of Carl Rogers, one of the most influential psychologists of the twentieth century. His person-centered approach to psychotherapy emphasized the importance of listening closely to deeply understand a client's experience—and then reflecting back that understanding. Many forms of intervention for helping people change have incorporated Rogers's reflective listening (also called "active listening"), including interventions for helping problem drinkers, adolescents and adults with intense emotions, and unmotivated students.[15] Careful listening helps kids feel heard, and several experts have pointed out that kids listen better *after* they are heard.[16] Also, when they feel understood—and, importantly, *accepted*—by their parents, it helps kids see their parents as the safe base they can come to, rather than run from, at times of stress.

Language that communicates careful listening when kids have strong emotions is similar to paraphrasing—but in a way that signals we are trying to understand their feelings. Psychologist and communication expert Eran Magen uses the helpful acronym WIG ("What I Got"—from what you said) to describe this kind of listening. Some examples of "WIG-ing":

- "*What I got* from what you said is that you feel like Erin betrayed you."

- "Am I getting this right—that the way she said it made you feel like she was trying to embarrass you?"

- "It sounds like you're pretty disappointed about your performance."

- "I think you're saying that your emotions were so strong in the moment that you freaked out."

- "Let me see if I'm understanding. Other kids were doing it, too, and you feel like your teacher singled you out and that it's not fair."

- "It sounds like you were really scared when I was late to pick you up."

- "You seem to be pretty mad about this."

One useful tip for asking questions: rather than ask a child why he is upset about something, ask, "How does that upset you?" For many kids, this phrasing sounds less challenging or accusatory than asking why.[17]

Through reflective listening, we can help kids see that we're trying to understand what they're going through. Magen says we win relationship "points" and make a deposit in our relational bank account every time a kid says "yeah" or "exactly" in response to our WIG.[18]

Language that expresses validation is similar—but adds the message that *I can see why you feel like that—your feeling is normal.*[19] Validating language shows a kid that he's not wrong to have his feelings, and that he is accepted and loved unconditionally. Some examples:

- "I'd be scared, too, if someone much bigger than me was threatening me."

- "That sounds like it would be painful."

- "That must have been hard for you."

- "I think I know how you feel."

- "I can see why you say you had a hard day."

- "I think most people would be upset by that."

- "I get scared sometimes, too."

Some Dos and Don'ts

Let's say your kid does poorly on a test that you know he didn't study for and blames his teacher for including questions on the test that weren't discussed in class. Here are some not-so-helpful and then some helpful responses:

Judgmental/Invalidating

- "You know you really didn't study very much."

- "What did you expect?"

- "Don't worry, you'll be able to make it up on the next test."

- "I think you need to study harder for the next test."

- "I don't know what you're upset about."

- "Ms. Coleman is an excellent teacher. I'm sure she wouldn't test you on material you hadn't been taught."

- "Maybe if you had/hadn't . . ."

Empathic/Validating

- "That must be frustrating, because I know you really want to do well in that class."

- "You sound pretty upset about your grade."

- "It sounds like you think Ms. Coleman was unfair."

- "I bet other kids were upset, too, when they saw material on the test that hadn't been covered in class."

Step 4: Explore—Ask Follow-up Questions

Once you've done the reflection and validation work of Step 3, your kids will feel heard and accepted. Since they no longer need to defend or justify themselves, they are more likely to admit their own role in a problem and can walk alongside you instead of fighting you. You can move on to an even greater place of curiosity. You can ask questions to better understand the child's experience and explore their openness to hearing advice, or considering ways to solve problems. Here's how one parent described the progression:

My sixteen-year-old son is at a top-notch independent school that specializes in helping kids with autism. I credit that school with saving his life. That said, he's never enjoyed school; it's very stressful for him. Every Sunday night for at least the last ten years, he would begin airing his grievances about the school—fussing about his classmates, his teachers, the work . . . everything.

Last April, at the end of spring break he started fussing at me about the fact that he didn't want to go back to school . . . I turned to him and said, "You know what? You have hated school for as long as I can remember. It sounds so hard to be going somewhere that you hate every single day." He visibly relaxed.

I then explained my perspective. "Here's the thing, kiddo. That school is the best I can do for you. I worked really hard to get you into that school. Remember how awful your previous school was for you?" He nodded. I continued, "So I'm starting to think that maybe this school thing is just not for you. Maybe what we need to do is start looking at how you can get the skills you need to do the work you want to do as an adult. And then we can just forget this whole school thing."

He opened his eyes wide, burst into tears, and ran into his room. I waited for about thirty minutes to give him some time to sit with the idea and went into his room. I opened his door, leaned in, and said, "Are you okay?" From under the covers, I heard a muffled "Yes." His head emerged, and he said, "You know what, Mom? My school is a great school. I just need to man up."

It's been nearly a year since then, and he hasn't complained about his school since. He will still fuss about situations that he is (reasonably) frustrated about, but he has thrown himself into his life at this school. He passed his state graduation exams and is starting to think about his next steps.

This mom meant everything she said—she wasn't manipulating her son to get him to stop complaining. And he was sixteen—it was reasonable for them to consider taking traditional school off the table. She was asking him genuine questions about alternatives, which he could hear and think about because she'd first made it clear that she heard him, she understood, and she empathized.

What Doesn't Work

Most parents have a pretty good idea what *doesn't* work to build connection, because our kids let us know by, well, tuning us out. Lecturing, scolding, criticizing, and nagging obviously provoke the "tune out" response. But so do these gems (and don't worry—we've all used them at some point or another):

- "It's not too cold to play outside." "How could you still be hungry?" These fall in the category of trying to talk a child out of their feelings, which isn't useful. "Don't be mad about that" is a frequent knee-jerk reaction when a kid's anger seems completely unjustifiable (for instance, when they didn't make a team because they didn't get in shape). If they're mad, they're mad. It doesn't actually work to tell them not to be.

- "You're just tired" or "You're just in a bad mood." Pointing out that a crabby kid is tired or crabby is never helpful. The very fact of being irritable means the person is less able to see themselves as irritable. The same is true for all relationships. After forty-three years of marriage, Bill's wife, Starr, has never once responded well to him telling her when she's mad about something that she's just tired. (And yet he is still learning not to say it!)

- *"Again?"* It doesn't matter what this is in response to—needing a larger item of clothing, spilling juice, missing the bus. "Again?" usually is felt as shaming, and shaming is never helpful.

- "Why didn't you hand in that assignment?" "Do you want to fail?" These aren't questions—they are accusations with a question mark—don't use them.

- "I'm sure it will be fine." This is otherwise known as dismissive positivity,[20] and it has the effect of minimizing a child's problems. We grasp why you might want to add the benefit of perspective when a child is making a huge deal out of something that you can see will pass quickly. After all, haven't we spent most of our lives learning not to sweat the small stuff? Don't we want our child to benefit from that wisdom? Sure we do, but not when it has the implication of delegitimizing how they feel, which, in the moment, it does. Cheerleading at the wrong moment doesn't make people feel met—it makes their pain feel discounted. It's also worth considering, are you being positive to help them feel better? Or to help yourself feel better?

- "That sucks. I'm going to call your coach [/director/teacher] and talk to him." This is an example of sympathy, not empathy, and it's particularly problematic when it crosses over into solving the child's problem. Empathy means just being with him in his pain, not pitying him or fixing it. Make no mistake: it is *hard* to sit silently, zip your lip, and just be present as your child "empties the trash." It seems simple but is deceptively difficult. Zipping your lip requires restraint, because it induces such a low sense of control in the listener. It makes you feel better to engage, solve the problem, reassure, or somehow make the child feel better. Zipping your lip is a way of signaling that it's not your life—it's theirs. And that's one of the most difficult notions for any parent to grasp.

- "That happened to me once." While sharing your experiences is great, be careful not to do it too soon. Magen calls this "taking the wheel." For the moment, your kid needs to be in the driver's seat. Magen also uses the metaphor of moving a spotlight. If your kid wants to vent about his completely, outrageously unfair teacher, it might not be the best moment to vent about your completely, outrageously unfair boss.

But What About . . . ?

One of the best parts of our work together is that we've had the chance to travel around the country, talking to parents and educators and hearing where people struggle to implement our advice. Here are some of the most common pushback questions we receive:

If I validate my daughter's feelings, she'll think her shouting at me is acceptable.

Recognize the difference between feelings and actions. Anger is a feeling that is a natural, expected part of the stress response. You can empathize with your daughter's anger and still make it clear that the action of shouting at you isn't okay. Your job isn't to sit and take it. You can say, "I know you're really angry right now, and I don't like it when people talk to me like that" or "I'm going to take a walk/go to my room for few minutes, and we can talk when things calm down. I need a few minutes to be ready to hear more."

What if my kid is feeling jealous or self-pitying? I don't want to validate those emotions, because they'll just become entrenched.

Empathy and validation don't mean that we agree with the child or condone everything he says or does; it's simply an effort to understand and accept the child's perspective.

Emotions don't become entrenched when they're validated. In fact, they tend to lighten. As Fred Rogers (of *Mister Rogers' Neighborhood*) said, if it's mentionable, it's manageable. And on the flip side, telling your kid that she should not feel jealous of her brother does not make that jealousy go away. If she stole her brother's cookie as a result of that jealousy, that's a behavior, it's not okay, and you should make that clear. But before you get into other ways she might have handled her jealousy, validate the emotion. John Gottman calls this emotional coaching, and through it, kids learn that emotions are acceptable, normal, and, yes, even manageable.

If you think about it, we all want to be met with this kind of empathy. If we screw something up—say we left water running and it created a big, expensive problem—we already feel terrible. We might have been tired or feeling stressed-out before we left the faucet on, which led to the absentmindedness in the first place. The last thing we want is someone chastising us for being thoughtless. ("How could you be so irresponsible?") We want compassion. "I know this is really stressful for you. You've got a lot going on." You need your emotions heard and understood, and then and only then can you turn to learning from the mistake. Or say that you're incredibly angry about something that happened at work. You want to vent that anger, not have someone minimize it or tell you that you shouldn't be feeling that way. You *are* feeling that way. What you're looking for in someone you feel close to is for them to hear that emotion, to empathize with the fact that—whether rightly or wrongly—you're mad.

What if you empathize and empathize, but your kid never breaks out of "woe is me"?

If that's the case, this is no longer an emotionally charged encounter, but a negative loop the kid has developed. Once you've expressed, "I hear how you're feeling," multiple times and it's clear that your empathy hasn't freed your kid, say something like, "This feels like a circle now. You say one thing and I counter with another. I want to break out of it. I love you, and if you're suffering I want to do everything I can to help you, but I don't think this pattern helps either one of us." Or you might say, "I call what you're doing self-torture, and I'm not going to contribute to it. I see it differently. If you'd like to hear my angle, I'd be happy to share it with you."

Obviously, there's more to it, though. If reflective listening is easy and effective, we'd all be doing it. So what's the catch?

The reason so few parents practice reflective listening is that, remember, it's *hard*. Reflective listening can often feel forced and inauthentic. Our kids might look at us like we've grown two heads or ask, "Why do you keep repeating what I say?" When they do, simply explain, "I'm trying to change the way we talk to each other" or "I don't want to fight and criticize, and I want to do my best to let you know I want to understand where you're coming from."

Reflective listening also requires pushing away all the many other demands on your time (Dinner! Getting out the door for this activity or class! Sending that last work email!). If you are in a state of mind where you cannot really focus, say "I really want to give you my full attention. Let me finish this, which should take me five or ten minutes, and then we'll talk." Then when you've reach that stopping point, put the phone down, close your laptop, and turn away from the other tasks occupying your brain. Reflective listening also requires not jumping to problem-solving. So often, we fall into the temptation of trying to make our kids feel better by solving their problems. Instead, reflective listening helps kids feel better and think more clearly, so they can solve their problems for themselves.

Finally, and most important of all, you have to push away fear ("What lesson do I need him to learn here?" "Am I communicating I approve of whatever he's saying if I don't freak out?") so you can be open to listening.

Empathy and discipline seem opposed to each other, though. Isn't discipline important, too?

It's more of a *with* than an *or*. You can absolutely discipline with empathy, and children who experience the two together do better over time socially, emotionally, and academically, and they have stronger self-regulation.[21]

Bill recently evaluated a seventh-grade boy named David who attended a school for students with learning disabilities. David is a sweet boy but one for whom many things are hard, as he has a language disorder, an attention disorder, learning disabilities, and social difficulties. Also, his stress response is so sensitive that he is highly anxious and very easily frustrated and angered. During Bill's initial interview with his parents, they reported that David is never happy and, in fact, is mad "all the time." They noted that he is remorseful and self-critical once he calms down, but his frequent emotional blowups were extremely stressful and wearing for David and his parents.

One day David's mother called Bill extremely upset. When classmates teased David about his choice of jeans, he responded with an ethnic slur in retaliation. He'd been suspended for a day. "How do I handle this?" she wanted to know. "What consequences can I give him so that he doesn't ever do this again?"

Bill first told David's mother that there is considerable evidence that punishment is not an effective disciplinary tool.[22] He also mentioned that, as Ross Greene has pointed out, the kids who get the most consequences often learn the least from them.[23] (We get more into this in Chapter 9.) He then reminded David's mother of their previous conversation about how discouraged David feels and how he often is so down on himself. It seemed unlikely that the best way to help him with this situation was to pile on more. As Jane Nelsen, the author of the classic parenting book *Positive Discipline*, put it, "Why did we ever think that to make kids feel better it was first necessary to make them feel worse?"

Bill applauded David's mother's decision not to allow him to play video games or do anything particularly fun on the day he served his suspension. But Bill's strongest recommendation was that, as much as possible, she express empathy for what David was feeling and try to understand what his experience was like when he used the offensive language. She could explain to him that the part of his brain that senses threat is extremely sensitive. She could explain that his outburst was related to the stress response—or fight-or-flight response—because, once we're stressed, we're supposed to protect ourselves by running or fighting. She might express understanding that when other kids were laughing at him, David understandably felt embarrassed, ashamed, and angry and that, with his stress response in full gear, he lashed out in a way that he thought would enable him to get back at the other kids. Helping him feel understood and that he is loved even when he does something stupid would be more effective than trying to make him feel even more discouraged, ashamed of himself, and isolated. It would be equally important for David's mother to talk about the unacceptable use of the slur, but he wouldn't hear any of that without empathy first. Discipline with empathy helps kids feel safe, heard, and accepted—unconditionally. And it helps their brains rebound from the setback.[24]

I'm completely on board with this philosophy, but I never get to show empathy or connection because my kid is such a closed book. How do I get him to open up to me?

To begin with, try spending time alone with kids who are more closed off. Don't put pressure on them to talk if they don't want to—but make the space for it in case they do. Don't expect your kid to start opening up the second you see each other at the end of the day. For a lot of kids, it takes time to transition—let them ease into it. Instead of asking "How was school?"—a question almost sure to be answered with a nondescript "fine"—you can simply say that you're happy to see them. Then you might follow up with, "Anything you want to share? Any highlights?" If not, let it go, give them time. Share details about your own day and they may reciprocate. Also, match their intensity as best you can. If you come at a kid who is taciturn with an abundance of charm and energy, it's not going to land. Lower your energy to meet his. He may hear you care, even if he doesn't care to acknowledge it at the time.

Also, arranging your nightly routine to have a few unpressured minutes to sit quietly on your kid's bed may help because, for many kids, the thirty minutes before bedtime is when they are most likely to open up. (It's also a wonderful time to give them the messages you really want them to internalize, like, "I love you no matter what," because the messages they hear just before falling asleep are the ones their brains are most likely to replay during the night.) When kids are older, look for opportunities to be alone together when their guard is most likely to be down. Ned's noticed that his son, Matthew, always talks more when he's moving—whether they're on a walk or throwing a Frisbee. While we've sung the praises of eye contact, there are also times when not making eye contact furthers honest discussion. Many parents talk about how their kid opens up when sitting in the back seat of a dark car. Ned remembers playing with a gadget as a kid while talking about something uncomfortable with his mom. She told him to look at her when he was talking, and he thought, *Okay, I can look at you or I can open up—you get one or the other.*

My child has an autism spectrum disorder, and lots of things that help other kids—like eye contact and hugging—don't work for him. What can I do to connect with my son?

Connection undoubtedly can be trickier for kids on the spectrum, although it's really important. Peter Vermeulen, one of the world's experts on autism, has recently emphasized the importance of helping kids with autism foster a strong sense of relatedness.[25] But feeling connected means different things to different people, including different people on the spectrum. It's all about sharing experiences in a way that communicates acceptance and respect. For some kids who are on the spectrum, feeling connected means being intimate and sharing feelings, as is the case for many neurotypical children and teens. Other kids feel connected when they engage in a task together, share their strong interests with an attentive adult, or play video games together.

With young children on the spectrum, one way of connecting and communicating unconditional love is through mirroring their actions—even something as simple as waving your arms when they do. Studies have shown that when adults imitate the behavior of children on the spectrum, it causes them to show more positive emotions, to be more socially responsive, and to decrease preservative behavior.[26] Mirroring is based on the idea that we feel closest to people who are most like ourselves (think identical twins). Even as a kid gets older, if they are sitting with their arms crossed, cross your own arms (in a relaxed way that doesn't make the kid feel like you're imitating them). Similarly, if they're sitting with their right foot crossed over their left, you can do that, too. Many therapists use this mirroring strategy to help their client feel safe and understood. It's a way of signaling, *I'm a lot like you, and I accept you as you are.*

My spouse is a great listener; me, not so much. What can I do if empathy doesn't come easily to me?

We're offering tools, not suggesting you need to change your personality. All the skills we've covered in this chapter *can* be learned, and we learn more every day ourselves. But also go easy on yourself if it doesn't come naturally. Start with curiosity, which lets your kid know you're interested, that you want to understand. Remember, your goal is for kids to feel listened to, not to have their problem solved. Ask questions, then more questions, all with an intent to understand something in your kid's day, or something she's upset about. Just keep at it, try different questions, observe what your spouse does that works, and do what feels right to you.

Putting It All Together: Sample Dialogue

When Alex picked her eleven-year-old daughter, Carey, up from school one evening, Carey launched into what a horrible day she'd had. The headline event was that a boy she knew had cornered her in the hallway on the way to lunch and kept nudging her with a stick he'd said he'd put in the toilet first. (Remember how charming eleven-year-old boys can be?) Alex expressed mortification on Carey's behalf, asked her how she'd dealt with it, and listened to how she was feeling now. Carey quickly moved on after "emptying her garbage." She didn't want her mom to fix it or respond to it—she just wanted to dump it so she wouldn't have to carry it anymore.

But throughout the rest of the evening, Carey was in a terrible mood.

Every little thing got under her skin, from her sister getting to choose the first hamburger, to not being permitted to order a calendar she wanted for her locker. She complained loudly when Alex mentioned they were having guests stay with them over a holiday weekend, saying, "Our house is turning into a motel!" She lamented how hard middle school was and blamed her elementary school for not preparing her well enough.

Here's what was going on in Alex's head throughout the evening:

Every time she's grumpy, she takes it out on her sister, and that's not okay.

She doesn't need a calendar—she has so much crap already that she doesn't use or take care of! I'm raising a materialist. I have to teach her better financial judgment or else she'll go into debt the first time she's offered a credit card.

I can't believe she's complaining about having weekend guests! I want my kids to learn generosity—what have I done wrong?

She's blaming her elementary school because she doesn't want to take accountability. Plus, she's being so negative—there were great things about her elementary school, just as there are great things about her middle school. I want to teach her how to view the world through a positive lens.

For the first part of the evening, Alex mostly kept these thoughts to herself. As the hours wore on, though, Alex grew impatient.

When the weekend guest issue rose again, she said, "Carey, it's really not a big deal. It's just a couple of nights out of 365 in a year. You can manage."

When Carey complained about school, Alex said, "Stop trashing your elementary school. You made great friends there and you loved it."

Carey's mood did not improve with Alex's comments. In fact, it worsened. Alex was already reaching her limit and her interactions with her daughter became tense. At last, Alex said, "Just go to bed! You've been in a foul mood for hours and I'm tired of it!" Tears and slamming of doors ensued. Alex felt like crap, and so did Carey.

While we completely get Alex's frustration, we want to play with what would have happened if she had used empathy in her communication instead.

The first thing she needed to do was calm herself and think of the bad mood as an opportunity to connect. Related to this, she needed to turn OFF the parental subtitles that narrated the values and attitude she felt she had to instill in her daughter. She also had to turn OFF her fears. There's a time and a place for guidance, but Carey clearly wasn't in the mood to accept any coaching.

Next, she needed to remind herself that Carey did not have the brain that Alex had. Sure, Alex could see that Carey was making mountains out of molehills, but Carey didn't see it that way. And in Carey's world, at least her world that evening, they *were* mountains. It helped Alex to remember—which when she took a step back, she vividly could—her own feelings of being completely misunderstood by her parents at that age.

It would have helped to remember what she'd done when Carey was a baby and had been upset about something. Back in the infancy days, Alex did what most parents do when their kid's upset: she investigated. Is she hungry? Is her diaper wet? Does she have to burp? Is she teething? Is she tired? Gassy? If Alex used those powers of investigation with Carey at eleven, she'd get a clearer picture of what was going on. The incident with the boy in the hallway had likely upset her more than she was able to communicate. It was early into middle school, so there'd been a lot of change in Carey's life. Carey liked order and routine, so the idea of having guests really was upsetting to her in the midst of so much else. There was social pressure at school, new to Carey, so the locker calendar might have had something to do with that. She was also tired, as it had been a long week with early mornings.

So, given this mental work she did first, let's say Alex handled the evening this way instead:

When Carey lashed out at her little sister, Alex corrected the bad behavior. Remember, we're not suggesting you be permissive. Bad behavior is bad behavior. A bad mood is something different.

When Carey complained about not being able to buy the calendar, Alex said, "I hear you. You're really frustrated by that." And then she let it go, understanding that Carey was just tossing out some more garbage.

When Carey complained about having guests, Alex said, "You've really had it with guests—it sounds like you're wanting more time with just our family." Carey then began to explain her feelings more, and Alex asked, "Tell me more about that. Why are you feeling like you don't want them?" And then she repeated back, "So what you're saying is. . . ."

When Carey complained about her elementary school, Alex said, "It sounds like you're really feeling worried about school. It's pretty tough, huh?"

Carey did not turn into a bundle of joy, but she felt met, and her temperature lowered with every understanding word and gesture from her mother. When Alex suggested that Carey looked tired and might benefit from getting to sleep a little earlier that night, Carey didn't agree. Alex, a little weary from Carey's mood, decided to remove herself instead. "Well, I am. I think I'm going to go up to my room and read for a bit."

Remember What It's All About

It seems to us that this is a chapter where the kids should have the last word. And so we conclude with a transcript from an interview we did with a high school student named Jay:

JAY: I feel closest to my dad.

US: What is it about your dad that makes you feel like you can talk to him about anything?

JAY: He doesn't judge me and he listens.

US: How can you tell?

JAY: If I've messed up, he won't throw it in my face or say, "You shouldn't have done that." He'll say, "I'm glad you learned from that. But this is what you can do so that you're not in that situation again."

US: Do you agree with what he says?

JAY: Yes.

US: Do you do it?

JAY: Sometimes.

With teenagers, "sometimes" is high praise indeed.

Chapter 2

The Language of a Parent Consultant

"If you want to be independent, you've got to listen to me."

—*Parent to his failure-to-launch twenty-six-year-old son*

I n 1964, Bob Dylan released "The Times They Are a-Changin'" and warned parents that "your sons and your daughters are beyond your command." In the same year, Rudolf Dreikurs published his classic book on child-rearing, *Children: The Challenge* (he got that right!), in which he argued that children raised in democratic societies eventually learn that their parents cannot truly make them do anything. Parents were in for an awakening. Family structures shifted, and Dad was no longer the de facto head of the household. Dreikurs purportedly told his students that "when Dad lost control of Mom, both parents lost control of the children,"[1] as without that power imbalance between Mom and Dad, kids no longer had a model of subservience. Meanwhile, authoritarian parenting, exemplified by the phrases "Because I told you to," and "Do it, or else," began to lose favor, as study after study found that children raised under this style were more likely to have low self-esteem, weak self-control, and poor social skills and, if yelled at, were more prone to behavioral problems and depression.[2] But a permissive or laissez-faire parenting style, exemplified by the phrase "Do what you will," was shown to be even worse.[3] What was a well-meaning parent to do?

What research has shown to work is an *authoritative* parenting style in which parents set standards and enforce limits but also treat children respectfully, seeking their opinions, encouraging them to make decisions, and helping them figure out the kind of life they want. Authoritative parenting is most likely to produce children who are successful, well-liked by others, empathetic, emotionally intelligent, generous, and self-reliant.[4]

The good news is that parents naturally have authority over kids. We're older, we're more experienced, and (hopefully) we have better self-control than our kids. While it might not always seem like it, kids do fundamentally grasp that we're the guides in our families.[5] The problem comes when we try to force this authority. Kids need limits to feel secure, and it's right for us to play our natural role as the authorities in our families. But if we repeatedly push kids to do things against their will, if we argue with them about the same things over and over, if we lose our temper and get into shouting matches, our natural authority goes down the toilet.[6] We're lowered to the same level as an out-of-control child. When a parent screams at a kid for screaming at his brother, in other words, the hypocrisy isn't lost on anyone.

We are big proponents of a parenting model firmly grounded in the authoritative philosophy: we call it the "parent as consultant" model, and we believe it's the most effective way to hold on to your natural authority and be a guiding support to your kids. Think about it—effective consultants don't argue with their clients about the same thing again and again, try to force their clients to change, tell their clients what to think or feel, criticize them harshly, do things for their clients that they can do for themselves, or work harder to help their clients change than the clients work. Consultants don't bring their own emotional baggage; their interest is the success of the client. They listen and ask good questions, first and foremost. Replace "clients" with "kids" and isn't this what we want our parenting to do—to help kids learn to run their own lives?

This approach works, in part, because it does wonders for the parent-child relationship. As the last chapter explained, when we're closer to our kids, they're more open to our influence and experience. It also works because ***kids and teenagers are much more capable than we give them credit for.*** If we consider the power of high school student activists, teen artists and musicians, kids with significant work or household responsibilities, and young people with a mission to do good in the world, it's hard to think that all they can be entrusted to do is go to school and play sports. It's also hard to imagine that they can't figure out the college search process without their parents driving it. (We know a mom who was clear with her kids that, while she was willing to help pay for college, she didn't want to be involved in the college search process. One of her sons was recently accepted to Stanford, and she hadn't even known where he'd applied.) We don't have to nag our kids all the time or make their decisions for them. And we shouldn't do for them what they can do for themselves.

Even young children are capable of much more than we think. An educator friend of ours recently observed an elementary school in Finland, where they have among the best educational outcomes in the world. In the middle of a lesson, a first-grade student received a call on her cell phone. She got up and motioned to her twin sister to come with her. The principal, who happened to be in the classroom, asked what was going on, and the girl and her sister explained to him that it was their dentist's office calling with a courtesy reminder that they had an appointment later that hour, which they walked to. Although admittedly the culture in Finland is very different, it's a simple example of what kids are capable of in the right circumstances.[7] Remember that kids have a brain in their heads and want their lives to work. They almost always step up to the plate when they are respectfully entrusted with responsibility.

The secret sauce of the parent-as-consultant model has these simple ingredients:

1. Offer help (like tutoring or psychotherapy) to kids, but don't push it on them (unless kids are seriously depressed, abusing drugs, or deeply in denial about their problems).

2. Offer to share your knowledge, experience, and wisdom, but don't try to lay it on kids whether they want to hear it or not.

3. So long as they are willing to consider other perspectives, encourage kids to make their own decisions, and go with their decisions unless almost any sensible person would say that they are crazy. A decision is not irrational simply because you don't agree with it!

4. Offer to help them solve their problems if they need it and provide emotional support when they're upset, but don't rush to rescue them. Kids develop resilience through experiencing stress, trying to cope with it, and then having time to recover. If we solve problems for them, we condition kids to look to us for solutions rather than within themselves.

In this chapter, we'll show you how to do these four things, giving you the language of the consultant to make your own.

Why Nagging, Scolding, Lecturing, and Forcing Don't Work

A memorable greeting card reads: "I want to give you some advice my mother gave me, because I sure as hell won't be using it!" Think about it. Have you ever seen someone act on—or be grateful for—advice that was forced down their throat? Catch yourself if you are trying to push your advice, or coerce your kid to do something through lecturing, repeating yourself, arguing, yelling, or intimidating. It may sometimes work in the short run—they may just give in and go along with you for the moment to get you off their backs—but it never works in the long run. Whenever you tell kids "You need to" or "You should," expect pushback.

When parents nag, it in fact has the opposite effect from what's intended. Nagging makes kids dig in their heels and feel less inclined to do what we want them to. "Whenever my parents ask me, 'Shouldn't you be doing your homework?'" said one of Ned's tutoring students, who was earning straight As at a competitive high school, "it makes me want to do it *less*."

Time and time again in interviews with kids, we hear that nagging is particularly grating around homework and chores. They're willing (if not exactly happy) to take out the garbage, kids say, but they want to be the ones who take ownership of when it's done. The second their parent asks them to do it, a resistance response kicks in. This most likely comes from our natural resistance to being told what to do—which can threaten our sense of control and our sense of self. *I thought I was doing okay*, the brain thinks, *and now I'm being told I'm not*.

Another troubling—and surprising—dynamic can come into play when parents nag: their kids come to depend on it. One high school senior, Angela, said, "I'm glad my mom forces me to get up in the morning and is constantly on me about school, because there's no way I would get up or do homework if she didn't." That doesn't mean Angela wasn't stressed about her grades. Many underachievers *seem* to spend very little time thinking about (and worrying about) their schoolwork, but it's an illusion. Most are actually deeply worried and employ the most common mechanism for dealing with anxiety: avoidance. By nagging our kids, checking their homework, and logging on to school portals to check their grades, we are actually reinforcing their use of this unhelpful coping technique. Nagging provided a beneficial short-term solution for both Angela and her mom: Mom eased her anxiety by nagging, Angela eased her anxiety by going deeper into avoidance. Then what? Angela was about to graduate from high school! She had no healthy way of dealing with her anxiety, and no practice taking care of her life by herself. Unless when she goes to college, she can find an *in loco nag-entis*.

We may know that nagging, lecturing, and scolding don't really work, but most parents have a hard time resisting the urge to check in. After all, these habits have long been the currency of "good" parenting. When parents tell us, "I keep telling him that," "I keep trying to get him to see," or "I've told him a hundred times," they're trying to signal they are doing the best they can to be good parents—to give their kids the right message.

This myth of the good parent as one who is vigilant and controlling goes pretty deep, societally, and is prevalent in many aspects of our lives—most especially in school. Many schools now have grades and assignments posted online, in real time. At back-to-school nights parents are encouraged to log on frequently, and to follow up with their child about any missing assignments. Even the parents who philosophically disagree with this approach might have a hard time ignoring it. (This was a particularly fraught issue during COVID-19, when distance learning pushed parents more into the role of teacher.) After all, *the teacher told them to*! We encourage parents to remember instead that there's a deeper, and we would argue dysfunctional, cycle going on in these instances. Teachers are concerned that if a student doesn't do well, the teacher will be blamed, so they push some responsibility for the student's performance to the parent. Parents are concerned that if their student doesn't do well, the teacher will blame their parenting, so they accept the role of homework hard-liner. And around and around it goes, with everyone pushing anxiety back and forth, like wiping a big spill with a paper towel until it's spread all over the place. Though research does support parental involvement in their kids' education,[8] we want parents to be involved in ways that strengthen the kid, not in ways that weaken them. Keeping track of a kid's assignments so they don't have to? That's not helping anyone grow.

Nagging and lecturing also calm us down. Instead of sitting on our hands, zipping our lips, and not doing anything, we are *doing* something. We are taking action, and that makes us feel better, because doing *something*—even if it's never proved to be helpful—is less stressful than doing nothing. The challenge is, while parenting this way is less stressful for us in the moment, it makes our kids *more* stressed.

Clinical psychologist and researcher Jessica Borelli and her colleagues have studied what they call parental overcontrol, which is characterized by high parental vigilance, excessive attempts to regulate children's thinking, emotions, and behavior, and inhibition of a child's motivation to solve problems independently.[9] In one study, Borelli and her colleagues gave children challenging puzzles to complete in view of their mothers and instructed the moms not to help unless the kids really needed it. Many moms in the study couldn't help themselves from premature intervention. And as they offered help, their stress levels decreased.[10] Makes sense, right? They were *doing* something. But as they offered help, their child's stress increased. The long-term impacts of parental overcontrol for kids include anxiety, perceived incompetence, a heightened belief that the world is a frightening place, and an inability to withstand stress.[11] So parents: while it's not easy to sit on your hands, do it anyway. One parent, who was trying to be less controlling of her teenaged children, said that her daughter told her, "I love you, Mom, and I can see that this is hard for you. I'm going to give you permission to trust me."

Change the Energy: May the Power of No-Force Be with You

The Sunday before the SAT, one of Ned's students, Jessie, was scheduled to take a practice test—but there was also a party she really wanted to go to on Saturday night. She asked her mom if she could, throwing the ball into Mom's court. Jessie's mom said no, that the practice test mattered too much. Jessie was furious. They were still fighting the morning of the practice test, which did not bode well for Jessie's score.

The truth is, Jessie's mom was screwed no matter what. If she'd given Jessie permission to go to the party, but then Jessie didn't do well on the test, Jessie'd probably blame her mom for that, too. Instead, when Jessie brought up going to the party, her mom might have said:

"First of all, Jessie, I can't *make* you stay home. I'm not going to put a lock on your door. I also know that your friends are important to you. You have great friends, and spending time with people you care about is really valuable.

"But I also know that you want to do well on this practice test. You might think about what helps you be in the right frame of mind to do well. Being more rested certainly helps. But mostly I hope you have a feeling of confidence when you enter the room. I don't think I should decide which is more important to you. What do you think makes sense? I'm happy to talk through the pros and cons and, if you decide to forgo social time for sleep, how to get some social time later."

In this scenario, Mom wins no matter what. She has voiced her suggestion, and if Jessie decides to skip the party, Jessie knows it was her own choice. No fighting or power struggles. If Jessie goes to the party, no matter how she does on the practice test, she's gotten the opportunity to reflect and test something out. How much sleep does she need? Does it affect her performance? Mom has the natural, unforced authority to help her reflect on whether the choice to go to the party, in the end, was a good one. She has changed the energy of the entire encounter.

Another line that completely changes the energy is, "I love you too much to fight with you about your homework; I'm willing to be your homework consultant. But I'm not willing to fight with you all the time or act like it's my job to make you do your work." While this approach is one of the more popular ones we've recommended, it's not intuitive to many parents, and it can be surprising to kids. One mom told us that when she used this line with her eighth-grade son, he smiled, then he hugged her, and then he nervously asked, "Is something wrong with you, Mom?"

"I love you too much to fight with you about your homework" is powerful for four reasons: (1) It acknowledges that it takes two to fight—and that if we don't want to fight repeatedly about something with our kids (which is always toxic to a relationship), we can decide not to.[12] (2) It signals that our relationship with our child is more important than however they are doing in school or in other aspects of their life. (3) It reminds us that when we give up the fight—and the role of the child's boss, manager, taskmaster, or the homework police—we have the freedom to consider another kind of relationship, one that we'll find much more satisfying. (4) It clarifies who's responsible for what.

Chase was a thirteen-year-old student who resisted taking medicine to treat his ADHD from the time he was diagnosed in second grade. Although he was able to do reasonably well socially and academically through the fifth grade, he began to struggle more in both domains when he entered middle school. Chase's mother was particularly concerned that his impulsivity was affecting him socially, as he tended to say and do things that turned other kids off. Also, his inattention caused him to miss social cues, and his low tolerance for frustration caused him to overreact to the things that his peers did. He also frequently failed to turn in assignments and made careless errors in his schoolwork. His mom's sense of urgency about his grades ramped up as he was about to apply to high school. His mother felt he was either unaware of—or in denial about—the extent to which his ADHD was affecting him socially and academically, as he insisted that he was doing fine in school and had a lot of friends. Chase had refused urging from his pediatrician to take medication a year earlier, and Chase's mom asked Bill to talk him into it.

Bill explained that he doesn't believe in trying to force kids to do things against their will. He did say, though, that he would talk to Chase and see if he could encourage him to see that trying the medication may be in his own best interest. Here's how the conversation went:

BILL: I don't want anybody to try to force you to take medication. Not only would it be psychologically unhealthy, but no one can really *make* you take it. Kids do all sorts of things to avoid medication, like hiding it under their tongue, or making themselves throw it up.

CHASE: I've never wanted to take it.

BILL: I know. And no one's going to make you, I promise. But I want kids to make informed choices about their own lives, and if it's okay, I'd like to share my perspective with you.

CHASE: Okay.

BILL: For many of the kids your age that I see, medication for ADHD significantly improves the quality of their life. Sometimes they say it's like turning on a light switch. Because of this, I usually recommend that they try medicine and see what it does, and *then* decide whether they want to use it or not. If you found medication to be extremely helpful, you would be under no obligation to take it. It may be useful to know, though, whether medication could help you get your grades up so you have a better chance of getting into the high school you want—and if it may help you keep up with the workload of the high schools you're applying to.

Predictably, when he did not feel forced, Chase readily agreed to a medication trial, which was life changing.

Get Buy-In

Once you've made the ground rules clear—that you're not forcing anything—the next step is getting buy-in from your kid. Do they want to hear your thoughts about a problem? After all, if you ask yourself whose problem it is, isn't it ultimately the child's?

One of the simplest ways to get buy-in from kids is simply to ask questions like, "Can we talk for a minute?" "I've got an idea about that, would you like to hear it?" or "May I share an opinion with you?"

Here's what buy-in looked like with Ned and his teenager, Matthew. The video game *Fortnite* has been a staple in their home for some time. Ned knew that if he was critical of the amount of time Matthew spent playing, Matthew would just shut him out. Of utmost importance to Ned was keeping a dialogue going, and for Matthew to come to the conclusion himself that he was playing too much. For several weekends, Ned bit his tongue as Matthew and the game were inseparable. Was this stressful for Ned? You betcha. Would it have felt better for him to coach Matthew on limiting his time on the game? Yep. But as Ned is uncommonly versed in the futility of this approach, he kept his thoughts to himself.

On a Thursday evening when Matthew had the next day off, Ned asked him what he planned to do with his day.

"Play *Fortnite*."

"Anything else?"

"I'm not sure. I'll think about it."

When Ned returned home from work Friday evening, he found Matthew parked in front of the computer, seemingly having a whale of a good time, still in his pajamas. A little irked, Ned asked Matthew whether he could kindly finish up his game and *get dressed!* as they had made plans to go out for pizza as a family.

"Oh, yeah. Sure thing."

Ned let the steam evaporate, bit his tongue, and enjoyed the family outing. Saturday, when Matthew found other ways to not do homework all day, Ned said nothing. Sunday morning, same thing. Sunday at around 5 p.m., Matthew bemoaned how he had "wasted the whole day Friday playing video games" and wished he had used part of that day to do some of the homework that he now faced. If ever there was an "I told you so!" moment, this was likely it. Instead, Ned said, "Yeah, I can see how frustrated you are. Can I ask a question?"

"Sure."

"How long do you think you spent playing *Fortnite*?"

"Maybe ten hours."

"Wow. Was it fun?"

"It was."

"As you reflect on it now, how many hours do you think would have been enough to get your *Fortnite* fix and still have had time to get some homework done and maybe play piano or something else?"

"Maybe four or five."

"In the future, would you want Mom or me to help you manage that?"

"Yeah, I think I'd like that."

By his senior year, Matthew accepted and appreciated the "tech consultant" role his parents offered to play. "I know you said you're trying to get that paper done by midday," Ned or Vanessa would say. "Would it help if I took your phone for the next few hours?"

"Yeah, that'd be great. If I need it, I'll come ask."

Ned's end goal was never to regulate Matthew's schedule or technology use. And in fact, Ned and Vanessa backed slowly away from their role as tech consultant, knowing that soon Matthew wouldn't be living at home anymore, and how much he played would be up to him. Helping him develop the skills to know when enough was enough was the best thing Ned could have done.

If you ask your kid if you can offer advice, they may say no. Respect it. If Matthew had said no, Ned would have backed off, because the conversation wouldn't have gone anywhere if Matthew had felt forced. Asking if you can discuss something is not code for "Here's how to make your kids listen to you." Sometimes they may not want to listen, sometimes they may just not be ready for input, and your backing off is the best and most respectful thing you can do. When the dad of one of

Ned's students wanted to quiz his daughter on vocabulary words, Ned suggested that he first ask her if she wanted such help. The dad said, "Okay, got it. If she says no, how do I get her to let me?" Alas, you don't. If you respect her wishes, though, you've not only shown her respect and supported her sense that she can handle things herself, but she's also much more likely to seek out your advice or ask for your opinion or help in another instance.

Bill's daughter, Jora, was very shy as a child. Although she was always a good student, she was slow to warm up to other kids and was reticent about volunteering during class discussions. Her teachers almost always commented that she was an excellent learner but should speak up more in class. Bill asked Jora at various times during her childhood and early adolescence: "Would you like to be less shy?" and "Would you like to have an easier time speaking up in class?" She consistently said no. Bill did not try to force help on her or try to coerce her with all the reasons why speaking up would help her, knowing that his words wouldn't be useful if she disagreed there was a problem in the first place. If she did not want to speak up more, that was her choice. She might recognize with time that there were drawbacks to her shyness, in which case she'd know she could reach out to Bill for help. Now grown, she's still an introvert, but she's a charming adult who handles interpersonal situations very well, is assertive, has great friends, and has the courage to take risks when she needs to.

One of the hardest things as a parent may be when we see our kids struggling, but they reject our offers to help. We just know that they'd feel better if they'd take our advice and get some exercise, or that they'd get the result they wanted with their friend if they just called her, or that they wouldn't worry so much if they just talked to their teacher about their grade. It's maddening, and all we can do is watch them needlessly struggle. But hang in there. Just because they don't want your help in the moment doesn't mean they never will, and there's nothing that says you can't leave the door open. And as you sit there fretting, remember that your job as a parent isn't to pave the way for your child so that there are no bumps in the road; it's to help them figure out the right way to handle those bumps themselves, and to grow from them.

Don't Rescue

We've covered the first three ingredients of parent as consultant: offering but not forcing help; offering but not forcing wisdom; and encouraging kids to make their own decisions. But as with so many recipes, if you leave a crucial ingredient out, the dish turns to mush. And this fourth ingredient might be the toughest: let kids solve their own problems. As parents, we want to rescue our kids—it's in our wiring. And yet it's in their wiring that they need to rescue themselves.

Steven Maier, one of the most prominent psychologists in the world, shows us just how critical it is for kids to fight their own fights. In one of his studies, Rat A and Rat B are in a box with a wheel they can turn, while their tails are outside the box. Both rats are administered a shock to the tail that, while not painful, is very annoying. Rat A finds that if he turns the wheel, the shock stops. Rat B finds that turning the wheel has no effect—and that he is dependent on Rat A's turning of the wheel for the shock to stop.

When Rat A turns the wheel, his prefrontal cortex (PFC), the "pilot" of the brain, activates, which calms down his stress response, and he goes into coping mode. Rat A develops strong connections between the PFC and the primitive stress system in his brain—and he then goes into coping mode whenever he is stressed (including when the wheel no longer works to stop the shock). Rat B, who doesn't learn a sense of control, becomes a nervous wreck who is easily stressed and, when stressed, panics or shuts down rather than coping.[13] In other situations, Rat A is curious, brave, and resilient, while Rat B cowers, hides, and avoids novelty and exploration. What Maier concluded from this and related studies is that the sense of control that Rat A acquired was like a vaccine that in-oculated him from the harmful effects of stressful situations. Being saved makes you grateful to be safe in that moment. Saving yourself makes you feel brave going forward.

When we rescue kids, then, we keep them from being inoculated. We take away their sense that they're in control and deprive them of the op-portunity to learn that they can handle things when they get hard. We also make it easier for kids to avoid dealing with stressful situations, rein-forcing avoidance habits. And there's still more harm: how people *reflect* on an experience is more important than the experience itself.[14] If we end a stressful experience at the peak, if we're effectively plucked out of the danger zone, we don't have the experience of coming down from it. It's like with yoga: yoga classes don't end with complicated balancing poses—they end with Savasana, or corpse pose. We remember the most intense part—"Wow, that was intense!"—and the end—"But it worked out fine." The brain isn't ready to move on after wiggling awkwardly like a tree—it needs to recover and let the body absorb the work it's done. When we rescue kids, they can't reflect on the recovery part of the experience, be-cause they didn't really have it. They just reflect on the peak of the scari-ness, and the event looms larger in their memory than it would otherwise. Their brain doesn't learn that it can handle stressful experiences.

"My seventh grader started telling me that he's the weakest, most pa-thetic person in PE," a mom shared with us. "He was actually fighting back tears. I could feel my pulse rising, and I wanted to tell him it wasn't true and start solving the problem for him.

"But I remembered . . . about staying calm in their storm and offering help without laying it on them—so I took a deep breath and said, 'Oh, I'm sorry you feel that way. I can see that you're really upset about it. You seem very fit to me, but I'm so glad you feel like you can talk to me about your feelings. I'm happy to help if I can.'" That was all she did, and the next day, her son came to her with his own plan about how he would improve his fitness.

We're not suggesting you should never bail a kid out. There are times as a parent, or if you're a teacher, when it's clear a kid is really struggling and needs a hand up out of the quicksand that only an adult with authority can offer. But watch that that hand up doesn't become a pattern. One dad we know agreed to excuse his son's school absence when the kid wasn't ready to turn in an assignment due that day. Then the same thing happened a month later. When the son asked a third time to stay at home so as not to be late with an assignment, the dad recognized that his son's procrastination and avoidance had become a pattern, and so had the dad's inclination to rescue him. "You know," he said, "I get that you're stressed about not being ready with this assignment. But I think you can tell your teacher that you need more time. You can handle it." The dad didn't want to reward his son's inclination not to face the music—the son needed to see that he could face his teacher, and that while stressful, it would be okay.

So What Do You Say?

A high school student told us that the person he confides in the most is a teacher at his school. He and a bunch of other kids go into her classroom during lunch, and he consistently seeks her input about problems. "We have conversations and I ask her what she thinks about this or that and she gives me great advice," he said. "She doesn't tell me to do stuff. She suggests stuff or gives me different examples instead of making me go on one path. She'll say, 'You could do this, that, or the other, and it will end up this, that, or the other.'" First of all, we bow down to this amazing teacher. There's a reason her classroom is such a mecca. Notably, she wasn't even this kid's teacher!

Second, how can we be like her? How can we ensure that our kids come to us for counsel and support? What language does this teacher use that is so effective? Part of it, undoubtedly, is that since the students are not her children, she doesn't have the weight or worry in the same way parents do. But also, this teacher didn't claim to be all-knowing. Likewise, parents curiously increase their credibility by acknowledging their limits. Admitting that you don't have all the answers, that you're not sure of the best next step, and that you have a lot to learn about their life and pressures does not disqualify you from having a valuable perspective. So don't be afraid to be humble.

Here are some of the most useful phrases of the parent as consultant:

The language of no-force

"I'm not going to try to force you; it probably wouldn't work very well if I did. You could just tell me you did one thing while doing the opposite. It would be hard for me to ever know."

"I have confidence you can figure this out on your own."

"I'm pretty sure you can handle it, but if you need me, I'll be there for you."

"I'm sorry I've been like a broken record about this. I realize that you can hear me and that you have a good brain in your head."

"I love the fact that this is your life and you get to figure it out."

"I imagine that the ideas you have are very similar to mine, although you may have ones I haven't thought of. No one has a monopoly on good ideas."

"I couldn't make you do that. All you'd have to do is close your eyes and flop to the floor in order not to do it. So let's talk about the best way to get this done."

"I'd appreciate if you . . ." Or "I'd like you to . . ." (Instead of "You need to . . .")

The language of seeking buy-in

"May I make a suggestion?"

"I've got an idea about that. Would you like to hear it?"

"Is that something you'd like to change?"

"Is that something you'd like help with?"

"I'm not going anyplace, let me know if I can . . ."

"Is it okay if I throw ideas your way when they occur to me?"

"Is there a way I can help?"

"I'm thinking about something and I'm wondering if it might be helpful to you."

"I don't want to bug you about this all the time. Would it help if I checked back in later, maybe in a few days?"

"Is it okay if I push you a bit—like a coach would?"

"I'm obviously not an expert on social media, vaping, cafeteria culture, and other stuff you're dealing with. But I'm trying to learn. Maybe my questions help even if my suggestions don't."

The language of problem-solving

"I wonder what would happen if you . . ."[15]

"I wonder how many approaches we can come up with, even if you choose not to try most of them."

"Have you thought about what other people might try or suggest?"

"I have some ideas that might be helpful, but I don't always know what's best for you."

"Would you be open to brainstorming about a Plan B?"

"I can sure see why you think that. Do you think there are other ways to look at it?"

"I can't take that thought away from you, but I see it differently."

"For whatever it's worth, you might want to try . . ."

"I know you think you're right and I think I'm right. I'm wondering if there's a way to study this situation to see if one of us is more right than the other."

The language of supporting decision-making

"I have confidence in your ability to make decisions about your own life and to learn from your mistakes, and I want you to have tons of practice making decisions before you go to college."

"There's a lot of information to gather before you make this decision, but ultimately it's going to be your call."

"Do you think you'll be able to know if it works or not?"

"If it doesn't work out as planned, do you have a plan for that?"

"It's kind of scary for me, but you know yourself better than anyone."

"Nobody else really knows what it's like to be you."

The language of being clear about who's responsible for what

"I don't want you to think that somebody other than you is responsible for your schoolwork."

"If I take responsibility for something that's truly yours, I'll feel like a terrible mother."

"If I work harder than you do (at homework/problem-solving/taking responsibility for possessions), I'll weaken you. I don't want to take responsibility for something that's yours. I'm willing to help in any way I can, but I don't want to act like it's my job to see that you get your work done."

But What About . . . ?

Aren't there some things we just have to force our kids to do? Like eat healthfully or brush their teeth? If they don't do these things, that affects us, financially and otherwise.

Child psychologist Ross Greene suggests categorizing your "asks" of your kids into three baskets.[16] Basket 1 involves issues that are worth enduring a meltdown over—usually safety-related, like wearing a helmet or a seat belt. Basket 2 consists of important issues for the long term, that are great material for a discussion but not a fight, like being more organized so that mornings are less chaotic, or brushing teeth every night. And Basket 3 involves issues that just aren't worth it, like a bed that doesn't ever seem to get made, or a mismatched outfit. Decide which basket your ask falls in.

For Basket 1, you do not say to your five-year-old, "Sure, if you insist on crossing the busy street without me, go for it. I'll be here if you need me." No way. You might give the child a choice between holding your hand or going straight home, but either way, he is not crossing that street unaccompanied. Also—and this is important—for a child who is addicted to drugs or alcohol, or severely depressed, you will take over more decisions because they are literally not in their right mind.

For Basket 2, you want to engage in some family problem-solving (which we discuss in Chapter 9). If you've explained that you can't force your child to brush his teeth, then you might ask if you could share why dental hygiene is important. If he says no, then let it go for the moment, but bring it up at a family meeting as something you're not comfortable with and that requires some problem-solving. Also consider having some other expert (pediatrician, teacher, coach, dentist) deliver the message. Experts seem always to come from a faraway land and rarely live under the same roof!

Basket 3 is the easy one—you just let it go. No one has ever been harmed by not making their bed. And mismatched clothes are the new style anyway. So empty that basket, and think no more about it.

What about the fact that teen brains haven't developed yet? Isn't it my obligation to step in to help fill the gaps in judgment?

A fair (and fairly common!) question, to which we have two answers. The first is that brains don't finish developing until the midtwenties or even the early thirties. So if you're planning to step in to fill the gaps in judgment, well, you'll be serving that role for much longer than you think, or than you want to! Second, brains develop according to how they're used. Practice using executive-functioning skills (including decision-making!) is the best way to bulk up that muscle. A nineteen-year-old who has had practice making decisions and managing their life will be a far more successful nineteen-year-old than the one whose parents have decided everything for them.[17]

My two-year-old had pneumonia and refused to take her antibiotics. My husband held her while I forced it down her throat. It sounds like you're saying I did the wrong thing, but how can that be?

No, you didn't do the wrong thing. Taking potentially lifesaving medicine falls into Basket 1, since it's about safety. While this wouldn't be a good long-term approach for a teenager taking medication for ADHD, you do what you have to do for a two-year-old facing a dangerous infection. (But when Ned forced his daughter, Katie, to take medicine when she was a toddler, she threw it up in his face. Parenting is full of unexpected challenges.)

I wanted my third grader to make the decision about where he'd go to school for fourth grade. After touring several, he told me he wanted to go to a certain school because it had gerbils in the classroom. My wife and I decided this wasn't solid reasoning, so we made the decision for him. He seemed really relieved not to have to make that decision. Aren't there times that kids WANT us to make the decision for them?

Yes, absolutely. Often kids don't want to make decisions, or it feels overwhelming for them to do so. In these cases, we recommend making the decision *alongside* them. This might look like telling them you'll make the decision, but if it were their decision to make, which would they choose? This takes the pressure off while still allowing them to flex their decision-making muscle. As they get older, you'll want to back further and further away from the process, so that they feel more confident. Ned almost always asks his high school students to decide whether the ACT or SAT is a better test for them. He goes with their call, unless he thinks they're missing something, in which case he just makes sure they consider that perspective before they make the decision.

It sounds like you're pushing the anti–tiger mom approach. But in my family, the tiger mom approach worked well.

The so-called tiger mom approach, where parents are highly controlling and invested in their children's achievement, has indeed been effective in raising some very accomplished people. Part of the reason for this is cultural. Whereas many kids raised with an overcontrolling approach don't feel close to their parents, that hasn't been true of many kids in second-generation families. The latter group knows just how important they are to their families, in part because of the ways they see their parents allocate their time and attention. Also, while the tiger mom approach will work for some kids, that doesn't mean it will work for all—or that it's the best approach even for the kids who don't fight it. High achievement is often believed to outweigh the emotional costs of chronic stress, a belief we don't share. Moreover, just because some kids did well under that system, it may be *in spite of*, not because of that approach. Additionally, for those who know of the tiger mom approach but didn't read the book that set off the frenzy, *Battle Hymn of the Tiger Mother*, it's worth noting that the author, Amy Chua, wrote, "This was *supposed* to be a story of how Chinese parents are better at raising kids than Western ones . . . But instead, it's about a bitter clash of cultures, a fleeting taste of glory, and how I was humbled by a thirteen-year-old."[18]

After reading your book, my partner and I tried to be hands-off with our daughter. She really struggled when she began sixth grade but said she could manage it on her own. It was pretty clear to us that she couldn't, and we helped her develop a system to manage her work—we insisted that we sit together and get the homework done between 4:30 and 6:30. She didn't fight us about it, and she did much better afterward, but it sounds like you'd say we did the wrong thing. Did we?

Not at all. If she had fought the help, then it would have been a waste of time, because, again, help that is forced rarely, er, helps. You might try something like, "I trust that you have this under control, but I admit that I get nervous. What if we picked a time or day when I can check in, just to backstop you? That way I won't hover, but we can both know I have your back if needed."

Or, if you see your kid is overwhelmed, you might say something like, "It looks to me like you're working so hard to keep your head above water, and it looks like you really need some help here. I want to help you structure things. Is that okay?" If the answer is no, then back off for the time being, but let her know you're there if she changes her mind.

Even when help is accepted, though, be careful. So often parents swoop in and bail out a struggling kid who is all too happy to take the help . . . forever! Instead, you want to make sure she has the tools and support she needs, but then, little by little, step back so that you're no longer needed.

I hear your argument that parents' nagging and moralizing rarely sticks. And yet, I think back all the time to the stuff my parents nagged me about ("Clean up your own mess!" "Do the hardest thing first." "Follow through if you've made a commitment."). I remember it annoying me at the time, but with age and distance, I can see how it shaped me. It did stick. How does moralizing differ from expressing family values?

Part of our responsibility as parents is teaching kids moral lessons, but there are many different ways to impart those lessons. "These are good ideas about life" sends a very different message than "My ideas about life are better than your ideas about life." Was nagging and moralizing the only way your parents could have expressed their values? Sure, you're on board with their values now, but perhaps if they'd been communicated in a better way, without your feeling forced or nagged, you would have adopted them more readily twenty years earlier.

I used to fight with my daughter all the time, and since reading The Self-Driven Child, *I've adopted the consultant approach. Our relationship is much better, but she's still really struggling in her life. It makes me think being a trusted adviser isn't enough.*

No, the consultant approach isn't always enough. (If it were, we'd have only one chapter in this book, not nine!) But it's an important piece of the puzzle. One dad we met developed a stronger relationship with his eleventh-grade son when he adopted the consultant approach. Even so, his son, who was really anxious, refused to go to school, even though it meant he'd get kicked off the baseball team he loved so much. His parents ended up enrolling him in a therapeutic wilderness program for three months, and when he came back, he was in a stronger frame of mind for everything. The takeaway here is that while the improved relationship wasn't enough to get the boy to solve really long-standing avoidance problems, imagine tackling those problems *without* the close relationship with Dad.

Inside the Brain

The teenage brain scares the hell out of most parents, and for legitimate reasons. Dopamine is the neurotransmitter for effort and "drive." Puberty triggers a dramatic increase in the concentration of dopamine receptors, especially in the circuits that carry messages about rewards from the emotional centers in the brain (in the limbic system) to the PFC, which decides what to do with this information. The increase in receptors for dopamine makes these pathways much more easily activated. This means that things that feel good feel even better during adolescence. Kids feel more alive, and they will go out of their way to seek novel, stimulating, and thrilling experiences.[19] This dopamine/limbic system lovefest means: (1) they're more likely to be impulsive; (2) they're at an increased risk for addiction (more on that later); and (3) they're prone to "hyper-rationality," or overemphasizing the potential positive outcomes of their behavior, because after all, what could go wrong?[20]

Yikes, right?

And there's more, because their brains are also more sensitive to relationships, especially with peers. For most teenagers, being with kids their age activates their brain's reward centers—and causes a spike in dopamine. Especially for young teens, it's like crack cocaine. Even just seeing pictures of other kids or thinking about their friendships causes a dopamine spurt. The presence of peers also increases serotonin and the bonding hormone oxytocin, which also make peer relationships particularly important. For this reason, being rejected or embarrassed by peers is more painful during adolescence than it is at any other time of life—and impressing your friends is more rewarding than ever. When teens think their friends are watching them (even if they're not), their reward center activates. It's not that kids aren't aware of the problems with risky behavior. The idea that adolescents think they're immortal and are unaware of potential dangers is a myth. It's just that the risk/reward ratio of risky behavior weighs much more heavily on the reward side in the teenage brain.

Parents have a tricky line to walk here. We don't want to stomp out adolescents' drive for novelty and stimulation altogether—it's part of what makes adolescents in any species adaptive, capable of trying new things and growing. Without this drive, we would never have moved on from being Neanderthals. What we do want to do is help kids stay safe enough to keep them from doing something with enormous consequences.

Toward this end, we can let our kids know we appreciate how important it is for them to be around their peers. We can explain to them that as they move through adolescence, they are sculpting their adult brain, and that they should embrace that responsibility. We should respectfully inform them about the effect of chemicals on the developing brain (see p. 145). We can encourage them to prioritize sleep, because sleeping enough will make them be less impulsive. And we can encourage them to become black belts in the art of stress management, because when kids aren't stressed, they make better decisions. Parents can also work to keep the relationship close—no easy task when teens act in rash ways. Finally, parents can remind their kids that ultimately, they have to police their own behavior. No kid wants to hurt someone in an accident or screw up their life.

Putting It All Together: Sample Dialogue

Luke is the father of a fifteen-year-old, Stephanie, who attends boarding school. The two of them talk three times a week, but often the discussions turn into arguments that leave both of them frustrated. Stephanie brings up a problem; Luke says, "You should do this or that"; she fights his suggestions; and the discussions routinely become unpleasant.

In their last conversation, Stephanie complained to her dad about how her history teacher gave her a bad grade on an essay, but she didn't know why, and she really didn't have a sense of what the teacher wanted. Luke wanted to check in directly with the teacher but knew it was better to encourage Stephanie to advocate for herself.

"Strange," Luke said. "Why don't you ask if you can talk to him about it?"

"Ugh, no, Dad! He's a jerk. And there's never time anyway."

"You just need to ask him when *would* be a good time. He's a teacher—it's his job to answer your questions."

The dialogue that followed was round after round of Stephanie rejecting Luke's suggestions, Luke feeling frustrated, and then finally yelling, "It sounds like you just want to be miserable about this! Why did you even bring it up to me if you don't want to hear what I have to say?"

"Fine, next time I won't!"

Needless to say, this was not the result that either of them wanted.

Imagine that it played out this way instead:

When Stephanie shared her complaint about her bad grade, Luke's mind was probably broadcasting running commentary of his perspective. *She needs to learn to advocate for herself! She needs to be assertive! She needs to take responsibility for her schoolwork, not just blame others.* His first step should be turning the commentary OFF. A consultant would keep a certain level of detachment, and Luke needed to, too.

"You sound pretty upset about that grade," he might have said. "From that, I gather that it's really important to you to do well in that class."

"Yeah," Stephanie said, "but it's not like Mr. Brighton makes it easy."

"No, it doesn't sound that way. I have some ideas that might be helpful, but I don't always know what's best for you. I also don't know Mr. Brighton or have a firm understanding about what goes on in his class. But would it help to talk through some ideas? It's mainly stuff that's worked for me when I've been in similar situations."

Perhaps Stephanie said no.

"Okay, fair enough," Luke said. "I'm not going anyplace, so let me know if you change your mind and want to talk about it."

Stephanie may come back to Luke about that issue—at which point she presumably wants to hear what he has to say. But she might not. Let's say the next time they talk, she brings up a problem she's having with some of her classmates. He can tell even by the way she describes it that Stephanie was in the wrong, but saying so obviously won't earn him any points. He's also not willing to assert she was right. But here's the thing: she didn't *ask* him. So instead he says, "Is there a way I could help?"

Stephanie immediately relaxes, knowing her dad won't be moralizing with her. She feels encouraged to open up more and to share her vulnerability, and even own what she thinks might have been her fault in the argument.

Remember What It's All About

To summarize what we know may feel like a lot of information, the most useful rules of thumb for being a consultant are:

- Before speaking, create the conditions for a receptive audience. Don't waste your breath if your kid's not listening. Say, "Can I run this by you?" then zip your lip unless they say yes.

- Don't tell them the same thing over and over again. If you tell kids something once, and possibly remind them once more, after that there is little chance that they will suddenly listen and thank you for persisting. Save your breath. Every time we ineffectually tell a kid something, it weakens our ability to communicate with them.

Instead, think of this wonderful Aesop fable about the North Wind and the Sun. The wind and sun were arguing about which was stronger, when a man came by wearing a cloak. They agreed that whichever of them removed his cloak would be the winner. The North Wind went first and blew heavy gales on the man, who only clutched his coat more tightly. Then the Sun warmed the earth, first gently, then more persistently, and the man grew so warm that he took the cloak off and rested in the shade.

The moral: Gentleness and kind persuasion win where force and bluster fail.

Our advice to you: Be the sun.

Chapter 3

Communicating a Nonanxious Presence

Fred Rogers was a master at communicating with kids. And as he told his friend the writer Jeanne Marie Laskas, he took more than a lesson or two from the way his grandfather communicated with him. "I remember one day my grandmother and my mother were telling me to get down, or not to climb, and my grandfather said: 'Let the kid climb on the wall! He's got to learn to do things for himself!' I heard that. I will never forget that. What a support that was. . . . And you can understand my mother and grandmother. They didn't want a scratched-up kid. They didn't want somebody with broken bones. No. But he knew there was something beyond that. He knew there was something more important than scratches and bones. . . . I climbed that wall. And then I ran on it. I will never forget that day."

Fred Rogers went on to create challenges for kids on *Mister Rogers' Neighborhood*, bringing up topics that were hard and sometimes scary, while giving children a safe landing, a calm presence, to return to. "If people are comfortable in that atmosphere," he said, "they can grow from there, in their own way."[1] Mr. Rogers communicated to kids what his grandfather communicated to him—a *nonanxious presence*[2] that radiated courage and confidence in the face of fear.

Given the unprecedented levels of anxiety and depression in young people, we suspect that this is not what's being communicated to many children and teens today. In fact, many of the kids we talked to for this book—and so many of our highly anxious clients—seem to feel that the main message they get from their parents (and other adults) is "be very afraid." When we talk with teachers in Seattle about second-grade students in full-on school refusal, with school counselors in Texas about fifth-grade boys having panic attacks due to the "pressure" of middle school, or with high school teachers in New York who say that *all* their students are anxious, we assume that kids are not getting messages from adults that instill confidence and courage. Similarly, when we talk with parents in the Washington, D.C., area who look at their kid's interest in soccer, or theater, or being with his friends, and think, *What's that going to get him? It's a waste of time if it doesn't improve his chances for getting into college*, we ask ourselves, is it any wonder that kids are so anxious?

Don't get us wrong—kids get anxiety-inducing messages from plenty of other places, too. Schools often reinforce a "scarcity mindset," which communicates that the path to a successful adult life is extremely narrow and treacherous—and that if kids ever fall off it, they're screwed. Schools pit students against one another for the top achievement awards and emphasize acceptance to the best colleges, as if only the top students who go to the most elite colleges will be able to create meaningful lives. Kids compete in their social lives and on sports teams. Social media brings constant comparison, competition, and often cruelty, the effects of which are exacerbated in the majority of children and teens by chronic sleep deprivation.

We want parents to move in the direction of being a nonanxious presence in their families. Families, like other organizations, work best if the leaders are not highly anxious and emotionally reactive, and if home is a safe base to which family members can return after a stressful day. The first response of many parents when they hear this message is, understandably, "Easy for you to say!" Parents may want to provide a safe home base from which kids can explore that proverbial wall, running on it, testing its limits, maybe even falling so that they know that they can, but what makes sense intellectually can be incredibly hard to actually adopt, and even harder to communicate. It's one thing to tell your kid to explore, to take risks, that it will be okay and you will be there waiting calmly no matter what happens. It's quite another to watch while they do it. Let's just call it like it is: Parenting can be terrifying. To love a child is to risk having your heart broken. You want them to make their own mistakes but please please please can they not get hurt when they do?

But being a nonanxious presence doesn't mean a Zen atmosphere 24/7. It doesn't mean that we're never supposed to worry or that you have to gleefully embrace standing on the sidelines. It also doesn't mean you have to make sure that your kids are never stressed. Creating an environment in which kids don't suffer from chronic stress doesn't mean avoiding disagreement or disharmony, hard stop. As we emphasized in Chapter 2, we can help create a stable, safe home by enabling our kids to deal with stressful situations from time to time so they develop emotional resilience and confidence in their ability to handle what life throws at them. Coping with challenges strengthens the connections between the PFC and the amygdala, and it turns out that strong connections between the PFC and the amygdala are the best neurological marker of resilience.[3]

Being a nonanxious presence means not being burdened by excessive worry or fearfulness, not being highly reactive emotionally, and having a courageous attitude toward dealing with life's challenges. When we can be a nonanxious presence, we're better able to support autonomy in our kids, to tolerate the stress we feel when they take on challenges or when they struggle, and to help them learn to manage their own anxiety.

When we can be a nonanxious presence, we help our kids develop brains that are capable of enjoying success. We can't tell you how many times we've heard parents say things like, "Kids need to be stressed if they're going to be successful," or "If my kid gets into a good enough college, all the stress and sleep deprivation will have been worth it." Oy, that's just not so. Young people won't be capable of enjoying their success if they are chronically tired, stressed, anxious, or, worse, depressed. No amount of achievement, money, or prestige is worth the price of lifelong vulnerability to anxiety and depression.

When we are a nonanxious presence, we help kids achieve *sustainable* self-development, by communicating messages such as:

"The world is actually a pretty safe place."

"Things usually work out okay."

"I love you no matter what you do or say or achieve."

"You're capable of managing your own life."

"You don't have to be good at everything to have a great life."

"Screwing stuff up is a necessary part of learning to do things well."

"I'm not worried about you. Everybody has to go through some hard stuff."

"There are thousands of ways to become successful in this world."

"Life isn't a race; the world is full of late bloomers."

And we're not suggesting that you have to be calm for the sole purpose of making your kids calm. Parenting is stressful enough, and the last thing we want to do is add an unattainable goal to your list. In fact, this advice shouldn't generate a to-do list at all but rather a to-be list. A nonanxious presence is a different way of looking at things, a way that will make *you* less likely to feel burned out and pressured. So, yes, the environment you create is for them, but these adaptations benefit you as well. Our goal is to make it easier for you to keep things in perspective, so that you radiate calm, courage, and confidence, rather than fear and doubt.

How We Communicate Fear and Anxiety— or Calm and Courage

Our Language

Let's start with the obvious. When we lecture, scold, yell, or criticize, when we say something positive but in a sarcastic tone, or when we try to make our kids feel guilty, it activates their amygdala, triggering their stress response and putting them into a defensive, rigid, reactive state. Even more basic, when we say *no* or *don't* (which young children hear dozens or even hundreds of times a day), it releases stress chemicals in our kids' brains (and in ours) that are associated with fear and anger. Functional brain imaging research has shown that even seeing the word *no* on a screen for less than a second while you're lying in an MRI scanner will cause your brain to suddenly release dozens of stress-producing hormones and neurotransmitters.[4] Conversely, positive words like *yes*, *love*, and *peace* activate systems in the prefrontal cortex (PFC) that are related to emotional regulation.[5] The problem is that negative words like *no* and *don't* have a more powerful effect on kids than positive words. For this reason, the researchers Suniya Luthar and John Gottman say that "*bad is stronger than good*" when it comes to communicating with children and teens.[6]

One of the implications of this research is that when negative words and negative interactions with our kids (or with our partner) outweigh positive ones, it's toxic for the relationship. John Gottman's research with couples has identified a "magic ratio" of positive to negative interactions for a healthy relationship: 5 to 1. This means that for every negative feeling or interaction between partners, there must be five positive feelings or interactions for the relationship to remain healthy.[7] It thus makes sense for us to *consciously use positive words* that signal love, care, trust, respect, and appreciation more than we might ordinarily, even if it means having to acquire a new habit. Some examples:

- "Have I ever told you that I'm crazy about you?"

- "How'd I get so lucky to have you two as my kids?"

- "I'm glad you're home."

- "That was really fun. Let's do that again soon."

- "Thanks for remembering to put your dishes in the dishwasher."

- "I really enjoyed watching your game last night."

- "I'm impressed that you've been able to get to bed on time with so much on your plate."

- "You're a great daughter."

- "Sometimes I take for granted how well you set the table. I really appreciate it."

Dr. Bonnie Zucker, one of the nation's experts on childhood anxiety, recommends reflecting back the positive personal qualities we see in our children, acting as the healthiest kind of mirror for them.[8] For example, "I noticed you let him go first. You're a pretty nice kid, you know," or "I loved that you were kind to that kid who was sitting alone," or even simply, "I loved talking with you yesterday." Bonnie tells her own clients who she knows are the most difficult at home, "I really look forward to Thursdays—because that's the day we have our sessions together." A parent we interviewed said she also makes sure her son overhears her saying good things about him when she's talking on the phone with her friends. And when a kid hears these positive comments over and over again, they begin to see themselves as you see them, with calm confidence.

Also, when your kids ask to do something, try finding ways of saying yes—or at least not saying no immediately. For example, say "Let's talk about it to see if we can make it work." Or: "Give me a few minutes to think about it and then we can talk." Or: "I'm not sure, but if I have to say no, I really want to try to find a Plan B that works for you."

Research on negative language also shows us that we should avoid talking with our kids when either we or they are highly stressed. When we're stressed or when our kids are stressed, stress hormones shut down the PFC, and the amygdala runs our brains. We're much more likely to use negative language, to have the same stupid argument over and over, or just to pick a fight with our kids. When we're stressed and our kid is stressed, we're communicating amygdala to amygdala—and nothing good comes out if it. So practice the mantra *Wait till I'm calm*. Remind yourself that if you're mad and want to let your kid have it, or if you're very worried and want to voice your concern, it's time to zip your lip, go for a walk, or meditate for a few minutes. If you wait, you'll deliver your message better—and to a more receptive audience. Putting off a discussion doesn't have to signal that you're only willing to be together when everyone's calm, just that you're only willing to *problem-solve* when cool heads rule the day.

Our Questions

Asking kids the same questions over and over again conveys worry, even if the questions themselves don't. Among the most common, of course, are "Don't you have homework?" or "Why didn't you turn in that assignment?" But let's say your kid has been having trouble with other kids at lunch. When you see her at the end of the day, it's completely logical to ask, "How was lunch today?" but such a question actually keeps the spotlight on something she may have moved on from or wants to move on from, or that she simply needs a break from. It also signals to her that you're worried. If you're a receptive ear, she'll tell you if there was a problem at lunch, whether or not you ask. You can always find the balance of attentiveness without stress by saying something like, "I know lunch has been hard for you, and I might want to periodically check in about it. Could we spend a few minutes talking about it on Wednesdays?"

Our Own Stress Level

There's another reason why being a nonanxious presence helps kids: stress is contagious. If the mother of an infant is given a stressful task to perform, her baby's stress level rises as the mother performs the task—and it spikes especially sharply if the mother touches the baby.[9] Similarly, John Gottman's lab has learned that they can measure the level of conflict between parents in two ways: (1) by asking the parents how much they argue and (2) by measuring the level of cortisol (a major stress hormone) in the urine of their *kids*.[10] In the same way that sitting next to an anxious person on a plane makes us feel more anxious than we otherwise would, or that watching someone do a stressful task makes us more stressed, when Mom and Dad are stressed, the kids "catch" it.[11] Kids even pick up our stress indirectly, because when we're stressed, we're less warm and affectionate, less encouraging, less attentive, more inclined to say no, and less supportive of autonomy—all of which hinder a kid's feeling of safety and calm.[12] Stressed parents are also more likely to overreact to their kids' setbacks or shortcomings, becoming more upset than the kid. A friend of ours still remembers his mother taking to her room for days on end whenever he went through a breakup. He'd be over it, but she wouldn't be.

Before you start beating yourself up about every time you've been stressed during your child's life, relax. In the same way it helps kids to accept their feelings, it helps us to accept ours. We're not saying you need never be anxious about your kids, which is an unlikely aspiration. Rather, just accept your feelings, and try whenever possible to communicate calm.

If parents can be present, radiating calm, that benign grounding helps kids take healthy risks.[13] Little kids will literally look to a parent's reaction and get the message, "I'm not afraid, and you don't need to be afraid, either." Ned's twin brother, a paramedic, is often in tough situations where family members of a sick or injured person are understandably freaking out. Steve will calmly say, "I'm not panicked about this, so I don't think you need to be. If you like, I can let you know if you should panic." In a similar vein, Navy SEALs, who are often thrown into some of the most stressful situations imaginable, use "calm is contagious" as a mantra.

Calm parents are also more likely to be warm and affectionate, which helps kids develop stress resilience. In a study of rats, the rat babies who were licked and groomed (in other words, nurtured) by their mothers after stressful experiences grew up to be almost impossible to stress—such that they were even nicknamed "California laid-back rats." This was true whether they were the biological offspring of the grooming mother or fostered by her. In other words, it wasn't genetics—it was the act of being soothed that created an aptitude for resilience.[14]

Our Pity

Many parents don't think there's anything problematic about feeling bad for kids. What if they have a serious illness or disability? What if they don't have any friends? What if they didn't make the basketball team when their two best friends did? What kind of monster *wouldn't* feel sorry for them? But we don't want kids to feel sorry for themselves, so perhaps we shouldn't feel sorry for them, either. We should strive to communicate courage, not fear or self-pity. As we said in Chapter 1, you can acknowledge and validate their feeling by saying things like, "Yeah, I hear that you're feeling really hurt about that." But underlying that acknowledgment is a calm confidence in them, that they can tackle it, that they can hurt, but that once the hurt has subsided—and it will—they can come out stronger at the other end. Empathy instead of pity also signals that we love and accept them as they are—no matter what.

When We Enable Avoidance

The major manifestation of anxiety is avoidance. The best-documented treatment for anxiety-related avoidance is exposure therapy, through which kids progressively are able to face their fears—and learn that they can handle what they previously thought would be overwhelming. The parents' role in this process is to be supportive and not to enable or accommodate avoidance. We've seen levelheaded parents accommodate their anxious children in a myriad of ways—from letting kids sleep in their bed, to asking a shy child's teacher not to call on her in class, to never being out of earshot of a twelve-year-old who is terrified of being alone. We talk much more about avoidance, accommodations, and a new program designed to help parents reduce accommodations, in Chapter 5.

A local expert on childhood anxiety, Jonathan Dalton, recommends that when kids are highly anxious, parents use a "bank teller voice" to validate the child's emotion ("I know that this makes you really anxious"), and then ask, "What can you tell yourself when you feel this way?" If parents give kids the coping language themselves ("One step at a time" or "I can do this"), the prompts will help the child temporarily, but that kind of coaching won't help the child develop the skills he needs to find the coping answers on his own.[15] Stepping back, though, is much easier said than done, because the stress of "doing nothing" while waiting for our child to go into coping mode can feel overwhelming. Becoming a nonanxious presence can make it much easier to do the hard things.

When We Model Distorted Ways of Thinking

According to cognitive behavioral therapy, most of the thinking that triggers anxiety is distorted or irrational, and much of it falls into three main categories.[16]

- Catastrophizing, or blowing things out of proportion. This can mean assuming that the worst-case scenario is the most likely, which means saying things like, "If you don't get into that algebra class, it could affect your whole life," or "If you keep getting into arguments, you could lose all your friends." The more we can keep things in perspective ourselves, the more we can help our kids learn to not overreact or to assume the worst.

- "Should-ing"[17] as in, "You are so smart, you really should do better than this," or "You should try harder at practice." "Should" according to whom? Where's it written? Much of mental health is replacing "I should" or "I have to" with "I want to." It's a transition from a fear-based mindset of obligation to one of choice, and if we use the language of choice, it will help our kids be less anxious.

- Fortune-telling, which involves saying things like, "Your whole future will be affected if you don't take a foreign language." At the end of the day, no one really knows—there's no crystal ball in parenting. Reminding ourselves—and our kids—that we don't know how things will turn out can lower the mental temperature in our family.

We all fall into these faulty models of thinking sometimes. So when you realize you're catastrophizing, "should-ing," or fortune-telling, point it out. Let your child hear you talking back to irrational thoughts. "I just found myself going down a rabbit hole of what would happen if. . . . That doesn't really make sense."

When We Try Too Hard to Cheer Them Up

There's nothing wrong with trying to cheer kids up, but doing so can backfire in a couple of ways. For instance, during the coronavirus lockdown, Ned's daughter, Katie, was pretty down in the dumps at dinner one night. Ned asked gently if there was anything he could help with or anything she'd like to discuss. She shook her head and shrugged her shoulders. Vanessa tried to turn her mood with good cheer, pointing out all the positives of lockdown. It was bait Katie didn't want to take. Ned walked over to Vanessa and gently said, "I can see how you're doing all you can to help her feel better. My hunch is right now she has a reason to feel sad or to want to feel sad. I don't think it's helping for us to try to take that away from her. Let's be okay with her being sad."

The movie *Inside Out* kept running through Ned's head in this moment, where the emotion "Joy" did everything short of cartwheels to keep "Sadness" at bay. But if we want kids to develop emotional resilience, we cannot be the ones who always pull them out of hard emotions. If as parents we steamroll, distract, or coerce through sadness, anger, or fear, our kids won't ever have to face those important feelings, feelings that also help them make sense of the world. We sometimes give messages that those feelings are problematic. We can unwittingly give our kids messages that "we don't like" those feelings, making it harder for them to bring those feelings to us when they really need to. What Ned and Vanessa really wanted was to keep the walls low between them and Katie, making it easier for her to peer over it when she needed help.

When We Watch Too Closely

One trend we find particularly worrisome is the increasing encroachment on kids' private lives, which has contributed to significantly lowering their sense of control. This started with the replacement of unsupervised play with adult-directed or supervised play (e.g., team sports) and electronic games, and it worsened when parents were encouraged to monitor their children's grades and school assignments online. Our most recent concern is the popularity of apps like Life360, whereby parents can track their kids' whereabouts at all hours. We've lectured at schools where most of the parents are tracking their kids, and we even know parents who are tracking their college students' every move—without the kids' knowledge or consent.

The reason most parents use these apps is that *they* feel less anxious when they can know where their child is at any moment. But as with other forms of parental overcontrol, the things we do to lower our own anxiety can make our kids more anxious. We suspect that monitoring kids' whereabouts gives us an illusion of control (which lowers our stress), because the truth is that, as hard as we try, we truly can't keep our kids safe. The two of us worry, though, that closely monitoring our kids makes them feel less safe by communicating messages such as:

- I don't trust you.

- The world is so dangerous I need to know where you are at every minute.

- I'm so anxious I couldn't go for ten minutes without knowing where you are.

- You can't be safe without my supervision.

Kids will feel safer—and less anxious—if we ease up on our monitoring and work on conveying the following:

- I trust that you can take care of yourself and can ask for help when you need it.

- I don't have to know where you are at all times.

- You don't need me monitoring you 24/7.

- I can't protect you from every negative thing that could possibly happen.

- Let's think together about the best ways of keeping yourself safe.

- There's always been a lot we *could* be afraid of, which doesn't mean we have to worry all the time.

Helping Kids with True Danger: Expressing
Concern *and* Courage

Fear might be contagious, but calm is, too.[18] You can express concern, and when you do so calmly, you build courage instead of fear. If the line between concern and fear seems thin, well, it is. We've found that much of the work isn't in the *what*, but the *how*. Consider this conversation between a teenager and his mom:

TEEN: Hey, Mom. Can I go bike outside?

MOM: I wouldn't. It's dark out.

TEEN: What if I wear a headlamp?

MOM: But your bike isn't lighted. Your sister's bike has lights on it, but yours doesn't. Your bike even says on it to *not* ride at night.

Everything the mom said was accurate; riding a bike at night can clearly be dangerous. But her response started with the conclusion of "no, because it's too dangerous," and then built a case for her position. She signaled to her son that he should be more afraid than he needed to be. Instead, we recommend collaboratively tackling the issues before coming to a conclusion. Rather than saying, "I wouldn't," she could have said, "Hmm. I have some concerns, but let's think them through together." In addition to expressing her love, she could also share that she respects his judgment, that he can be trusted.

Ned was hiking in Arizona when he came across a family doing the same hike, and they all walked together and chatted for a distance. While the conversation was light and interesting, the mom punctuated every other sentence by telling her elementary school-aged kids, "Be careful!"

Although Arizona has some dangerous hiking trails, this one was quite safe. There were no steep drop-offs, just some branches to climb over and streams to cross. If she had said something more specific like, "Oh, let's all focus as we cross the stream" or "Note this branch sticking out," she would have taken generalized anxiety and transformed it into the guidance of a more experienced hiker. Again, the *how* makes an important difference.

Black parents told us they particularly struggle to express concern without unduly inducing fear in their kids, and for very good reason. For one, they worry about expectations, that teachers won't hold their kids to the same standards as everyone else or will think an average performance from a kid is "just fine." Studies show that even when teachers have the best of intentions, harmful stereotyping still happens.[19]

"We have to be twice as good to be taken half as seriously" is a common refrain we heard. One Black mom remembered taking her daughter to a school admissions interview at the same time as a white family. The white family was dressed down—the dad wore a baseball cap, the son wore Converse. In contrast, "My daughter had a ballerina bun in her hair and wore a church dress." The daughter asked why she had to dress up when the others didn't. And so the mom sat down to explain. "I had this conversation with my daughter when she was in third grade," the mom said. "I told her that sometimes people have this thought, way back in their head, about who you are, and they don't even know you. I didn't want to paint a picture that the world was an unsafe place, but I didn't have the luxury not to have that conversation."

These conversations undoubtedly bring a weight. "I haven't had that conversation with my child," said another Black parent. "I remember it being drummed in [when I was a child]. I remember the weight that I always had to be so perfect and to do so much more."

Yet we've also heard that addressing this painful, even traumatic, terrain isn't something many feel they can avoid, given the stakes. These parents have expressed that, as say, a parent of a Black male teenager, do you *not* talk about what could happen if he gets pulled over? Sure, it would be great if we lived in a world where parents felt they could tell him to relax, and feel relaxed yourself, but that's not reality. How do you tell your son that the rules for what he wears are different without telling him why you think that? This is obviously an incredibly complex question that many brilliant books grapple with. (We recommend *Whistling Vivaldi*, *So You Want to Talk about Race*, and *Biased* as good places to start for nonfiction . . . and *The Hate U Give* in the fiction realm.)

A Black mom named Sophie suggested one possible solution. She said that when there's a news report of a shooting of an unarmed Black man, she's started making it a point to watch the reporting with her kids—who are in sixth, seventh, and ninth grades—and use it as a teaching moment. Sophie's ninth grader wondered why she hadn't shared news like this with him years before. "I kind of get why you didn't," he said. "But share with me what you think I should be prepared for." This openness goes back to Fred Rogers's strategy: kids learn about something scary, and home is the safe base from which to sort it all out. Safety doesn't mean being Pollyannaish and assuring kids they are immune from threat, but rather, saying, "This happens and it's not fair, but I believe you can handle it. Here are tools and techniques you can be aware of."

"I don't think it sunk in the first time I had 'the talk' with him last year," Sophie said of her son. "But this year, the first time he went to the mall, he asked me, 'Should I wear a hoodie?' It's in the back of his head, and that's not a bad place for it."

Making Home a Safe Base

One of parents' most important roles is to make home a safe place where kids can regroup and recover before going out into the world. You can't control what bullies they'll encounter or what disappointments they'll suffer, but there's a lot you can do to give them a safe landing at home.

Build in recovery time. Emotional resilience develops through experiencing something stressful, coping with it, and then having a time and a place to recover from the stress. It's similar to strengthening a muscle—you push it, you breathe through it, and you drink chocolate milk and eat bananas afterward. Make room for that recovery time, in whatever form that takes. One fretful mom said of her daughter's finals week, "She's spending all this time after testing with her friends—what good is that going to do her?" Friends are like the chocolate milk and bananas. She needs them to recover. You can push yourself harder in the moment if you know that a break is coming, and when.

Reframe short-term and mild stress as positive. Again, while chronic and extreme stress are terrible for the brain and body, some stress is okay—and even necessary for optimal performance. So when your kid is feeling stressed, and stressed about feeling stressed, let them know that stress has good features, too. A study from the University of Wisconsin that analyzed data from a large health survey concluded that the less we worry about being stressed and anxious, the less harmful the effects of stress and anxiety will be.[20] And as psychologist Alicia Clark says, if we fear anxiety less and embrace it more, it can be an ally for us. Dr. Clark recommends three ways to "hack" your anxiety—or to take control of how you view anxiety so you can use it as a resource. First, think of anxiety as a helpful signal that an issue needs to be addressed. Second, label the feeling as a way of taking control of your experience. This could involve, for example, reframing anxiety about a performance review as excitement—or as your brain's effort to get you into optimal performance mode. Third, aim for the sweet spot between crippling anxiety and lacking adequate stress to get motivated.[21]

Introduce humor. When Ned's kids are upset, he often tells or texts stupid knock-knock jokes—or even slides them under their closed doors. The jokes aren't necessarily all that funny, but sometimes elicit a chuckle, or just a laugh at Ned's willingness to be so corny. We don't want to chronically talk kids out of being unhappy, but it's been said for eons that laughter is medicine, and we agree.[22] When we "read the room," it's often clear that delivering an earnest sonnet about how much we care won't be as effective as joking around together, simply lightening the load. Sharing a laugh also reinforces connection, reminding kids we're there for them, that they're not alone on this crazy journey of life.

Enjoy your kids as they are. We gave this advice in our previous book, and it remains among our most popular guidance for parents. Remember the way you looked at your kids when they were babies? You were full of awe and wonder. It's the most natural way to give the message, "I love you as you are, unconditionally, and you don't need to change or improve for me to be crazy about you." This simple reminder doesn't involve a script for what to say or how to be, although it might be helpful to look back at early photos of your kids so you can tap into that feeling more easily.

Remind kids that they have control over their own emotional reactions. Eleanor Roosevelt famously said, "No one can make you feel inferior without your consent." Her wisdom emphasizes the degree of choice we have in our emotional responses to the events in our life—and thus our responsibility for our own emotions. This is one of the key insights of cognitive behavioral therapy, which is that much of our anxiety and emotional distress is rooted in our own (often irrational or distorted) thinking about the things that happen to us, or that *might* happen to us. Eleanor's pithy line also serves to remind us that our emotional reactions can vary according to how tired or well-rested we are—and that our reactions are not the only possible ones, as other people may very well react differently than we do.

As you'd guess from Chapter 1, we're not at all suggesting that you try to talk a child out of feelings. When a child says, "You made me angry," we certainly want to validate their feeling in the moment. But over time, we can also teach our child that other people don't make us angry, that we actually make ourselves angry through what we tell ourselves about the things that other people say or do.

When your kids are really struggling and you don't know what to say, don't say anything. Take the pressure off yourself to always say the right thing, direct the right course of action, or heal the pain. Often the best thing you can do is just sit with your kids, bearing witness to whatever it is they're dealing with, but saying nothing.

The Most Important Work Is on Yourself

Over the last few years, the majority of children Bill has evaluated have been diagnosed with an anxiety disorder, often along with attention, learning, or social problems. When parents ask what they can do to help, it rarely occurs to them that one of the most important things they can do is manage their own anxiety as effectively as possible. Indeed, when kids are not doing well, our most important work is often on ourselves. A study out of Johns Hopkins University demonstrated that if you include the whole family—including the parents—in an intervention to reduce stress, the kids are much less likely to develop an anxiety disorder.[23] It's pretty clear that while our kids' anxiety is not our fault, there's a lot of work we can do on ourselves that will help them manage it. (Again, more on this in Chapter 5.) Wayne Dyer, the late, great self-help psychologist, used to say that when we are happier, the less likely it will be that our children will feel the need to worry about us or have a sense that they are responsible for our happiness. Plus, we'll transmit our calm to them.

When we really work at it, calm becomes like a layer of skin—it's always on us, even when we don't realize it. Many people have commented to Bill in the years since he began meditating that he has a calm presence—even when he doesn't feel particularly calm inside. But when you practice being calm enough, you begin to radiate it, and that calms the environment, and the people, around you.

There are multiple ways to manage your anxiety. You probably know the basics: sleep, exercise, and generally try to take care of yourself. If you have a partner, also put energy into *that* relationship. It's at least as important as what we're asking you to do for kids. We're also strong proponents of meditation. A peaceful family requires peaceful people. Bill and his wife, Starr, practiced Transcendental Meditation regularly when their children were growing up, and while their children were at times embarrassed about their "weird" parents, Bill's son recently said that when he thinks of his childhood home, he remembers it as being so calm *because* his parents meditated. In fact, numerous studies have shown that the practice of TM lowers stress, aggression, and crime in the larger environment.[24]

A thirteen-year-old boy we know had a very conflicted relationship with his father for years. A year ago, the father learned to meditate, which he said transformed his relationship with his son. According to the dad, "The things he did that used to set me off didn't set me off anymore. It was weird at first. I'd think, 'I need to react to that so he knows it's not acceptable.' However, after a few months of not being so reactive, the behaviors that bothered me so much just kind of dropped off. I guess meditation helped me change our pattern." Kids notice the change in their parents, too. A teenage boy with autism learned TM with his mother and several months later was asked by a reporter what he noticed from meditating. The boy answered, "TM calms the mind and it calms the mom."

Separating your own happiness from your child's is a lifelong pursuit, but it's one of the best practices you can begin for your own benefit and for your child's. Among the most important advice given to parents of teens and young adults with substance abuse problems is to work toward separating their own happiness from whether the child chooses to use or not. We have found that this "emotional separation" is equally important for parents whose kids have less serious problems. It's never easy, and there's truth to the saying, "You're only as happy as your least happy child." But if we believe that our mental state is inextricably linked to theirs, it leads to enmeshment or codependency—and can allow kids' challenges to use up way too much of a family's oxygen. Separating your happiness takes work and vigilance, and then some more of it. There's a temptation to think, *If my child is struggling, what does that say about me?* But remember, your children are raised by you, but they are not you. Your identity needs to be multipronged for everyone's sake. If your happiness cannot begin until your kid is happy, you might push your kids to "get better now," fraying your relationship and your ability to help.

It's why we recommend talking to *yourself* before you say a single word to your kid. Divide your self-talk into four key reminders that we've broken down into the acronym W.A.V.E.

Self-Talk: How to W.A.V.E.

Whose life is it? You might add to this, "Whose responsibility is it?" and "Whose problem is it?" Remember, your kid's problems are *his* problems, and it's okay if you don't take them on as your own. We've known many parents who wouldn't go out and enjoy themselves if their kid was struggling, because they felt they had to be at home and always available. Just recently we heard a mom who doesn't work say she's devoting her life to her son—he needs her full-time attention—which did not strike us as a healthy message to give her son. If you feel similarly, change your practice. Get out. Laugh, see friends, and give yourself permission to be carefree for a while. You will be stronger when you return home.[25] Have a date night and keep it even if your kids are working on a big project—or maybe even playing in a game. Focusing on your relationship with your partner, maintaining your own interests, and taking care of yourself are among the best things you can do for your kids.

Accompany. You do have a role to play as a parent, and it's an important one. You are there to help, but not to direct.

View with perspective. Remind yourself what's really important by taking the long view. In the big picture, your child wants her life to work out, too. Progress might not be at the pace you'd like, but trust her.

Explore your angst. When you're feeling anxious, worried, or sad about your child, we encourage asking yourself the following questions that Barry Neil Kaufman posed in his book *To Love Is to Be Happy With*: "What are you unhappy (or worried or mad) about?" "What about that makes you unhappy?" "What are you afraid would happen if you weren't so upset about this?"[26]

For years, Bill asked parents this last question. Invariably, they answered by saying things like, "If I wasn't so worried, it would mean that I am a completely insensitive mom with no empathy." Or "If I wasn't so upset, I wouldn't be motivated to try to help him." Bill would then ask, "Is it really true that if you weren't so worried, you'd be completely lacking in empathy?" Or "Are you saying you wouldn't do everything possible to help your child just out of love?" In every case, parents realized that they didn't need the burden of negative emotions to be a good parent to a child they loved immeasurably.

The two of us do this work on ourselves, still, all the time, when we're feeling pressured, or fearful, or upset. We did it when we were worried about missing our deadline for this book, in fact. It helped to break it down to our core value, which is to share what we've learned to as wide an audience as possible, not necessarily to hit every deadline. Likewise, break your own core motive down: *My job as a parent is to love my kid and help them figure out who they want to be and the kind of life they want to live—and how to get there.* When you focus on your values this way, it lowers stress and helps you get out of fear-based thinking. We tend to feel happiest and most fulfilled when we have a larger perspective on things. We can remind ourselves about our highest values and core motives, which can give us broader perspective and remind us that it's not a big deal, it's a little deal.

But What About . . . ?

I don't want to make my kids anxious, but I can't deny that I'm really stressed-out right now. First there was the coronavirus quarantine, which was rough on us, and we are still really struggling to pay our bills. I don't know how to hide all of my worries from them.

When you feel stressed (and who in your circumstances *wouldn't*?) it's best to be up front about it with your kids. When your face and your words don't align, it's deeply unsettling. Even your best attempts to disguise your stress fail, so you might as well name it and explain what you're doing to cope with it. The CDC guide on communicating during crises, in fact, holds credibility as one of its top six rules.[27] It may be that the best thing you can do is to double down on your efforts to manage your stress—which is invaluable modeling for your kids.

We are also strong proponents of a philosophy known as radical acceptance, which focuses on accepting that, for all we know, the world is as it should be. One of the basic ideas is that there's no evidence that the world is supposed to be different than it is. That doesn't mean we don't attempt to make the world better—for that is also as it should be. As author and speaker Byron Katie said, "I am a lover of what is, not because I'm a spiritual person, but because it hurts when I argue with reality." Radical acceptance suggests the best thing you can do is to make peace with what is right now, because we can't predict the future, and for all we know, what seems like a disaster can lead to an opportunity. A single paragraph within a multichaptered book obviously can't do justice to a philosophy that is a lifelong practice, which is why we recommend reading the works of Byron Katie, in particular her book *Loving What Is*.

Are you saying I can never get mad at my kid, or I'll stress him out? 'Cause that's unlikely to happen.

Not at all. A safe base does not mean that you have to play chanting music, or that you can't ever grumble at your kid to pick up after himself, for fear that you'll stress him out. Kids need experience dealing with strong emotions. So by all means, get mad when he leaves his dirty dishes in the sink! Just remember the mantra, "Wait till I'm calm." Always aim, as we mentioned in Chapter 1, to communicate PFC to PFC. Also, apologize if you lose your temper. It's an enormously powerful way to communicate love and respect.

My seven-year-old is so sensitive and anxious, and she knows she worries about things that don't seem to bother her friends. How can I explain anxiety in a way that she can understand?

We'd suggest saying something like, "You're a really sensitive kid, which means you deeply feel your own feelings and other people's, too. This makes you an incredible human being! But it can be hard to be sensitive, too, because it means you get stressed really easily. You have this part of your brain called the amygdala that can't think—it just senses if there's anything that might be scary. It's like a smoke alarm that will go off even if there's not really any smoke. Everyone has one, but yours is more sensitive. There's this other part of your brain called the prefrontal cortex that you might think of like a pilot. The pilot is great at solving problems, and calming you down, but when you get stressed it doesn't work very well. So the trick is trying to make sure the pilot is monitoring the alarm system. There are some things you can do that will help, like getting enough sleep and moving your body. And it can help just to say, 'Hey, smoke alarm! There's no smoke!' or to ask, 'What's the worst that could happen? If that happened, could I handle it?' Because you can!"

Putting It All Together: Sample Dialogues

Kevin's a seventh grader who had an incredibly busy week of play rehearsal and soccer practice. He didn't get home one evening until after 9 p.m. and was too tired to write the essay his English teacher assigned, so his mom, Kendra, suggested he go to sleep and that she wake him up early the next morning.

The next morning, Kendra woke Kevin up early as promised, then bustled around helping her other two kids get ready for school. As in most households, mornings were a busy time.

Kevin got out his notebook and said, slightly panicked, "I didn't write down the question for the essay I'm supposed to write."

Kendra, who still hadn't finished her first cup of coffee, said, "You're just realizing this NOW, when you have to leave for school in thirty minutes?"

Kevin said, "It's not my fault. Ms. Brown has terrible time management, and she wrote it down at the very end of the period."

"Kevin, don't blame Ms. Brown. You messed up. Are you saying that no other kids in the class were able to do their homework? When are you going to start taking some responsibility?" Kendra was anxious. She had a million things to do and simply didn't have time for this. She also thought of her sister, Beth, as she often did when Kevin messed up. Beth always blamed other people when she was late, or when she lost things she'd borrowed, or when she otherwise screwed up. Kendra firmly believed it was because their parents never held Beth accountable when she was a kid. Kendra was determined not to make the same mistakes with Kevin.

Kevin was now stressed about not finishing his homework, and his mom's energy and lecture made everything worse. His PFC went completely off-line as his amygdala took over. The scene devolved from there. Homework was not completed, yelling ensued, and Kevin's siblings "caught" the stress. In the end, everyone was late for the day and in a rotten mood.

Imagine if it had gone this way instead:

Kevin said, slightly panicked, "I didn't write down the question for the essay I'm supposed to write."

Kendra sipped her coffee. She thought to herself, *How could he not have thought of this last night? Then again, he doesn't have the brain of a forty-five-year-old woman. I can't expect he's going to think like me. And anyway, this is his problem, not mine.* She didn't share any of her internal dialogue with him, but instead said, "Ugh. You must be feeling stressed."

"Yeah, and I'm mad, too. Ms. Brown has terrible time management, and she wrote the question down at the very end of the period. I didn't have time to write it down."

Kendra did not like that Kevin wasn't taking responsibility for his mistake. But she stopped herself from projecting what his future might be like as a person who never takes responsibility for himself. There was no evidence he would turn out like his aunt Beth, and that line of thought just wouldn't help in the moment. Over dinner that night, she'd ask him if he wanted help with his organizational skills. She wanted to assist Kevin, but not rescue him. And what she really didn't want to do was create a mess of the morning by getting mad, which wouldn't serve anyone's purpose.

"Hmm," she said, calmly. "I wonder if there's a way you can get the question. Call one of your classmates, maybe? Any ideas?"

Because Kendra was calm, she helped Kevin access the prefrontal cortex part of his brain. Kevin thought for a minute, then said, "I bet Ms. Brown posted it on the class forum. Can I borrow your phone to look it up?"

Kendra lent her phone, and sure enough, Kevin found the question. He wrote the essay in fifteen minutes, and no one was late or more stressed than they needed to be.

———

The Franklin family went away one winter weekend, and their daughter, eight-year-old Maddie, begged to go to a tubing hill on the way home. The parents were reluctant because it would add an hour to their already long drive home, but they ultimately agreed. They arrived at the tubing hill and bought Maddie a ticket. She went down once and promptly started crying. "That was so scary," she said. "I hated it. Let's go home."

Maddie's dad, Ben, was annoyed. "We drove an hour out of our way to get here!" he said. "And we just bought your ticket." He was also frustrated that Maddie was always so cautious. As the dad, wasn't it his job to toughen her up? To push her, even if it meant she was uncomfortable? He didn't want her to be an adult who never took risks, who was fearful when she should be confident. "Look, Maddie, four-year-olds are going down this hill. You can do this. Get back up there."

Maddie started wailing and refused.

Imagine if it had gone this way instead:

"That was so scary," Maddie said after her first ride. "I hated it. Let's go home."

Ben felt really annoyed about the time and the expense. He asked her to wait a minute while he went to the bathroom, and then they could talk about it. Really he wanted to give himself time to calm his irritation and think through his approach. He reminded himself not to be a fortune-teller projecting her whole life based on this one incident.

When he returned, he said, "I'd love for you not to be afraid of this, Maddie. I have a feeling that when you try it for a second time, it won't be as frightening. I understand you wouldn't have wanted to come here if you'd known tubing was so scary, but the more you do it, the less frightening it will be.

"And I'm not mad at you, but I am frustrated because we drove far out of our way, and we just bought your ticket. I'm not going to make you go down this hill again, but if you don't, I feel like you should pay me back for the price of the ticket."

Maddie was angry, but she didn't argue his point as she considered what to do. Ben let it sit for a minute, then said, "Do you want to think of some things we can do to make it less scary?"

Maddie nodded and suggested they watch the other kids for a while. Ben agreed and also suggested that he could tie his own tube to Maddie's so she'd feel more secure.

Remember What It's All About

In a cherished scene from *Winnie-the-Pooh*, Pooh and Piglet are taking a walk and Piglet asks:

> "Supposing a tree fell down, Pooh, when we were underneath it?"
> "Supposing it didn't," said Pooh.
> Piglet was comforted by this. . . .[28]

Some of our most important work as parents is to be like Pooh, and to teach our children to be like Pooh, too. Ned was literal in his interpretation as he advised a student who was very anxious and fearful to go on a walk and take note of every tree that didn't fall, in order to rewire his attention. Or, as William James observed, "My experience is what I agree to attend to."[29] When we teach our kids these lessons, it's ultimately their own voice they hear saying:

"I have confidence I can handle this."

"This is a setback, but I'm about much more than this."

"I'm fine just as I am."

"Sure, maybe the tree will fall, but maybe it won't."

Chapter 4

Pep Talks: Talking to Help Kids Find Their Own Motivation

When the coronavirus hit in the winter of 2020, schools across the country were shuttered and parents—thrust into the role of distance-learning support staff—got a whole new insight into their kids' motivational styles. It's not that parents were clueless before—we've been speaking to their frustrations about motivation for years. But suddenly, finding the language to motivate kids felt imperative to getting through each day.

We asked teachers and parents to share their angst, and here's what some said:

"I teach ninth grade, and what I hear all the time from parents is 'My kid just doesn't care. I've tried taking away all of their devices and privileges and they still won't do anything.'"

"I have smart, talented kids who just don't seem to care about doing anything beyond the bare minimum (if that). I honestly worry about how they're going to survive in the real world—and what great stuff they're going to miss out on—because they're not interested in making an effort. If it sounds like hard work, or really any work, forget it. I feel I've failed in teaching them how good it feels when you work hard and do a great job and enjoy the results."

"I have a kid who does the bare minimum (but gets it done without much nagging), another who is such a perfectionist that before or during his work he will get so frustrated that it's not going to turn out exactly the way he imagined that he just gives up, and another who is pretty internally motivated but also responds well to incentives. I like to think we parent them all somewhat similarly, but maybe we shouldn't."

"My kids are only six and four. One morning I said, 'Girls, I want to do something fun with you tonight after school and work are done, but first I want you to clean up your toys.' When the girls finished school that afternoon, one said, 'Let's clean up our toys so we can do something fun with Daddy tonight.' And the other answered, 'Let's just do something boring with Daddy so we don't have to clean up.'"

Welcome to the world of motivation, friends, where styles wildly differ, carrots and sticks are relics of the past, kids are motivated for some things but not for others, and parents frequently pull their hair out trying to figure out the right things to say and do.

Before going any further, know that your job isn't to motivate your kids at all. Rather, you want to help them foster their own sense of internal motivation. **The end goal is not to get them to do well. It's for them to *want to do* well.**

The fact is that you really can't instill motivation in your kids, primarily because you can't make them want what they don't want—or not want what they want. What matters to kids may not matter to parents, and vice versa. You could offer incentives (like $50 for every A) or make threats (no video games for the next marking period if you don't have all Bs or better), which may work for a short while—although remember the ninth-grade teacher's comment suggesting it often doesn't. But over the long run, carrots and sticks do not develop the kind of self-drive that leads to long-term success. What we want is for kids to hit the motivational sweet spot—between the extremes of perfectionism (which we'll talk much more about in Chapter 6) and a sense of pointlessness in even trying. The key to hitting that sweet spot is the promotion of intrinsic, or autonomous, motivation.

"Intrinsic motivation" is just a fancy way of saying behavior that's driven by curiosity, interest, the pursuit of challenge, or the desire to develop skills. It's the opposite of behavior inspired by rewards like grades or by the desire to avoid punishment. We would much rather kids have a *little* intrinsic motivation each day as opposed to a lot of the extrinsic kind. Quality, it turns out, matters much more than quantity.[1]

Intrinsically motivated students study harder, pay more attention in class, ask more questions, get better grades, and are more likely to accomplish their goals.[2] Intrinsic motivation *automatically* produces effort and desire for a strong performance. This is due, in part, to increased availability in the brain of dopamine. In other words, when motivated intrinsically, kids don't have to expend energy forcing themselves to do anything.[3] The "let's get to it!" energy is there in spades. Also, when children and teenagers are intrinsically motivated, they are less defensive, willing to acknowledge personal shortcomings, and receptive to corrective feedback. They have heightened attention to possible mistakes, which shows up in brain wave activity, presumably because they care more about doing well than if they're working for a reward.[4] The challenge is that most schools rely on *extrinsic* motivation, which is why so many parents were tearing their hair out during COVID-19—especially when grades were taken out of the picture, as happened at many schools.

A friend of ours, Wendy, decided she'd been put in an impossible position during the school closures. Her sixth grader, Kelly, already had little interest in learning about ancient world history, which she struggled in. Without the teacher standing before her, and without the incentive of seeing her friends at school and getting to go to drama class (which she loved) right after history, what was the point? Wendy pushed Kelly for the first few weeks, and there were arguments aplenty, but when schools announced that all kids would get a passing grade no matter what—thus taking away the carrot and stick—Wendy thought *screw it.* Wendy asked, "What do you *want* to learn about? What questions do you want to answer?"[5] Kelly decided to study the Renaissance. They worked on a syllabus together, which included reading twenty nonfiction articles and two historical novels, watching two movies, sketching Renaissance-wear, and hosting a Renaissance evening for her family, complete with Renaissance food, costumes, and games.

The point of this story isn't that we should all homeschool our kids or become education disrupters (although we won't stop you on the latter!), but rather the huge shift Wendy noticed in her daughter: "It was such a dramatic difference," she said. "Before we made the change, I had to be on top of her, checking in to make sure she logged in to her classroom Zooms, sitting *beside her* as she got her work done because she said she couldn't do it alone. We fought, I was frustrated by her lack of ownership, and the word *lazy* was on the tip of my tongue all the time, though I knew better than to say it. Then when we came up with the idea that she'd create her own plans and study something she was interested in, she was all in. She downloaded two Renaissance novels from the library app without my even asking her. She wore an old Renaissance Halloween costume as she worked the first few days. And she talked nonstop at dinner about the class divisions of the Renaissance era and how unfair Henry VIII was to his wives." In fact, Kelly went beyond the requirements they'd agreed on—creating backstories for each guest to study in advance of the Renaissance evening.

Wendy didn't realize it, but she had employed the foundational theory of intrinsic motivation: self-determination theory (SDT). Developed by the eminent psychologists Edward Deci and Richard Ryan, SDT holds that intrinsic motivation requires that three deep human needs be fulfilled: (1) a sense of relatedness (which, once Wendy and her daughter stopped fighting, was restored), (2) a sense of competence (Kelly no longer felt lost or helpless in history class), and (3) a sense of autonomy (the whole project and its intermittent goals were determined by Kelly).[6] Self-determination theory is like a three-legged stool. For many young people today, the stool is not balanced, as so much emphasis is placed on promoting their competence that it weakens their sense of relatedness (especially to their parents) and their sense of autonomy. We need to balance the stool. And if we do nothing else as parents, addressing all three of these basic needs in our kids will powerfully help them to discover their own motivations.

SDT is not the be-all and end-all of motivation, but it lays down a constant drumbeat. Layered on top is the science of working hard and playing hard, as well as the science of change, which helps us talk with kids who don't seem to be motivated to do better. We'll cover all this in this chapter and the next, and give you some language you can use to turn up the volume.

What Not to Say

Bill recently attended a meeting at an independent K–8 school about Jeffrey, a bright eighth grader with ADHD and learning disabilities. School was hard for Jeffrey. He found the work to be extremely difficult, and he had trouble motivating himself to complete his assignments, which often felt overwhelming. The school's learning specialist said that it took the efforts of herself, two tutors, and Jeffrey's mom "being on him continually" for him to get any work done. The intense focus on getting Jeffrey to work reinforced his perceived lack of competence, wreaked havoc on his sense of autonomy, and caused a lot of conflict in his relationship with his parents and others who were only trying to help him. Bill thus advised them to stop these efforts immediately, because as long as adults were spending ninety units of energy trying to make

Jeffrey work, he would spend ten. Bill recommended that the learning specialist and the tutors not work harder than Jeffrey worked to help himself. (The teachers later told Bill, "We're only doing so much so that Jeffrey's mother will be less anxious!")

The school principal (who is excellent) then talked about how important it was for Jeffrey to improve his academic performance quickly. Jeffrey would be applying to independent high schools, and unless he turned things around soon, his choices would be severely limited. His performance was thus affecting a "four-year decision." "Jeffrey doesn't understand the long-term implications of his not working," said the principal. "That's why we need to continue to try to persuade him—to show him how important it is to do better." In fact, the principal attested that he'd already had two conversations with Jeffrey about the importance of buckling down and exerting more effort.

Bill said, "If telling Jeffrey how important it is that he work harder didn't 'take' the first or second time he was told, it's unlikely to motivate him the third, fourth, or fifth time." (Intrinsic motivation is not born of repetition!) Every time Jeffrey was reminded of how important it was that he perform better, it made him feel more stressed, anxious, discouraged, and resentful. He almost certainly had *tried* to do better because *he* wanted to go to a good high school, but due to his learning issues, his efforts often didn't result in high grades. Jeffrey often tried to avoid a primary source of his stress and anxiety—his schoolwork. It was unlikely that trying to make him even more scared about what would happen if he didn't work harder would produce results.

Bill suggested that Jeffrey would be much more likely to work hard if he didn't feel the burden and the excessive stress of feeling that he *had to*: "I have to, but I can't" takes away all sense of control. Bill recommended (a) telling Jeffrey that where he goes to high school is relatively unimportant in the larger scheme of things and (b) communicating a way forward that didn't require Jeffrey to do something he felt incapable of doing. Kids like Jeffrey—all kids, for that matter—benefit enormously from the sense of safety that comes from hearing, "I can see plenty of ways for your life to work out."

Jeffrey's team agreed to give it a shot. They eased off all the "doomsday is coming!" pressure and stopped pushing him. Their go-to spiel:

I want you to work hard, and I know that if you do, you can do a lot better. You don't have to turn things around immediately. If you don't get into the school you want, you can work hard as a ninth grader and apply to transfer, which a lot of kids do. I'm happy to help and support you, but I'm not willing to work harder than you do because I care too much about you to weaken you.

That they stuck to this script was impressive, because many parents and educators worry that if kids know they don't *have* to, they won't be motivated to do things that are hard. We haven't found this to be true. In fact, the first thing we tell the underachieving students we work with is, "I couldn't care less about your grades." We emphasize that there's no need to turn things around immediately, but that there may be some reasons for them to work harder and some ways for them to do better if they want to.

When the adults talked with Jeffrey about not wanting to work harder than he did, the energy in their relationship started to change, and when the pressure of having to turn things around "now" was lifted, everyone was less stressed. Quite predictably, when Jeffrey experienced encouragement instead of threats, he was increasingly able to give his all without fear that his all wasn't good enough. It wasn't a miraculous, throw-away-the-crutches kind of turnaround, but Jeffrey slowly stopped resisting the help of his tutors and the learning specialist, started to call a friend if he missed an assignment, and began asking for help when it was time to study for an exam. He wisely chose to apply to a high school that has an excellent learning support program, was accepted to the school, and is doing strikingly well as a student athlete in ninth grade. He even told his mom that he doesn't think he'll be able to play football again in tenth grade because of the increased academic demands—and is looking for a less time-consuming sport.

Trying to Motivate Through Fear, Guilt, or Anger

The dynamic initially at play with Jeffrey's skilled and well-meaning team is one we see all the time. Adults worry, a lot (see previous chapter!), and think that inducing fear will shake a kid out of his seeming passivity, that it will make a kid like Jeffrey see what he needs to do, at last. The problem is that when we try to light a fire under them by repeatedly explaining the gravity of their situation, it almost always increases their anxiety and shuts them down further. It also undermines our connection with our kids, in part, because they come to think that their achievement is more important to us than they are. With a weakened connection, we have less authority, and the hope of getting anywhere on motivation is pointless. Years ago, the parent of one of Ned's students insisted that Ned "put the fear of god" into her daughter so that she would take her test preparation seriously. Ned explained that, absent a lightning bolt from Zeus, he didn't think that was likely to work. We want to have *influence*, not *power*, over kids. Influence grows with mutual respect, whereas with power, it's a zero-sum game. Also, when we make threats that don't quickly materialize, we are reduced to the parents who cry wolf. One high schooler told us that her parents warned her that if she didn't pass a community college class she was taking, she could forget about college. When she didn't pass it, her parents said, "Don't think for one second this means you don't have to go to college."

So our advice: Don't repeat messages over and over, or raise your voice louder and louder. And give up on language that's meant to make your kid afraid or ashamed, including messages like this:

- "If you don't start studying more, I hope you'll enjoy working at McDonald's your whole life."

- "If you don't learn to work hard now, how will you ever be successful when it really matters?"

- "If you don't stick with the piano, you'll always regret it."

- "If you don't practice harder, you won't make the travel team again."

- "I know you could do it if you would just try."

- "You could have gotten all As if you'd worked a little harder."

- "I expect you to do better."

- "You don't work hard at anything!"

- "If you don't get your grades up, no college is going to want you."

One of the reasons phrases like these—especially the last one—don't work is that the context is beyond kids' understanding. Trying to get a seventh grader, for instance, to stick with swimming or with Spanish because it will look good on college applications is much like saying, "Now that you're in middle school, we believe it's time to have a serious conversation about a 401(k) plan for you." Kids aren't capable of thinking ahead the way adults are—that's what makes them kids.

But rest assured, if you've said any of these things, it doesn't mean you're a bad parent. At many of our lectures, a parent will raise their hand within the first fifteen minutes and ask, "What if I've already screwed up my kid?" To that we say don't worry. Kids can figure out their lives regardless of how they're raised. Some forms of child-rearing just make it easier. Parenting is frustrating—we get it. As one parent wrote us, "Why did no one tell us this was so *hard*????"

Just Do Your Best

Most parents want their kids to know that they care more about *them* than they do about their grades, but they still want to motivate them to work hard. So parents say things like, "All we insist on is that you do your best (or try your hardest)." Although they're trying to communicate caring and respect for the child, they're still setting an impossible standard that invites a character judgment—and can make the kid feel guilty if he doesn't give his full effort. If we're honest, most of us do not do our best in every situation. **Nor, really, should we. Part of the battle is knowing when we have done enough.** And anyway, who gets to decide what a child's best is? One of our favorite cartoons shows a kid looking up at his parent and asking, "Did I do my best?" Ned constantly sees parents move the goalposts on kids as to what their "best" might be. A student will reach a test score goal (stated by the student, his parents, his teacher, his prospective college) only to have parents ask, "But don't you think you could get a [. . . one level higher]?" It is deeply dispiriting and kind of unnerving, like swimming toward a shore that is always just out of reach.

"We just want him to do his best" is also often read as conditional approval. We've known many kids who will shoot us a meaningful *Uh-huh. Yeah, right*, expression as their parents say this. Ned was recently called by parents who wanted to begin a conversation about future test preparation— for their *eighth grader*. "We're not typical D.C. parents," the mom said (a reference to the striving intensity D.C. parents are often labeled with), thereby offering the surest evidence that they are. She then went on to explain that, yes, her daughter has an anxiety disorder, and, yes, she has ADHD, and, yes, they pay her for grades—but the only message they were trying to give her was that she "do her best" and that "the difference between a B and an A is only another hour of work a night." No wonder kids handicap themselves! What if they give their all and are found to be lacking? That's a much scarier proposition than giving less, yet knowing you *could have* done more, that you left some in the tank.

Along these lines, we're not big fans of teachers grading kids for their effort. How do you measure effort, really? For some kids, making an effort doesn't require any effort at all.[7] Bill's six-year-old granddaughter Charlotte recently finished a packet of schoolwork in two hours that she and her fellow first graders were given two weeks to complete. She *loves* worksheets, handwriting practice, word-finds, and math puzzles, which a lot of kids find to be mind-numbingly boring. Or imagine that two kids are tasked with reading a dry, dull passage. Their critique of the text might be the same (it's boring!), but due to human neurodiversity, these kids' brains work entirely differently. One kid is able to quite easily make herself read it, expending, say, three units of energy in the process. The other kid's brain panics and straight-up rebels. The mere idea of reading the text is terrifying to her. She stares and stares and stares at it, and even though she expends ten units of energy, she can't get through it. Perhaps her teacher tells her to focus, but especially if she has ADHD, that admonishment can actually make it harder for her brain to activate. No one can *see* her effort. That's why we worry that effort grades become judgments about a child's character that are drawn mainly in the dark.

The Science of Working Hard

Luckily, just as motivational science tells us what *not* to say, it also tells us what *to* say.

Many readers may already be familiar with the work of psychologist Dr. Carol Dweck, who has researched children's motivation for decades. According to Dweck's theory, some children have a growth mindset, reflected by the belief that they can improve their abilities through their own efforts. Kids with a growth mindset are said to see setbacks as part of the learning process and bounce back from them by increasing their effort.[8] When things get harder, they gear up rather than give up. Because they're motivated by interest in learning, not by grades, they see effort as crucial for their development and are open to feedback. Some research shows that, because kids with a growth mindset are intrinsically motivated, they have increased availability of dopamine and heightened sensitivity to errors.[9] In contrast, some kids have a fixed mindset, reflecting the belief that they were born with a certain amount of innate ability that is "fixed." They seek external recognition, avoid all situations in which they could look stupid or inept (and thus shy away from challenges), and see the need for effort as evidence that they really aren't very smart, or athletic, or musically talented.[10]

Dweck's work has generated numerous interventions for promoting a growth mindset in students. But several recent studies have concluded that getting kids to change mindsets isn't easy, at least through school-based interventions—and that even when they do, they may not show improvements in cognitive and academic performance or increased focus on learning rather than grades. Some elements of mindset interventions can even be *counterproductive*.[11] For example, you don't want to tell kids they can do anything they set their mind to, when really, that's not the case.

To be sure, there appear to be limitations in growth mindset theory. But there's still a lot to like in Dweck's work, and we suspect that parents may be more powerful in nurturing a growth mindset than school programs. So we'll focus on what we find to be most helpful for nurturing kids' confidence in their ability to get better and better and their willingness to take on challenges.

Emphasize the Value of Working Hard to Get Better

Bill tells the kids he sees, "Every time you work hard to get better at something, like reading, more and more brain cells work together—and become part of the 'reading team,' which is how effort changes your brain." When he tests kids who are sensitive to perceived failure and tend to give up quickly, Bill looks for any tests on which they try hard on relatively challenging items. Once he sees this effort, he says something like, "You seem like somebody who likes to do hard stuff and to solve hard problems. A lot of kids I see would have given up on those test questions—but you didn't. Even if you weren't sure of an answer, you tried really hard to think of a good one. I'm really glad to see that, because that's what makes people successful."

A parent might say something like, "Man, you really worked hard on that project!" Or, if their child is daunted by a task, the parent might say, "Yes, it's definitely a challenge. But I think that if you work really hard on it, you'll have more confidence that you can face challenges like this, and you'll feel really good." Or "I remember the first year you played baseball and you weren't such a great hitter. After seeing you get three hits today, I'm just appreciating how powerful practice and hard work are."

Inside the Brain

Possibly the most useful thing for anyone to know about the brain is that it develops, in part, according to how it's used. It's the most "plastic," or malleable, during early childhood and adolescence. The brain connections practiced frequently get stronger and stronger, whereas the ones that are not will eventually go away through a process called pruning.[12] In other words, kids—and especially teenagers—have a lot of power to shape their brains in ways that can make them smarter, emotionally stronger, and healthier.[13]

Here's what it looks like under a figurative microscope: As you learn and develop skills, the brain recruits more and more neurons

to fire together—a process called long-term potentiation. Synapses—
which, you might remember from high school biology, are the connection points between neurons—strengthen their connections to
one another, coding an event, a stimulus, or an idea.

Each time two neurons fire together, they tend to do it more, and
their combined energy triggers neighboring cells to join in the fun.
Eventually, the party permanently binds neurons together so that
slight activity in one will trigger the whole block, consolidating a
memory or skill and making the memory more easily retrievable and
the skill more automatic. Neurons that fire together wire together.
Even just sixty minutes after, say, learning to play a new piece on
the piano, electron microscopes will show how branching contact
points between nerves (dendrites) have grown and formed new ex-
tensions.

Any time your kid practices a skill or learns something new, more
and more brain cells fire together, which is why they get better and
better when they work at things, even those that are hard for them.
Bill makes this point as a way of encouraging kids with learning disabilities to "gear up" and work really hard at reading or writing, even
though these skills don't come easily to them, as well as at things
that do come easily. (He recommends working hard for short periods, interspersed with brief periods of "downtime" in order to allow
the brain to consolidate the new learning or skill.)

The other process that makes kids' brains so malleable is the creation of myelin. Think of myelin like the insulation around a wire.
Your neurons are connected together through fibers (axons, if you
want to dork out with us). Myelin is a fatty white substance that
coats those fibers and makes communication between neurons
fast—up to two hundred times faster than before the myelin formed
around the axon. These become the brain's white matter tracks.
Practice can actually increase the rate of myelination, which is
partly why it's easier to read, do calculations, and think the more

you practice, and why this chapter is taking much less time for us to write than Chapter 1 did.[14]

That kids and teenagers are neuron-firing, myelin-creating work-horses is useful to know, and so we should let them in on it.

Provide positive feedback for persistence, progress, and the strategies kids use to solve problems. Positive feedback can help support intrinsic motivation by raising a child's sense of competence. (Remember the three-legged stool!) However, Dr. Dweck cautions against telling kids that they're smart, a great athlete, or a gifted musician because it tends to foster a fixed mindset, by putting attention on their innate abilities. We see it somewhat differently—which we'll get into in a minute. That said, it's also fantastic to encourage the development of skills that don't necessarily come easily, by saying things such as:

- "I noticed how you stuck with that problem even though you were frustrated."

- "I know that a lot of kids would have given up, but you didn't. That's pretty cool."

- "I'm blown away by the way you solved that problem. I never would have thought of that approach myself."

- "When I was looking at the illustrations you made for science, I was thinking about the incredible progress you've made from practicing your drawing. I guess there's a reason they say that practice makes perfect."

- "It looks like all your hard work is paying off."

- "I remember when this used to be really hard for you—and now it seems so easy!"

- "I know that reading isn't as easy for you yet as you want it to be. When I think about how far you've come, though, it looks to me like you've made a lot of progress. I don't see any reason why you won't get even better the more you work at it."

Embrace the word *yet*. It's a tiny little word, but added to the end of a sentence, it practically sings out "growth mindset"! Some examples:

- "Most of us are not equally as good at everything, and virtually anyone can get better at something they practice. Are you open to the idea that, when it comes to algebra [or any challenging skill], you may not be very good *yet*—but with enough practice you could get quite good?"

- "It's true, you haven't learned to play that song . . . yet."

- "You haven't mastered dividing by nine, yet. But you can. Look how far you've come already!"

Dig into specifics that empower. There's a big difference between "You did a great job—I'm so proud of you!" and "It's pretty impressive how hard you worked on that—it looks like you made several revisions before you got it the way you wanted it." The latter promotes a growth mindset, whereas the former promotes a pleaser mindset. We like to think of positive feedback as the language of encouragement—rather than praise. We want to be clear that we're paying attention to our kids and noticing the great stuff they do, but we also don't want them to be all about pleasing us. It's more about making progress on their own goals.[15] Some empowering examples:

- "I love the incredible detail in your sketch—the creases in her hands are so spot-on."

- "You went beyond just summarizing the story. You offered a really interesting insight into why the father had to leave his family."

- "That was really cool. How did you figure out just which part wasn't working?"

- "I appreciate the care you took on this. You didn't rush, and you gave yourself enough time to do the job well."

- [If a teacher or tutor] "Wow, you are the first person to get that right in a long time. Do you know *how* you got that right—or what you were doing or thinking when you realized the solution?"

Because kids learn from observing their parents, it makes sense for us to *model* a growth mindset for our kids. For example, you could try making comments like this:

"I'm so glad I rehearsed the presentation I gave today. Every time I practiced it, it got easier."

"When I was trying to fix the sink this morning, I was tempted to quit because I started to feel like an idiot. I reminded myself that if I stick with it—and study the YouTube video again—I could probably figure it out, and I did."

"I have to learn something new for my job next month. I know I'll feel kind of foolish when I start to learn it, but if I keep at it, I'm pretty sure that I'll get it eventually."

Some Caveats

As with all things, moderation is the name of the game. If you comment every time your kid works hard at something, it may drive him a little crazy or make him suspicious that you've been reading a book like this one (would that be so bad?). Remember, a little can go a long way.[16]

Even though we've emphasized commenting on the *process*, not the *product*, that doesn't mean you *never* say anything about the actual result. If your child makes a heartfelt drawing, builds an impressive Lego structure, produces a good essay, or does a nice job of performing in a

play, it's fine to say, "That's beautiful," "Amazing," or "You were terrific tonight!" Also, though Dweck's work doesn't cover this, we love it
when parents validate positive *traits* like curiosity, kindness, and stick-to-
itiveness, which can cause kids to turn their attention inward to what's
intrinsic, realizing, *Hey, I **am** really curious about how things work*; *I **do**
notice small details that others miss*; *I **do** care about doing things the right
way*; or *I am nice to people.*

Another important caveat: We agree that just telling a kid "you're so
smart" is not such a good idea, in part because no one is smart in every
skill area. (If Bill had to make a living using his visual-spatial ability, he'd
be homeless; and if Ned had a job where he had to be detail-oriented,
he'd be living right alongside Bill.) However, we all want our kids to
think that they're intelligent, and if they struggle in school, we want to
reassure them even more. It's not so great for kids to think that they
aren't smart or, worse, to think that they're stupid, which is the case for
a lot of the kids Bill tests. Also, studies have shown that for Black students, many of whom have never been told that they're smart, simply
telling them they are is one of the most powerful ways to improve their
academic performance.[17] So when Bill works with kids who doubt their
ability, he doesn't lay on praise about their brilliance—for one, they probably wouldn't believe it. But he does tell them a greater truth: that they are
"smart *enough*" to do something useful and important in this world. He
adds, "I'm grateful for all the people in my field who are smarter than I
am, because they make up the theories that guide my thinking and make
up the tests that I get to use. But I'm smart *enough* to do something that's
very interesting and rewarding. You are, too." (This is also a good message
to kids who are bothered by the fact that there's always someone in their
class who's smarter than they are.)

Ned worked with a student, Lauren, who was impulsive, hyperactive,
and a completely terrific human. She told Ned that half of her teachers
adored her but half hated her. The ones who adored her thought they
could "fix" her; when they couldn't, they got frustrated. Lauren was

smart and worked hard, but some subjects just would not click for her, no matter what she did. So she concluded she must just be stupid. But Ned told her she's smart *enough*. Then he added, "I'm sorry you're grinding for grades and not getting the ones you want. If I may, I'd love for you to think about your hard work as what you're doing to develop yourself—not to get a certain grade. School is hard for you, no doubt, but I'm dying to see how you figure out how to contribute to the world with this exceptional brain and personality of yours."

When Ned gets kids who cling to the idea that they're stupid, he will say, "I'd like you to be open to the idea that you are really quite capable. It may not seem that way to you now. And you don't have to change your mind. I'd just ask that you keep an open mind because that's certainly the way that I see you."

With kids who have significant language disorders, marked difficulty with math, or severe learning disabilities in other areas that could make obtaining a college degree very challenging, Bill often says, "You're smart enough to do what you want to do as an adult." He'll then add something like, "Because you don't like to read and write, it's probably safe to say that you aren't going to want a job where you have to read and write all day. And you probably don't want a job that's too hard for you. That would suck. But you're smart enough to learn skills that will allow to you to make a living and to make a positive contribution to this world. From my point of view, that's the most important thing."

We also believe that it's important for kids—and especially teenagers—to be aware of their strengths, including the things they're naturally good at. For many kids, being told that they have talent in a specific area or that there's something they can do a lot better than most kids their age is enormously motivating—and gives them the confidence to stretch themselves. So after Bill tests kids, he tells them about their strengths in verbal reasoning, visual-spatial organization, math, or reading, and he always adds (even if it's not always *entirely* true), "The cool thing about you is that you work hard to get better and better. There are a lot of bright and talented people who don't contribute much to the world because they don't work hard enough to become really good at what naturally comes easily to them." It's a dual message—(1) you're smart enough and/or have talent *and* (2) you work hard to get better and better.

Inside the Brain

There are two systems in the left part of the brain that are specialized for reading words: one for sounding out words you've never seen before, and one for recognizing familiar words or "sight words." In kids with dyslexia, these systems are less active than they are in kids who learn to read easily. There's also a pathway that connects the back part of the brain, the visual part of the brain that processes the "ink on the page," with the left front part of the brain, which is where the names and sounds of letters and syllables come from. For kids with dyslexia, this tends to be a slow pathway. With practice and maturation, this pathway gets faster because the "cables" that connect the back and the front parts of the brain become covered in a kind of insulation (this is the myelin we talked about earlier) that increases the rate information travels.[18]

A dyslexic brain might have difficulty learning to read, but it tends to function better than other brains in important ways in adult life. Share this with your kids. Tell them research has found that individuals with dyslexia have stronger visual-spatial skills, higher creativity, greater entrepreneurial and financial success, and better skills in certain kinds of scientific thinking.[19] Because learning differences are rooted in genetics, you can also point out well-loved family members who share this trait with them.

Play Hard: Language That Promotes Flow

After a lecture we gave in Chicago, the father of a third grader came over to talk to us. The conversation started out great because he told us that his son loves to plays tennis and usually plays five or six hours a week. It became more complicated when he said, "The problem is that the kids in our community who are becoming elite tennis players are playing twenty to thirty hours a week. How can I make my son want to practice twenty or thirty hours so he can become an elite athlete?"

Yeah, this dad was pretty extreme (thirty hours of tennis for an eight-year-old?), but we get lower-key variations of this question all the time, usually around academics ("How do I motivate my kid to do better?" "What do I say to my kid to make him want to work hard?"). We think that what this boy's father—and many parents—miss is the enormous benefit that kids get from the joy of playing hard at something they love.

When a child or adult is intensely involved in a game of tennis with someone who's as good as they are, they often have the experience of "flow." The concept of flow was developed by Mihaly Csikszentmihalyi, who asked experts in dozens of fields about the times in their lives when they felt and performed the best. They all described the experience of flow, which happens when you're engaged voluntarily in a task that's challenging but manageable, tackle a series of goals, continuously process feedback about your progress, and adjust your action based on the feedback.[20] It's the being "in the zone" that kids (and their parents) can experience when they are deeply engaged in a sport or game, playing music, dancing, making art, solving a challenging problem, or learning something of high interest. Csikszentmihalyi writes, "The best moments of our lives are not the passive, receptive, relaxing times . . . The best moments usually occur if a person's body or mind is stretched to its limits in a voluntary effort to accomplish something difficult and worthwhile."[21]

Some of the best news for parents about motivation comes from the research of Reed Larson, a student of flow theory and adolescent development. Larson concluded from his research on motivational development that children become self-motivated adolescents and adults not through dutifully doing their homework, but through what he called the passionate pursuit of pastimes (he indicated years ago that video games don't count, which we'll discuss in Chapter 8).[22] Larson reported that the combination of high internal motivation, concentrated attention, and positive emotion that kids experience at these times reinforces their strong effort in a way that cannot be achieved by any other means.[23] According to Larson, when kids and teens frequently experience a brain state that combines high focus, high effort, high determination, and low stress, they are sculpting a brain that is capable of great focus. What this means is that, instead of holding back your exasperation when your kid wants to spend all his time on music, realize that what he's doing is extremely good for his brain and his development. Your kid is happy because he's doing something he loves, and you're happy because you know it's helping him develop motivation. It's a win-win.

When Bill's kids took an interest in baseball and softball, he was thrilled to support them in building up their skills—not because he cared whether they were excellent players, but because he knew that working hard to get better and better at something that was important to them was so good for their brain development. Bill spent hundreds of hours coaching and practicing with them, and he sometimes hired a college player who would give them exercises and drills to do at home—which the kids did with enthusiasm. It was never meant as a way for his kids to get ahead of other kids or to get a college scholarship in baseball. Bill's son, Elliott, became an excellent player but didn't make the baseball team in college. When they talked about it later, Elliott said that the only thing he felt bad about was that Bill had invested so much time and money in the sport. Bill was surprised to hear this and told Elliott, "It was never about baseball, it was about helping you get better at something because you wanted to, and it was about spending time together. I wouldn't have traded that for anything."

Ned's had experiences like this with his kids, too. One day when his son, Matthew, had a half day off, he spent an hour on his homework, then five hours teaching himself how to play a complicated song on the piano. Ned frequently hears Matthew play a certain phrase a hundred times trying to get it just right, and while he doesn't apply that discipline to his studies all the time, Ned always feels reassured that the kid knows how to work hard.

Some language for supporting the play-hard mindset:

- "I love watching you play."

- "I just want you to know that [pastime] is as important to me as what you're doing in school, because I know it's so good for your brain."

- "Even though you're not a star student, I don't worry about you because I know that through your commitment to art, you're sculpting a brain that will be able to go pedal to the metal when working hard in school is important to you."

This is an area where sometimes actions speak louder than words. Simply sitting and appreciatively watching your kids engaged in their passion—whatever that passion is—might indeed be the best way to encourage its pursuit. Your child is unlikely to ever forget what that felt like.

But What About . . . ?

My parents always communicated to me that I should stick to the things I was good at and stay away from things that I wasn't good at. I feel like I've almost done the opposite with my kids—encouraged them to stick with and work harder at the things that don't come as easily. I want them to have grit, after all, and sticking around when the going gets tough seems like an important life lesson. Is that wrong?

It's not wrong, precisely, but telling kids they're just going to have to learn to do things they don't want to do isn't likely to work. The life lesson you're after is much more readily learned when there's something that they *want* to do or accomplish, but that requires doing some things they aren't thrilled about. So a kid who loves swim team but hates the butterfly stroke that his coach insists on, for instance, will figure out how to muscle through that part of practice. It's extremely unlikely they'll miss this lesson altogether; life is long and kids have so many experiences and influences outside of their family.

That's not to say that we've never encountered a slacker adult—of course we have. Many of them didn't have the experience growing up of facing the reality that they'll get out of life what they put into it. Often they've been rescued or bailed out over and over; or other people have been on them constantly to perform; or parents and others have made accommodations, so they've never had to face things that make them feel uncomfortable.

If you're worried about your kid becoming an adult slacker, we have two suggestions: First, ask yourself, if this was to happen, could you handle it? (Of course you could.) Second, remind yourself that it's extremely unlikely that your kid will always be undermotivated. We've even seen some pretty impressive slackers pull it together in their mid-to-late twenties. This may be because of brain maturation (emotional regulation systems in the PFC aren't fully mature until the age of thirty-two, plus or minus a few years), or the experience of meeting a girl who doesn't want a slacker boyfriend. Bill tested a kid years ago whose father had been homeless for several years in his twenties and thirties but was a successful businessman and a good father in his midforties. For some reason, he wanted a better life. A relative gave him a chance, and it took. Never say never.

Inside the Brain

The brain is not born with a Han Solo–style pilot at the helm. The most important thing we have learned about the brain is that the PFC is slow to develop. Research in the early 1990s found a dramatic growth spurt in the PFC between the ages of seventeen and twenty. Later studies have shown that the PFC systems that regulate cognitive functions such as planning, organization, and working memory are not fully mature until about the age of twenty-five, while the emotional regulation systems (which help you calm yourself down when you need to) keep developing until about the age of thirty-two.[24] Now, that doesn't mean you have to wait until you're in your thirties to get your stuff together. But maturity does take time, and there's a good place in this world for late bloomers. This knowledge has helped Bill to reassure thousands of parents—and almost all his friends—that their kids would turn out okay in the long run. We want to be patient with our kids and we want them to be patient with themselves, to understand that life isn't a race to age eighteen.

While your suggestions about motivation might have made sense a few years ago, we're now living in an ever-more-competitive environment, where kids are going up against students from all over the world. They need to know that, even if it's scary. It sucks that the stakes are so high, even in middle school, but they are.

We understand the fear behind this comment, but we strongly disagree with the conclusion. You simply cannot help a child hit the sweet spot of motivation with a mindset of fear and scarcity. Imagine saying to an eighth grader, "Hey, you know you're competing not only with eighth graders in the U.S., but also with eighth graders all over the world. You have to step up." That kid will likely respond in one of two ways: either they'll panic, and their anxiety will drive their decisions; or they'll rebel and think, *So? I can't win anyway, so I might as well not try.* The truth is that there are many ways to be happy and successful in this world—and, at least in America, how you do in eighth grade has little bearing on whether you find your place.

It's true that fear *can* be a good short-term motivator, and there's nothing wrong with giving kids information that might make them anxious if we think it's important for them to have it. For example, if you express concern that if your kid doesn't finish a term paper it could lower their GPA enough that they might not get into one of the schools their friends are going to, it may give them the drive to work hard for a day or even a week. But it won't drive them to work hard for a whole semester, because fear-based motivation is stressful and very hard to sustain.

My kid has ADHD and is highly anxious, and rewards help him get himself to school in the morning and get his schoolwork done. Am I doing the wrong thing by rewarding him for these things?

Although they should not be a major tool in our parenting toolbox, we are not completely opposed to rewards. In cognitive behavioral therapy for anxiety, for example, kids are rewarded for taking the steps necessary to face their fears and thus rewards are an important part of the treatment. We also think it's great to spontaneously take kids out for ice cream or bring home a treat as a way of showing appreciation when they do a good job with things like carrying out their chores, getting ready for school on time, or finishing their homework on their own. If used respectfully and without controlling language, rewards are less likely to undermine intrinsic motivation. In this case, you might praise his work ethic and explain that many kids with ADHD need a little extra boost to get them to do things that they know they need to do but can't get themselves to. The key is to prioritize his autonomy—offering incentives to help the child meet his goals is much less likely to undermine his intrinsic motivation than bribing him to meet yours.

Inside the Brain

ADHD is chemical, not character, and yet it's hard not to become infuriated when you've asked your kid to do two things and they can't for the life of them stay focused on either. It's easy to think that they're just not paying attention, that they don't respect you, or that they're being willfully lazy. In actuality, it's just harder for them to make themselves do things they don't want to and to focus on things that don't grab their interest. From a brain point of view, kids with ADHD have a lower baseline level of the get-up-and-go neurotransmitter dopamine, and their dopamine system doesn't work as efficiently as it does for other kids.[25] Also, the prefrontal cortex of kids with ADHD tends to be three to five years less mature than the PFCs of kids without ADHD.[26]

ADHD is very genetic, running in families, and tends to show up differently in boys and in girls. While boys usually get diagnosed early, as they're more likely to be bouncing off the walls, girls are more likely to be inattentive, finding their own ideas or thoughts more interesting than whatever the teacher is saying.

ADHD is most frequently helped through the use of medications like Ritalin, but exercise can also help raise dopamine levels, as can a little bit of stress (the healthy kind!). Time, though, may be the greatest help. As the prefrontal cortex matures, it functions more efficiently, and it becomes connected with more and more systems in the brain, which means that it becomes increasingly involved in cognitive and emotional processes that used to be handled by different parts of the brain. For example, one of the tests Bill gives involves asking kids to say all of the words they can think of that begin with the letter *b*. When eleven-year-olds do this task, the sides of the brain (the right and left temporal lobes) activate. When they're sixteen and seventeen, the left temporal region activates most, with some slight activation in the prefrontal cortex. Three or four years later, the primary activation is in the PFC, and young adults can think of *b* words much more efficiently because the prefrontal cortex can think of strategies to organize the generation of words.[27] This is partly why a twenty-four-year-old can find a solution to a problem or find a way to compensate for a learning disability that had never occurred to them before.

It's also important to note that while physical development of the PFC is slower in kids with ADHD, this doesn't mean that they can't do well in school or be successful in sports or anything else. It just means that they may have to work particularly hard and be particularly patient. There is no need to rush to a finish line. (Bill didn't even know he was going to be a psychologist until he was thirty, and he didn't have his first job as one until thirty-four.) We also want to point out that some of the features of ADHD can also help make kids supercreative. And they have the opportunity to learn earlier than most the importance of slowing down and being careful—a trait that will serve them throughout life. It's also true that stress hormones raise the level of dopamine in the brain. For many people, this leads to too much dopamine and a PFC that can barely function. However, for kids with ADHD, a moderate degree of stress can optimize PFC functioning, which is why many grow up to be very successful in careers that involve high-pressure situations, like EMTs, courtroom lawyers, or emergency room doctors.

My kid hates seventh grade. He likes his band class, but hates everything else. He's not doing well, either, and I worry he's getting the message from his teachers that he's just lazy. What can I say to him?

One of the most important things to share with your son is that you're not worried about him. Say something like, "A lot of kids hate seventh grade, and nobody's even going to care about your seventh-grade report cards. You know, I [or another family member] was a straight C student in seventh grade, and it hasn't hurt me/them at all."

Then you might address the "lazy" label head-on, by saying something like, "You aren't a lazy person—I know this because I see how hard you work in band. Your struggles with your schoolwork are about your brain chemistry, not your character. For some kids, working really hard in school is easy. It's because of their brain chemistry—not their willpower. You probably just don't have enough of a chemical called dopamine—which is critical for motivation—working for you. One of the things that can help you get more dopamine going is to offer yourself a reward once you're done doing something you don't want to do. I'm happy to help with this. Maybe we could pick a show we watch together after you finish your homework? And the way the brain works, the more of a handle you get on the material, the more you'll see how it's possible to improve if you work hard, and the easier it will be, so it will be a reinforcing cycle."

Other ideas you might share are working with a friend so it's not as boring, or finding an older kid to come over and be a homework coach. A lot of kids find it easier to be motivated if they're working for someone else. Finally, you might suggest that he keep working hard on his instrument. "Playing music, because you love it, increases the dopamine in your brain, and it gives your brain the experience of being really focused, putting in lots of effort, and being happy at the same time. This can train your brain to work hard at anything that's important to you."

Putting It All Together: Sample Dialogue

Penny has two sons. Josh came out of the womb intrinsically motivated. He's seven now and doesn't like to watch TV or stay in his pajamas on the weekends because he wants to be productive. Penny gets this, because she was the same way herself as a kid. Her other son, Hugo, is twelve, and would be happy never to leave the house or get dressed. A weekend in bed, tasked with doing nothing, is heaven to him, and he'll stay in his pajamas drawing anime characters for hours. He often doesn't stop to eat because he doesn't want to hassle with going down to the kitchen. Penny understands that Hugo's brain works differently than hers. But it frustrates her to no end that Hugo is never motivated to go anywhere, do anything, or finish a job he's started. Penny appreciates her son's amazing creativity, but she also wants him to understand the value of working hard at things you don't necessarily love.

One day, when Hugo's teacher sent an email about how behind he was, Penny pleaded with Hugo to apply himself. She had a lot of work to do and didn't have the time to oversee his studies. Her stress and frustration levels, needless to say, were high.

"Sometimes," she said . . . well, yelled, "you just have to do stuff you don't want to do. I don't have the bandwidth to be on you all the time. You need to get it together, or you're going to drive everyone from your roommate to your boss to your partner crazy one day. You're driving *me* crazy now. And, Hugo, I'm only saying this because you're so naturally brilliant."

Hugo felt guilty—his mom was working really hard, after all—so in an effort to please her, he did what he was supposed to. But the next day, they were right back where they started.

(Hugo's reaction might also have been the opposite. He might have shut down, completely annoyed with his mother, who clearly just didn't get how boring the work was or how stupid his teacher was.)

Let's say it went this way instead:

Penny was beyond frustrated with Hugo, and she knew it. The very first thing she did was suggest that the two of them find time to talk later in the day when she'd be able to think more clearly. As she went on with her day, she reminded herself not to be a fortune-teller. Hugo at twelve was not who Hugo would be at sixteen, eighteen, or twenty-two. She didn't know that he would be a slacker. In fact, if she was honest, it was pretty unlikely he would be. Then she reminded herself to love the brain Hugo had—it was the brain that enabled him to get lost in sketching. He was different from his brother, and operated differently than she did, but his dreaminess was one of the things that made Hugo who he was, and she loved it about him.

When they talked later, it went like this:

PENNY: I want to apologize for something. I know that I've been lecturing you about having to do things you don't want to do. I just realized that I've been on you about this so much because, at some level, I'm worried that you might not figure out that if something is really important to you, you may have to do some things you don't love in order to accomplish it. I realize that's pretty crazy, and I'm confident that in time, you'll figure that out.

HUGO: Are you okay, Mom?

PENNY: Yes! I mean, I do think that it's important to do things you don't want to do, like clean up after yourself, or, you know, attend school even if you don't feel like it one day. But that's a long-term goal we can work on together.

HUGO: Okay. I think?

PENNY: I was thinking it might make sense to start having family meetings every Sunday, where we talk about what's working for us and what's not, and try to help each other with some long-term goals.

HUGO: (rolls eyes)

PENNY: Just give it a chance this one Sunday, okay? We can get takeout for dinner to make it more fun.

HUGO: I do love pad thai.

Remember What It's All About

Let's assume you've read and reread these first four chapters, and so far as you can tell, you're doing everything right. You've got a close relationship with your kid. You practice empathy, and you try your best to play the role of a supportive consultant. You also use a lot of the language from this chapter—yet you've still got a big problem. Your kid is failing most of his classes, vaping tobacco and whatever else, or is overweight, and you know it bothers him. Though you're supportive, and don't pressure, this apparently self-destructive behavior continues, as he doesn't seem to lift a finger to make his situation any better. There doesn't seem to be a positive pastime in the picture, and encouraging hard work isn't cutting it. What else can you do to try to reach him?

As we said, the landscape of motivation is rocky indeed. Sometimes relying on the science of motivation isn't enough—and, as you'll see in the next chapter, you need to use the science of change.

Chapter 5

The Language—and Silence—of Change: Understanding Ambivalence

Why do people so often have trouble making healthy changes? It's a question that's stumped business consultants, teachers, dietitians, parents, doctors, and therapists for years. A "science of change" field has emerged to tackle this issue, and those at its forefront have figured out some techniques that *do* work. As it pertains to parents and their kids, the best techniques are based on the timeless wisdom that you can't change others; you can only change yourself.

This chapter encourages you to think about your interactions with your kids as a dance (like a waltz or tango—not the latest TikTok sensation). If you're dancing and all you do is step on each other's feet, you can't really make your partner shape up and follow your steps. All you can do is change your own steps so that you work in more synchronicity. There's a great sense of power and calm in changing your own steps, by the way. It gives you a sense of control that you desperately need—we all do.

You don't have to be a passive observer, destined to watch your child self-destruct. Because while you can't change your child or make them want to change, you can help them find their own reasons for changing—and to that end we'll cover an effective practice called *motivational interviewing* (MI). If you have an anxious, unmotivated, or resistant child, trying to force them to face their fears, to work harder, or to comply with you is destined to be a waste of time, but you can adjust your response to their behaviors in ways that result in change.

As you'll see, sometimes the greatest power comes from simply looking at your own feet—not directing theirs.

Making It about What *They* Want: The Language of Motivational Interviewing

William Miller is a psychologist who worked with problem drinkers in the 1980s and noticed that when he tried to help by pointing out the logical benefits of drinking less, it didn't help at all. His clients were deeply entrenched in denial. Miller knew a lot about addiction, but he was also interested in the science of change. And so instead of trying to change his clients' minds, he helped them explore their own experience of alcohol use and how it affected their lives. He expressed empathy and affirmation and guided them in examining possible reasons for change. It turned out that this strategy opened up far more capacity for changes in behavior, as his clients often reduced their drinking without any actual treatment. Miller and his colleague, Stephen Rollnick, went on to develop motivational interviewing (MI), a guiding style of conversation that puts intrinsic motivation front and center.[1]

A great insight of MI is that most people are ambivalent about changing, even when their problems are tearing their lives apart. For example, an overweight adult is usually well aware they'd benefit from losing weight—but is also aware that doing so would take a lot of restraint, deprivation, and self-discipline, which could be painful. They also know that they could try and fail—and then feel like they're in an even deeper hole than they were before. Similarly, underachieving students usually know that doing better in school would be a good thing, and most would like to be better students. At the same time, they're aware that even if they try as hard as they can, they still might not do well, which can be pretty disheartening. They also know that doing better in school could give their parents and teachers the satisfaction of saying, "I told you so," or could lead to the expectation that they will always commit Herculean effort to their work. Ned once tutored a teenager named Henry who never wanted to push himself in anything. Ned didn't fully understand until he met Henry's dad, who was prone to saying things like, "You always do this. You always wuss out." Although Henry's father hoped that comments like these would shame Henry into working harder, Henry clearly had the impression that no matter what he did or how he performed, it would not be good enough for his dad.

Or consider a kid who refuses to go to school at all. On one end of the scale, they *want* their life to work and know that they're missing out on learning that may be important to them. On the other end of the scale, they may have anxiety, fear of not being able to accomplish their goals, and fear of not being able to handle things if they do. When the parents' "righting reflex" gets activated, they focus on the end of the scale that pushes them to make their life work ("School is important!"). The kid will then predictably voice the other side of their ambivalence and defend the status quo ("It's no big deal"; "School is stupid anyway"). They will cling to the other end in order to maintain balance. Miller and Rollnick found the same thing with their clients: if they argued one side of a client's ambivalence about drinking, the client would argue the other side.[2] The plain truth is that it's exhausting to feel ambivalent, to have mixed feelings about anything important to you. It's much easier to think you want one outcome definitively, or that you definitely don't, than to wrestle with feeling both ways. But we all—including our kids— have to do just that. When someone—say, a parent—tries to rush that process, all it does is get in the way, push us to extremes, and slow down the clarity that will come in its own time.

Although MI involves a complex set of skills that require training to use in a clinical setting, many of its tools can be used by parents who want to help their kids sort out their ambivalence and find their own motivation to change. At the very least, parents can avoid digging the holes their children are in deeper—by not continually arguing one side of their ambivalence and strengthening their resistance to change. Using these tools effectively requires patience and continual effort to "check" the righting reflex. But they can really help kids decide to move in a healthier direction.

A boy we know was starting to become a bit of a couch potato. His mom was concerned about his unwillingness to get any exercise. She also worried about his self-confidence and about what she suspected may be the onset of depression, so at every opportunity she could find, she encouraged him to go running, or to move his body somehow, in order to get an endorphin high and generally improve his health. She was an avid biker herself, and she told him repeatedly how good it made her feel when she went on a long ride. The boy consistently resisted her encouragement, and it drove her crazy. Why would he resist something that would so obviously help him? He clearly had enough time, he had learned in a science class about the importance of exercise for the brain, and he *wanted* to feel better. So why couldn't he motivate himself to do it? Exercise became a point of tension between them, at a time when they needed to be closer than ever.

Eventually, she tried a different approach. She took her son for dinner at their favorite local pizza place, and said, "Listen, I want to apologize to you for something. I've been pressuring you a lot to exercise, and that's not really fair to you. And it's probably pretty annoying. I love to exercise because it helps me handle the stresses of life better and makes me feel better about myself and the world when I do it. I want that for you, too. But I also get that exercise can be unpleasant. You get sweaty, it's uncomfortable, and it can be really hard. I understand why you may not want to do it, and I'm not going to bring it up again. You know your body better than anyone and know what you want, so you should do what feels right to you. But if you decide you do want to get more exercise, I'm happy to help in any way I can."

Her son appreciated her apology. As the weeks and months went on, his mom kept her word and stopped nagging him to exercise. He wanted to exercise, because he believed his mom that it would make him feel better, and he wanted to lose some weight and be healthy. But he also detested exercising, so a large part of him *didn't* want to. He never actually articulated his desire to change with his mom, but he did fire up the family's exercise bike on occasion, something he never would have done before. After some time had passed, he also asked his mom for money to join a health program where he'd get recipes and a personalized training routine sent to him each day. When he didn't feel triggered by his mom's righting reflex, he could work through his ambivalence on his own.

Step One: Ask Questions

There are some crucial keys to MI, starting with the idea that we should listen more and talk less (thus the "silence" in this chapter's title). Ask questions that encourage self-reflection, help kids clarify the values and goals that are so crucial to motivation, and help to elicit what MI calls *change talk*—or talk about how and why change might happen. This is important because the more kids *hear themselves* say why and how they might change, the more likely they are to change. Start with *what, how,* or *why*, such as, "If you wanted to, how might you get yourself to work harder?" or "What do you think might help you stick with things longer?" or "Where would you like to see yourself at the end of the year?"

Other open-ended prompts include:

- "How are you feeling about your relationship with your coach?"

- "How do you see yourself making it through the next few weeks?"

- "What sorts of things have you done in the past that have helped you?"

- "What could be some of the benefits for you if you were to go to bed at 10:30 instead of 11:30?"

- "Can you tell me more about it?"

- "Can you explain to me how . . . ?"

- "How do you feel that went?"

- "How hard do you think you want to work?"

- "How prepared would you like to be when you go in to take a test?"

- "How well do you feel your grades reflect your effort?"

- "Why do you think remembering to take out the trash is so hard?"

Refrain from directing the answer. Motivational interviewing is like playing a game of twenty questions—you're looking for information, not trying to dictate the outcome. "Why didn't you spend more time on this?" will often come across as "You should have worked harder and done better!" While open-ended questions usually work better, yes/no questions can work, too, by inspiring longer conversations. Some good ones:

- "Are you working as hard as you would like to?"

- "Are you satisfied with your level of effort and preparation?"

- "Are your grades about right for the work you did?"

- "Do you know why this is important to you?" (versus "Why do you want to do this?")

- "Do you think that's about near the top of your range?"

- "Is this something that matters enough to you to spend more time on?"

- "Did you do as well on that as you expected to?"

- "Do you wish you had a reason to put more effort into this?"

Step Two: Listen and Validate

Use the reflective listening and validation skills from Chapter 1 to let your child know you're trying to understand them—not judge them. These could include comments like:

- "You were really upset. That must have made you feel even more frustrated."

- "So you're wondering why you decided to do that."

- "What I got from what you said is that you're pretty worried about whether you're ready to go to college."

- "That would have taken a lot of courage."

- "You're someone who wants loyal friends because you're a loyal person."

- "You're determined to change things."

- "It's obvious that you really worked hard on that assignment, and I can see why you're disappointed."

- "Despite the fact that it complicates your social life, you don't want to do things that aren't consistent with your values."

As you listen, keep an ear out for "change talk." For example, a struggling and apparently unmotivated high school student may admit that he's worried about not being eligible to play basketball if he doesn't get his grades up. Or a fifth-grade girl who gives up when anything gets hard may say with disappointment that her friends are getting better at soccer or drawing than she is. When kids voice awareness of reasons why it might be good for them to change, keep listening and validating—rather than pouncing to enthusiastically reinforce this side of their ambivalence.

Sharing Your Ambivalence

One of the best ways to show your kids you grapple with ambivalence, too, is to verbalize it. "I really don't want to drink as much soda as I do. But I love it. It gives me energy, it tastes good—it's exactly what I want on a hot day. I'm worried that if I didn't drink soda, I'd be grumpy or tired. On the other hand, my dentist has told me to cut down, and I don't want stained teeth all the time—and I don't want to get diabetes from all the corn syrup." The more open you are about working through your own ambivalence, the more they'll start to recognize how ambivalence plays a role in their decisions, too.

You can also emphasize the importance of working through problems on one's own, such as, "A colleague told me about a problem he was having. I almost started to tell him what to do but thought better of it. That was for him to work through. So I asked how I could help."

You can always model coping techniques by verbalizing when something frightens you and how you deal with it. Perhaps it's public speaking, which plenty of adults fear (most more than death). "I really don't want to make a speech, but I also don't want to be afraid of doing it," you might say. "So, when I'm feeling really anxious about it, I think I'll tell myself that the worst thing that could happen is that I would embarrass myself, but I'd be able to handle it." Or "Maybe I'll arrange to have someone in the audience I can look at who will give me courage." Or "Maybe I'll treat myself to a piece of chocolate cake afterward."

Step Three: Put on Your Consultant Hat

Once you're pretty sure that your child is open to considering changing, you can use the consulting language we discussed in Chapter 2. You can ask more questions to help the child find their own solutions, like, "How do you think you might be able to pull that off?" Or "What kind of pushback do you think you might get from your friends?" And when you think you've got buy-in, you can offer advice or make suggestions about possible ways to change. Use phrases like, "It may be worth considering if it would work if you . . ." or "I wonder if it would helpful if you . . ." MI uses the framework "elicit-provide-elicit": (1) elicit what the child wants to know or would like to know (in other words, get buy-in), (2) provide information tailored to their needs, and (3) elicit what sense they make of it. The adult does not tell the child what to do or how to interpret the information. Instead, elicit-provide-elicit evokes from kids what sense *they* make of it.

Nicole Brady, a social worker at a large high school, uses MI with her students almost every day. She recently worked with a student named Jenny who had been smoking weed heavily and using party drugs for several years, a habit that dramatically affected her grades and her relationship with her family, though Jenny would never acknowledge it. Her family reached out to Nicole for help.

In one of her talks with Jenny, Nicole started by saying "I'm not here to tell you what to do. I'm sure you have plenty of people who tell you what to do." Jenny visibly relaxed with this disavowal of the "righting" reflex.

Then Nicole asked, "If you had to tell me between 1 and 10, what's your willingness to stop using?"

"Oh no, no," Jenny said, as even 0 seemed to be too much. "I'm going to keep using. I can't stop."

"Okay," Nicole said. She knew that telling Jenny, "Here's what's going to happen to your brain and your life if you keep smoking so much pot," wouldn't work at all. As Nicole told us, "She'd either say, 'No, that might happen to other people's brains, but not mine.' Or she'd say, 'Okay, maybe, but I don't care.'"

Instead, they talked for a while about Jenny's life and her pot usage, and why she liked smoking so much. She liked how it made her relax and that it made it easier to talk to people she felt nervous around. There were a lot of benefits to pot in Jenny's book, and each time she explained one, Nicole didn't try to talk her out of it. She just nodded and reflected back what Jenny said, showing her she heard her, without passing judgment. She kept asking more open-ended questions, listening for "change" language. At one point, when Jenny was seemingly done singing pot's virtues, she said, "It is getting kind of expensive, though."

"Oh?" Nicole asked. This was the change language she'd been waiting for. "Let's say you weren't spending so much money on it. What would you spend that money on?"

Jenny became animated. "I could get my hair done. I could get these cool shoes."

"What might happen if you decided you would buy weed only once a week instead of twice? Would that leave you with enough money to get your hair done?" Jenny just shrugged, and Nicole left it alone.

At their next meeting Jenny said, "Look, Ms. Brady! I got my nails done."

Nicole asked her how she'd managed to pay for it, and Jenny said she'd bought weed only once that week.

"Cool," Nicole said. "How did that feel for you, to get your nails done?"

"I loved it!"

Nicole had discovered Jenny's currency, something that motivated her as much as pot.

Jenny met with Nicole regularly, and little by little, Jenny started using less. Nicole started charting Jenny's grades with her; she didn't pass judgment on what the grades were, she just suggested they write everything down. While Jenny had always been convinced that her pot usage didn't affect her performance in school, she could see for herself quite clearly that her grades improved when her usage went down, and she really did care about her grades. Like all kids, she wanted her life to work out.

Clearly, it's much harder for parents to have this kind of calm, non-judgmental discussion with a child who they suspect is using drugs, in part because most kids who are using lie about it when confronted, and because some parents are so anxious that it's hard to remember to listen. There are also teens whose drug use is impairing enough to warrant treatment, even if it's against their will. If parents are concerned about their child's possible drug use, we strongly recommend consulting with a pediatrician or an expert in teen substance use. However, if parents find drugs or paraphernalia, or otherwise suspect use, starting out a conversation about it in a calm, inquisitive, nonjudgmental way—using tools from MI—can work better than angry confrontation and accusation. When parents try to understand their child's experience, rather than leaping to judgment, it usually leads to a closer relationship and greater influence.

Learning to Stop Accommodations— and Handle the Backlash

We need to talk about anxiety for a minute, both because it's so highly prevalent in kids, and because how we handle an anxious kid has much to teach us about changing behavior. Anxious kids are usually ambivalent about becoming less anxious because to do so means they have to face their fears.

Even before the coronavirus pandemic, studies concluded that approximately one-third of teenagers between thirteen and eighteen would develop an anxiety disorder at some point during adolescence. Stop for a second to really take that in—*one-third*! We also know that 80 percent of the kids with high anxiety will never get help.[3]

A lot of anxious kids don't want to have anything to do with therapy. The parents can see that their child is suffering, but the child doesn't want to deal with it—either because they're not motivated to change or because they're too anxious to participate in an activity that will require them face their fears. Even if a kid goes to therapy, they often won't do the "homework" required to make progress. Many a parent has turned to accommodating their kids because they simply don't know what else they can do.

In many ways, evolutionary forces aren't kind to parents. When our children are young, it's in our wiring to protect them and to soothe them when they're upset. And it's in our children's wiring to look to us when they're upset. We wake when they cry, and we fuss about whether they're too hot or too cold. New parents are likened to fierce bears when something looks like it will harm their child. We would not have survived as a species if we didn't have these instincts. But then as kids get older, we have to wrestle with these impulses. We have to be sure that our instinct to protect and to soothe does not turn into what psychologists call accommodation.

Accommodations are the things you do to prevent your kid from getting upset, or to calm them down when they are upset, and they come in two shapes: *active participation* in anxiety symptoms, and *modification* of family routines. The most common form of active participation is answering the same questions over and over to reassure anxious kids (we know a parent who had to tell her child every single night that there were no chickens around!) or sleeping next to a child with separation anxiety. Modifications might look like maintaining a rigid schedule, accompanying a child so they never have to be alone in a room at home, or avoiding a certain street where a dog-phobic child once saw a dog. Research suggests that 95 to 100 percent of parents make accommodations to their children's anxiety, which is how anxiety becomes a systemic problem—

by which we mean, the whole family seems trapped in a pattern that isn't serving any of them.[4] Accommodating lowers parents' stress by increasing their sense of control. It can also enable them to get a full night's sleep (in the case of kids who are afraid of sleeping in their own bed), and it lowers the emotional wear and tear on the household. Accommodating also makes anxious kids feel better in the short run, but it reinforces their avoidance.

A program called SPACE (Supportive Parenting for Anxious Childhood Emotions), created by Eli Lebowitz of the Yale University Child Study Center, holds a lot of promise for parents.[5] SPACE has been shown to be just as effective in decreasing children's anxiety as cognitive behavioral therapy (CBT), and it's aimed exclusively at *parents*, not kids.[6] The tools it teaches are based on the premise that "we simply can't make someone different unless they ask us to help them change." If you try to change someone's behavior without their wanting to change, all you're doing is escalating conflict. What parents can do (surprise, surprise!) is change their responses to a child's anxiety.

The SPACE program has two main goals. The first is to increase parents' ability to demonstrate acceptance of their anxious child through the use of supportive statements that combine (a) an expression of empathy and validation and (b) communication of confidence that the child can handle their challenges. Supportive statements could include, "I know that this is really scary, but I'm 100 percent confident that you can handle it," or "I know that this is hard for you, and I know that you have the ability to manage hard stuff." The second is to decrease accommodations.

SPACE asks parents to practice making supportive statements before making any change in accommodations. It then asks them to identify the various ways they are accommodating their child's anxiety and, over time, to decide which accommodations to stop. Once a plan is developed for discontinuing an accommodation, the parents inform the child of the plan by reading a written statement, ideally at a time when parent and child are reasonably calm. Parents may, for instance, inform their anxious daughter that they will no longer be alerting her as to where they are in the house at all times. The written statement starts with empathy, explains how the specific accommodation has not been helpful, lets the child know how the parents will be changing their behavior, and expresses confidence in the child's ability to handle their anxious feelings. Importantly, the statement focuses on the ways in which the parents' behavior is going to change—and does not focus at all on changing the child.

The SPACE program also includes tools for helping parents manage stress and anxiety. The SPACE manual suggests that, as parents are learning tools for managing their own anxiety, they communicate messages like, "I didn't used to think that you could cope with anxiety. I would get very afraid for you, and I know that made you more afraid as well. Now I understand that you're stronger than I thought. I've become sure that you can cope. So now, when I feel afraid for you, I take a deep breath and that helps me to calm down. I tell myself that you're strong. I would like to help you use tools like that as well."[7] This is an area where it's okay to offer a reward, as it can often help if kids get some sort of reinforcement for working through their worries without your help. But primarily, your main focus is on your own behavior.

Not surprisingly, when parents begin to reduce the accommodations they've been making for months or years, the kids don't tend to take it very well. They can become extremely anxious, hysterical, and demanding—and even threatening, toward themselves or their parents. You have to stay strong in the face of this opposition, without escalating conflict or responding in kind. You can't shout, argue, or engage in power struggles. All you can do is hold your ground.

The SPACE program takes seriously how *hard* this is. It's emotional, it's counterintuitive, and it requires an intense amount of self-control. Parents need tools to help them "anchor" themselves when faced with their child's distress, so that they can in turn be an anchor for their child.

SPACE found that some of the best ways to do this come from nonviolent resistance (NVR)—an approach that Mahatma Gandhi used to bring the British empire to its knees in India, and that Martin Luther King, Jr., used to help increase racial equality in America. It may seem discordant at first—how is any of this relevant to an anxious kid?—but attitudes and strategies from NVR have been adapted to work with parents by Israeli psychologist Haim Omer, who initially used NVR in work with violent and self-destructive children.[8] These tools reduce the sense of helplessness that parents often feel when their kids' emotions are out of control.

Here's what it looks like:

When it's time to act—say, you need to go to your bedroom and want your child to stay in the living room (a frightening prospect for them)—you might say, "I'm going to go into the bedroom by myself. I'll come out in ten minutes and congratulate you on being so brave." Use a calm, even voice as you explain the plan.

As the child inevitably begins to resist (*Why is Mom doing this? She always lets me come with her!*), you might say, "I'm taking a deep breath. I'm telling myself you're strong. You might do that, too." Remember not to do the work for them. They need to experience going from not knowing how to cope to knowing. They need to create a neural pathway they can use again.

It's probably not hard to imagine what happens next. Your child freaks out. You're mad, because you have things to do and you don't have the time to watch your kid melt down. You probably just want to shout, "I'm ten feet away! Get over it!," slam the door behind you, and let them wail without your having to hear it. Or you may want to soothe them. Or you want to give in and let them come along. But using NVR, you don't do any of these things. You engage as minimally as possible. You restate calmly what you are doing and why (although only once! Less is more!), and you can remain present while they work through it. If the child becomes extremely upset or aggressive, however, it is usually best to go into your bedroom and let the child deal with their feelings. One of the important features of the SPACE program is the inclusion of supporters who can help the parents in their efforts to not accommodate the child. The supporters may support the child verbally ("I'm so proud of you"), for instance, or come over when the parents leave the house—and stay for a while with a child who has separation anxiety.

A scene in the film *Ray*, a biopic of the late, great Ray Charles, offers another great example. In this scene, a young Ray, who has just begun to cope with life as a blind child, trips over a rocking chair. He cries for his mother to help him. His mother stands just a few feet away, but she resists going to him, and watches him silently instead. After a few seconds, he sits up and begins to follow sounds he hears: a passing train and then a cricket in the house, which he tracks, picks up, and holds to his ear. He then says, "I can hear you, too, Mama"—and cautiously walks toward her, finds her, and hugs her, whereupon she starts weeping. When Ray asks why she's crying, she says, "Because I'm happy."[9]

Any parent would understand if Ray's mother went to him. He was little, he was scared, and he was clearly disadvantaged. But if his mother pitied him and rescued him so that he could avoid facing his fear of a dark world, she would have made him feel like an object of pity or a being in need of rescue. If she went to him each time he fell, he wouldn't learn all the incredible resources he actually had available to him. By standing there alongside him, but not interfering as he struggled to cope, she communicated confidence.

Changing our own behavior to help our children can be very challenging, and parents of anxious kids will usually need more support than can be offered here. Parents can start with Lebowitz's new book, *Breaking Free of Child Anxiety and OCD: A Scientifically Proven Program for Parents*. If more support is needed, they can seek out a psychotherapist who has been trained in the SPACE program. The SPACE website, spacetreatment.net, has a list of trained therapists in each state.

As Kids Get Older . . .

So far, we've talked a lot about helping younger kids face their fears. But what about older ones? What do SPACE and NVR look like when a "kid" is eighteen, twenty, or, as in the case of one of Bill's clients, twenty-three?

Bill had seen Charlie off and on since he was six. Charlie had ADHD but did pretty well in his teenage years in a highly structured boarding school. After high school, though, he really floundered. He made several failed attempts at taking college classes, and he quit or was fired from numerous jobs. When he came to see Bill as a failure-to-launch twenty-three-year-old, Charlie routinely got up at noon and played video games and smoked pot in his parents' basement until 4:00 a.m. Bill didn't have to work very hard to help Charlie get to "change talk." Charlie expressed great sadness and shame that he had experienced so much failure and was "doing nothing" with his life. Bill and Charlie talked through some changes Charlie wanted to make, though it would not be easy. Bill gave him names of therapists he might reach out to for help with his addictions, but Charlie didn't call them.

Bill also talked with Charlie's parents who, as you might guess, were exceedingly frustrated by—and fearful for—their son. They didn't want him living the life he was, but they didn't want to kick him out, either. They felt like they were all that stood between him and homelessness. Bill advised Charlie's parents to tell him that they supported any efforts he wanted to make to develop himself—but that he would not be allowed to freeload at home, because that would be the worst thing for him. Note that Bill would not have made this recommendation without making sure that Charlie had access to mental health support if he wanted it, nor without being confident that Charlie was not mentally ill, in which case he might well have ended up on the street.

Charlie's parents stopped the lecturing and scolding pattern they'd gotten into with him, changing the energy of the relationship. They also told him that he would have to move out if he wasn't engaged full time in some kind of employment, education, or volunteer work. This is a hard line for parents to take, and a hard line for young adults like Charlie to hear. Charlie understood, but he angrily challenged their timeline a few times, saying that if he couldn't stay longer, he'd end up on the street. Throughout all Charlie's pleas and protestations, throughout their own fear, his parents stayed strong. They asked themselves, "How can we stand by our own beliefs without attacking or giving up?" They didn't want to enable their son. They didn't want to attack him. And they didn't want to "save" him, because they knew that wouldn't help him at all. After Charlie's parents made themselves clear and held their line, Charlie called one of the addiction therapists that Bill had suggested weeks before.

Over a year later, Charlie's father told Bill he was cautiously optimistic. Charlie had started working with an addictions counselor and was able to give up pot and greatly restrict his time on video games. The counselor also supported Charlie in developing a healthy sleep-wake cycle. Charlie had completed more than a year of community college courses and was holding down a part-time job. Approximately two years later, Charlie's parents emailed Bill: "You won't believe this." They went on to explain that Charlie was in his last semester of college and completing a major in electrical engineering. They also reported that he was driving fifty miles each way to an engineering-related job, which he was performing successfully, and that he had a steady girlfriend who was crazy about him. Bill most recently heard from Charlie's parents a year after that, and they said that Charlie had finished his degree, had a very successful career as an engineer, and had recently gotten married. Although Charlie was still working to raise the low self-esteem he experienced due to so much failure as a young adult, they said he was an incredibly kind, motivated, and determined young man who was simply a joy to be around (after having driven his parents crazy for years!).

There are many reasons to feel encouraged about these very effective ways of changing the patterns we're in with our kids. But we also want to be clear that for kids—no matter their age—who suffer from extreme anxiety, professional help is critical. And if they refuse that professional help, while not ideal, there is still a silver lining: through programs like SPACE, parents can seek help for themselves—and help their child in the process.

Inside the Brain

The long-ago ad campaign "This is your brain. This is your brain on drugs" with the fried egg was pretty accurate. The short-term effects of drugs and alcohol include compromised cognition, slower processing speed, and impaired memory, coordination, and emotional functioning. The long-term effects of alcohol use by adolescents is even worse, as it has lasting effects on the adult brain. Research with rats suggests that heavy use of cannabis during adolescence also shapes the development of the adult brain in ways that impair later functioning.[10] For credibility purposes, though, it's important to be honest about the limits of our understanding about the long-term effects of alcohol and pot on the brain,[11] because we can't do studies where we assign some teenagers to a "heavy user" group and some to an "abstinence group." This can make it difficult to tell what's cause and what's effect.[12]

Research and plain common sense, though, show that the way we grow up emotionally—and develop high stress tolerance and resilience—is by feeling our feelings and dealing with them, and by successfully handling stressful situations.[13] Kids who smoke pot chronically and/or use alcohol to avoid feeling their feelings thus deprive themselves of the experiences that allow them to grow up emotionally.

While we could fill an entire book with information about drugs and the teenage brain, here are the five points we find most compelling:

1. Puberty makes the brain more "plastic" and thus more easily aroused by pleasurable stimuli—and the adolescent brain is more affected by stress hormones, drugs, and alcohol than the adult brain.[14] It's also more vulnerable to addiction, and the vast majority of addictions start in adolescence.[15] A strikingly high percentage of regular young pot users become highly dependent on marijuana and can't stop using, even if they want to.[16] (Fortunately, there is evidence that the young brain can recover from heavy pot use, at least to some extent. In a study of regular marijuana users age sixteen to twenty-five, those who stopped using for four weeks showed significant improvement in verbal memory, especially in the first week.[17])

2. Even short-term marijuana use is a problem. It can lead to school difficulties, due, in part, to problems with memory and concentration. The THC in pot alters the functioning of the hippocampus (the brain's major memory center) and impairs the ability to create memories. (Persistent use likely affects the important "sculpting" of the brain that occurs as adolescents shape their adult brain.) Pot also affects the functioning of the orbital prefrontal cortex, impairing students' ability to think, learn, and perform cognitive tasks. Furthermore, it disrupts brain systems that mediate balance, coordination, and reaction time, which can affect athletic performance and driving safety.[18] Persistent use is further associated with increased aggression, use of other drugs or alcohol, risky sexual behaviors, worsening of underlying mental health problems, and interference with prescribed medication.[19]

3. Many young people use marijuana to cope with anxiety, especially those with social anxiety disorder.[20] (Bill's teenage clients often tell him that they do better when they smoke pot, which usually means that they don't worry as much about all the things they aren't accomplishing.) While pot does offer short-term relief from anxiety in some young people, well-controlled studies show that its long-term use is connected with *increased* anxiety over time.[21]

4. Alcohol is simply terrible for the developing brain. Repeated exposure to alcohol in animal and human adolescents affects the development and functioning of the brain's white matter (which allows brain cells to communicate with each other), especially in the prefrontal cortex and circuits for emotional regulation.[22] Also, the earlier a person starts drinking, the greater the likelihood that they will develop a substance use disorder later in life.[23]

5. Bingeing is particularly brain-toxic, specifically the drying-out period that happens afterward. If you have five drinks over the course of the day, it may not be great for your liver, but it wouldn't affect your brain as much. And yet when given the chance, adolescents (including adolescent lab animals) consume more alcohol at one time than adults. Over 90 percent of the alcohol consumed by teens and young adults is in the form of binge drinking, which is defined as four drinks in a row for females in a two-hour period, and five for males.[24] Bottom line: They're at higher risk for using alcohol in the worst way.

Perhaps the best message that we can give kids about drugs and alcohol is that if they do choose to use, they should delay as long as they can.[25] Unfortunately, educational programs designed to help teenagers make better choices about drugs and alcohol haven't worked.[26] Knowing facts like the ones we've shared here doesn't actually decrease the biological drive for risk taking, novelty, and pleasure, and the desire to alleviate stress through substance use. In our experience, though, *parents* can be more effective at talking with their kids about drugs and alcohol, so long as they do so in a respectful way, offer themselves as resources, share the kind of information that's in this box, and encourage kids to talk to them or other trusted adults. Because so much of substance abuse is tied to stress, *how* adults talk to kids (serving as trusted advisers, not overly informed scolds) may be even more important than what they say.[27]

But What About . . . ?

Our twelve-year-old daughter is healthy, outgoing, and friendly. She is very smart and responsible, and her grades are good. But she won't try new things, especially if she thinks that she might not be good at them. She won't try out for sports, even ones she loves, and she won't be in a play if she has to audition for it. Is there a way we can help her develop the courage to take risks?

We'd initially approach this from the perspective of motivational interviewing. You could start by asking open-ended questions like, "How are you feeling about trying out for soccer this year?" Or "What kinds of things are you thinking about doing this summer?" Then use reflective listening to let her know you're trying to understand—and not judging her. As you ask questions and affirm, listen for talk that reflects any openness to change—or dissatisfaction with her current situation. If she does comment that she'd like to be in the school play, reflect back her feeling and ask a question like, "What would keep you from being in the school play?" If she talks about her fear of auditioning or anxiety about not knowing all the kids, you could ask questions like, "What would it be like for you if you were sure to get a part in the play or a place on the team? Would you want to try out?" or "Would you like to feel less worried about trying new things?" Affirm the fear behind her reluctance: "That would be really scary, to put yourself out there that way. What do you think would happen if you got rejected?" Remember to ask questions without endorsing a candidate for the win. Note that you are not providing answers to her fears. Rather, you are using MI to help her identify her motivation. First she needs motivation, then she'll find or create solutions to obstacles.

If she expresses a desire to be less anxious, consider using a book like Dr. Bonnie Zucker's *Anxiety-Free Kids* to help her face her fears, or offer the option of working with a therapist who specializes in the treatment of anxiety. If she is resistant, fair enough—just be sure you're not enabling her avoidance by accommodating her in any way. You can't and shouldn't force her to try out for anything. But do notice if her avoidance behavior crosses over into your family life in a way that you have inadvertently supported, and think about seeking out a therapist who is trained in the SPACE program.

If I have so much power by changing my steps, does this mean that my child's anxiety (or other problems) is my fault?

No, absolutely not. We're not interested in parents punishing themselves. Anyone who has more than one kid knows that kids are different, and some are more vulnerable than others. However, the way we respond to their anxiety affects how long the anxiety persists. While we are always in favor of apologizing to kids and of showing them our fallibility (a great life lesson), the most important thing to do is focus on changing your steps in the present.

All my eighth-grade son cares about are sports and being with his friends. He puts the absolute minimum effort into his schoolwork. He says he wants to play baseball on his high school team, but I'm afraid that he won't have the grades to play. How can I help him without being on him all the time?

Motivational interviewing is ideal for this scenario. Remember the elicit-provide-elicit framework. You can ask questions like, "Are you working as hard as you want to? How's this going for you?" Then provide information, by saying things like, "Let's look at the high school's rules on academic eligibility." Let him connect the dots himself, then say something like, "If there's any way I can support you, let me know." If his grades are such that he can't play, empathize with his disappointment (rather than saying "I told you so"). It will be tough to see his pain, but remember it's an important life lesson. You can offer to help him meet eligibility requirements for the next season, and keep engaging with elicit-provide-elicit conversations. If, however, he gets on the team and is still struggling, call the coach. Ask the coach to be the one who talks about academics with your son, instead of you.

Putting It All Together: Sample Dialogues

Zenobie was a good student throughout elementary and middle school, but when she started high school, her grades began to slip. Her parents didn't want to get too involved, but they watched the pattern nervously. They noticed that Zenobie complained a lot about her teachers—especially her science teacher—and dashed off her assignments instead of putting any real effort into them. *What happened?* her parents wondered. *She used to care about her grades, now she just refuses when it comes to doing anything she doesn't want to.* They ruled out the two most common causes of a rapid decline in motivation: (1) she wasn't using pot or other drugs (she was the kind of kid who wouldn't even have a sip of caffeine) and (2) she didn't appear to be depressed. So what was going on with her?

The more Zenobie's parents queried her about her schoolwork, the more defensive she got. She insisted that Cs were an average grade, so all it meant was that she was an average student, which was fine with her. Her parents knew they shouldn't make it about character, but they also knew how capable their daughter was, and it drove them crazy that she wasn't applying herself. Their arguments involved a lot of phrases like "lazy," "lack of effort," and, from Zenobie's perspective, "overly controlling."

Then Zenobie's dad tried changing his steps in the dance. "I really want to change the dynamic between us when it comes to your schoolwork," he said. "Your grades aren't nearly as important to us as you are. Let's not fight about this anymore."

"Sounds good to me," Zenobie said.

"Despite what it might seem like," he added, "we really don't care very much about your grades. What we care about is that you're learning what kind of life you want. And that you're learning how to get yourself to do the things you need to do to get that life."

"That sounds like you're saying I need to buckle down and study."

"No, that's not it. Being a B or a C student will not doom you in life, or mean that you can't get a higher education if you want it."

"Yeah, right."

"No, really," he insisted. "If you're happy with Bs and Cs, then you're happy with them. But I've never really asked you how you feel about them."

"Are you asking if I'm happy with Bs and Cs? I mean, I guess. I'm happy enough. I can't get As, so what's the point of this?"

"That would be frustrating, to feel like you wanted to get As but couldn't. That would suck."

"Yeah, it does."

"Do you know what keeps you from getting As? And remember, honey, it's not a problem for me. I'm just curious."

The conversation veered to talking about Zenobie's teachers, some of whom she really couldn't stand. She just couldn't feel motivated to work hard for her science teacher because she disliked him so much. Her dad expressed empathy, and they went on to talk about reasons she might work hard on science that had nothing to do with her teacher. Then Zenobie talked about how she had fallen behind in history, and trying to catch up would be too hard. Her dad again expressed empathy. He kept asking questions to get her to explore how she'd feel if she did push through and got caught up, why that effort might be worth it, and why it might not be. Zenobie didn't become an A student that semester. But she felt safer talking to her parents about how school was hard, and they helped her figure out how to make it better.

Teddy was an anxious nine-year-old boy who had shared a room with his twelve-year-old brother for most of his life. When his family moved to a new house, Teddy and his brother got their own rooms. Although Teddy's older brother loved his new privacy, Teddy felt frightened lying in his bedroom alone and found it very hard to sleep by himself. His parents wanted to be sure he got a good night's sleep, and so they agreed to sit in his room until he fell asleep for the first few nights, thinking that, once he got used to the new house, he would feel comfortable sleeping on his own. When Teddy was in bed, they assured him that there was nothing to be afraid of, as they would just be downstairs or in the next room, but it didn't seem to help. They also tried to encourage him by pointing out that a lot of nine-year-olds can fall asleep on their own. This didn't seem to help much, either. They then worked with Teddy to try to find something that could help him feel less afraid. He tried listening to music and audiobooks, mindful breathing, and a guided meditation, and he even tried counting the stars on his ceiling made by a cool night light. But while these strategies work great for many kids and seemed to help Teddy feel calmer, he still panicked when his parents tried to leave the room and insisted that he couldn't fall asleep without them.

They continued sitting in Teddy's room until he fell asleep, even though his nighttime anxiety got worse rather than better. They recognized this new normal was a big problem, because they didn't feel they could get a babysitter and spend an evening out. They missed their freedom and worried about Teddy's growing fears.

Fortunately, Teddy's mom read that sometimes children's biggest fear is about their ability to handle their own anxiety, which seemed like it may be true for Teddy. So one day when Teddy was playing in his room, his parents joined him to talk.

Mom: "We know you're really scared about falling asleep on your own. A lot of kids your age have that same fear. And still, we think it will be good for you to be able to sleep on your own. And we realize that sitting in your room with you hasn't made your anxiety better—in fact, it seems to have made it worse. So, starting this weekend, we aren't going to be sitting in your room while you fall asleep. We're happy to check in with you every half hour until you're asleep—but not to stay with you. We know you're strong, and we have 100 percent confidence that you can make it through the night without us."

Teddy: "But I can't do that! I need you or daddy to be able to fall asleep!"

Mom: "We know it feels that way now, and we can work on this together."

At this point, Teddy and his parents worked on a plan with him where he could sleep outside their open door—and then go into his own room later in the night if he wanted to.

The first night did not go well. Teddy cried and shouted that he wouldn't be able to sleep. Several times he went downstairs to where his parents were watching TV, insisting that they sit with him while he fell asleep.

Mom: "Teddy, I used to be afraid of your worries, too, but I'm not anymore because I know you can handle a lot more than you think you can. So, Daddy and I are going to continue watching our show. We'll check on you every thirty minutes like we agreed."

Teddy continued to plead, but his parents worked to stay calm so that they could help him see that they could handle his anxiety. Still, he refused to go to sleep until his parents went to bed, but he eventually did fall asleep in the hallway outside their door, which is where they found him in the morning.

The same thing happened the next night, although Teddy's cries and pleas were less impassioned. His parents checked on him every half hour, but he still waited until they went to bed before falling asleep in the hall.

Teddy was tired the next couple of days—they all were. But his parents told him they were proud of him, that he made it through the night because he is brave. They told him he could sleep outside their door as long as he needed to. After a week of sleeping on the floor outside their room, Teddy fell asleep in his own bed for the first time, apparently after recognizing that his bed was more comfortable! His parents noticed that he was turning on the night light—and maybe counting the stars—and that he seemed to be learning that he could manage his own worries and fears.

Remember What It's All About

If you are struggling with a child who is anxious, or who is floundering and does not seem willing to change, we know how awful it feels. As we've said, few things are more stressful than seeing someone you love struggle and not having a sense that you can do anything about it. Take solace in the idea that you *can* do something, just not what you thought. Remember that what we *don't* do for our kids can be as powerful as what we *do* do for them.

There is power in silence, and in listening. There is power in not getting stuck in a repetitive loop with our kids, so that they have the freedom to make a change for themselves. Think about the power of being silent and strong, the power of communicating: *I'm not going anywhere, and I'm not going to fight about this anymore.*

Chapter 6

"What if I don't want to live up to my potential?": Communicating Healthy Expectations

"They tell him what to do without asking him what he wants, and so there's nothing at all he really does want."

—*Tove Jansson*, The Summer Book

Years ago, Ned tutored a young woman named Mimi who, at seventeen, was completely stressed-out by her life and everything she felt she needed to do in a day. Her parents, she said, expected her to get straight As, earn high scores on standardized tests, and make sure she had plenty of extracurriculars on her résumé for college. She believed that her teachers, too, expected this of her. Trying to break through a little, to get to know what made her tick, Ned asked her what she was interested in.

She thought about it for a minute, then said, "You know what? I have no idea."

"None at all?" Ned pressed.

"I haven't thought about it," she said with a shrug. "I'm too busy trying to meet the expectations everyone else has of me." It brings to mind a favorite cartoon of ours (as you can tell, we're serious fans of funnies). In it, two parents begin a sit-down with their teenage daughter by saying, "We've been thinking a lot about what we want to do with your life."

"Well," Ned told Mimi, "I'm not trying to add to your to-do list, but *your* interests may be something you just might want to think about."

A few weeks later, he learned there was a big fashion show coming up at school, and Mimi was participating. Mimi and several other students had designed and sewn outfits and were modeling them for the big show. Ned attended and ended up sitting right behind Mimi's mother. The whole time that Mimi's designs were being displayed, her mother was nose down on her phone. Ned wondered if Mimi's interest in fashion had ever been noticed, let alone celebrated, at home.

Mimi found her own way to a more authentic life, but it took some time. After a year or so at a college that hadn't been her first choice, she transferred to a fashion school and ended up studying the business of fashion. Her interest had been there all along—but no one, including Mimi herself, had really listened. The cacophony of expectations was just too loud.

In this chapter we ask, what does it mean to say that we have expectations for our children? And what does it mean when a child says, "My parents have such high expectations for me"? Does this mean that their parents have *confidence* in their ability to meet *the parents'* goals—or *their own* goals? Does this mean that parents believe their child *can* do well—or that they insist that the child *must* do well? Does it mean that parents always know what's right or best for kids? If so, at what age does this stop? We ask, in part, because it so often turns out that what parents expect from their children is ultimately not what the children want for themselves.

Two Kinds of Expectations: A Tale of Two Sweatshirts

In his book *A Hope in the Unseen*, Pulitzer Prize–winning journalist Ron Suskind described a mother in a very low-income community who bought her son a Harvard sweatshirt as a symbol of her hope for—and confidence in—him. This act was celebrated for emphasizing what he was capable of, and for fighting stereotypes or assumptions that might have held him back. In a different environment, though, a similar move can be toxic. We recently visited an independent school in the Southwest where elementary- and middle-school-aged children were encouraged to wear sweatshirts from the colleges they hoped to attend. The school counselors were rightly concerned about the mental health consequences for many of the kids wearing the sweatshirts of Yale or Stanford (where their parents had been students) who, most likely, will not be able to get in. Simply put, expectations can be healthy or they can be toxic. Our challenge as parents and teachers is to recognize, hold, and communicate the healthy ones.

The mom who bought the Harvard sweatshirt was communicating a healthy expectation, and there are reams of research on the power of expectations like hers.[1] Studies have found that the extent to which parents regularly communicate high academic expectations for their children ("You can do well" not "you must do well") had a *far* greater effect on the kids' academic performance than any other parental behavior, including how strictly parents supervised their children's free time or monitored their homework. As to the why of all this, look no further than the placebo effect, where research consistently finds that belief or expectations play a powerful role in physical and emotional healing.[2] More positive news: research shows that the under-fourteen crowd responds more to placebos than adults do—they are more likely to report reduced pain, for instance, after using a placebo cream.[3]

The most well-known research on the power of adult expectations on kids has involved studies of teachers' expectations—one of which led to the discovery of the Rosenthal effect or Pygmalion effect, wherein it was shown that students performed better when teachers held higher expectations of them. Though conducted in the 1960s, the studies have implications that still reverberate. When we interview parents of color, one of their primary concerns is that their kids' teachers may be biased about what their kids can do. In the words of one parent, "I have a problem with my kid's teacher being okay with Bs if my kid could, with encouragement, get As." We get that, and it's why we recommend that teachers operate with a set of two assumptions in mind about all their students: (1) that they're currently doing the best they can, *and* (2) that they can get even better.

The implications of the Rosenthal effect are hugely helpful for Ned, whose work is to help students raise test scores. One of Ned's favorite kids was an eleventh grader at a highly selective school. Although she was a good student, her sister was an academic rock star, and this girl perceived that her friends, like her sister, were all much more academically capable than she was. At one point in her work, she got a math problem right that was particularly tough, not just for her but for everyone. Casually, Ned muttered, "That was pretty geeky."

"What?" she asked, head snapping up from her work.

"Well, it's just that most people don't get that right. I guess you're a closet geek."

The corners of her mouth curled up in a tentative smile, and she put her head back down, working hard (maybe harder) on the next questions in her assignment.

After she graduated, she sent Ned a handwritten note, letting him know how much she was enjoying college, and expressing gratitude "for making me a geek." In actuality, she made *herself* a geek through her hard work. But Ned's casually dropped comment communicated his positive expectations of her.

The Rosenthal effect is trickier for Bill, whose work is to accurately reflect how kids perform on a series of tests that measure cognitive and academic abilities. Bill knows that if he inflated their scores, the kids would have higher expectations of themselves going forward and would therefore probably *do* better . . . So ever since he learned about the Rosenthal effect in graduate school, he's had to resist that urge. What he does do, however, when he wants kids to give their full effort on difficult test items, is say, "I'm almost positive that you can get this if you stick with it." And no surprise, it works.

But here's where the plot thickens: he says the *opposite* when kids seem to be reluctant to try the harder test items because they're afraid of failure. He'll say, "The items you're working on now are actually for older kids. You've already done the ones for kids your own age. I don't expect you to get these, but you've earned the right to try them, and I'd love to see you give them a shot." After hearing this message, 100 percent of Bill's clients give enormous effort to solve problems they are not expected to solve. Ned uses this approach, too, when he works with students who are particularly fearful of failure. That's why he's often referred to as a test prep therapist, rather than a tutor.

On the surface, it seems that statements like these communicate low expectations, right? But actually what they do is lessen the feeling of threat. We've known for over thirty years that the best learning environment for kids is one of high challenge, but low threat. This means that kids learn, and perform, best when they feel challenged (and not bored), and when parents and teachers express confidence in their abilities—but when it's safe to make mistakes, to not understand at first, or to struggle a bit.[4] When kids are fearful, the main task is to take that threat away. Communicate confidence, but not rigid requirements for performance or achievement. Emphasize both "I believe in you" and "you're safe—you'll be okay no matter how you do."

Well-meaning parents unwittingly stumble with this issue all the time. For instance, in a study of German—and later American—secondary students and their parents, parents were asked, "How much do you want your kids to get good grades?" They were also asked, "How confident are you that your child can achieve good grades?" When aspirations exceeded expectations, kids' achievement declined proportionally. The price of excessive expectations can be worse performance, but, as we mentioned in Chapter 1, it can also be much more serious, as students who grow up with excessive performance expectations are at strikingly high risk for mental health problems in adolescence and young adulthood.[5] So a first step, as a parent or a teacher, is to figure out where the kid *is*. Are they feeling expectations that aren't there? Are they feeling fearful of failure? The best way to get to these answers is simple: ask them.

The Language of Healthy Expectations

"When I was a little girl," said Kirsten Beeksma, who graduated from the University of Washington and now has three kids of her own, "my dad would always say things like 'I love how your mind works, honey, and how you can figure anything out' and 'Your brain is always working so cleverly' and 'You are such a deep thinker.' And I always felt like he thought I was smart and capable of anything. I struggled at times in high school and only graduated with a 3.4, but I always felt like I was smart. And in college I started to notice trends of difficulty, but again I never took it personally and graduated with a 3.5. But at forty years old I found out I was dyslexic. When I was diagnosed, I was asked about my feelings around school growing up. I said, 'I always loved school and felt like I could do anything, even though school wasn't easy, and my grades never really reflected how capable I thought I was.' The doctor who gave me the diagnosis said my feelings were nearly unheard of in cases like mine. Most undiagnosed dyslexics report feeling dumb and hating school and don't tend to finish college. And that's when I realized that my dad's belief in me was stronger than any test result or report card I received. His belief in me carried me when I needed it most."

When parents, coaches, and teachers use language like, "I want to see you get those Bs up to As," "If you'd only work a little harder, you could have gotten an A," and "You'll never be a starter, because you just don't work that hard," they are communicating toxic expectations. There is a sense of threat inherent in the language. But more subtly, even when parents communicate "I believe in you," that belief has to be realistic. I believe in you to what? Become a Supreme Court justice? Or live up to your potential? Both are problematic.

Case in point: Pippa is a brilliant girl with a history of ADHD, anxiety, and obsessive tendencies. When Bill tested Pippa most recently, she was an eleventh-grade student in an elite boarding school. At one point during a clinical interview, Pippa confided to Bill that she felt like a failure because she was struggling to earn Bs despite the fact that her verbal-intellectual ability is above the 99th percentile. She reported that she torments herself because she knows she is not living up to what she has been told is her extraordinary potential—and thus to the expectations of her parents and teachers. In response, Bill said to Pippa, "Screw your potential." (Actually, he used another profanity instead of *screw*, which, coming from Bill, gets attention.)

"Being as bright as you are is cool, in part because it allows you to do many things very well," he said. "As you figure out how you want to use your talents, you're going to be able to do something interesting and rewarding for a living. However, your talent will be of no use if you feel that you have to wear it like a hundred-pound weight."

"People know I'm smart and anything less than an A is like a failure to them," she said.

Bill asked, "Do you feel that way, too?"

Pippa answered, "All the time."

"You're going to be eighteen in five months," Bill pointed out. "Do you think that, once you're an adult, it would be okay for you to focus more on what you want for yourself—instead of how you're letting other people down?"

"Yes."

"Would it make sense to start now?" Bill asked. "I'd like you to think about two questions: 'How can I use my strengths to do good in this world?' And 'If I'm on this planet for a purpose, what might my purpose be?' It's possible that your purpose doesn't require you to use all 147 of your IQ points at all times."

We see kids like Pippa all the time, whose parents worry that if they're not pushed constantly they won't reach their potential. The idea behind this worry is that if someone does well on tests of ability, it would be a tragedy if they became a teacher rather than a physician. We believe this type of thinking largely underlies the drive to have kids busy all the time during the school year and to make sure they're doing something productive in the summer. While we want kids to have enough going on in their lives that they're not bored or getting into trouble, we don't want them to live in fear of not living up to their potential. And anyway, kids maximize that potential by creating a life they *want*. We also want to make sure that any pressure put on our kid—to stay at a particular school, or not to quit a certain sport—isn't actually about us, and the communities we've become invested in.

Parents can set the tone for healthy expectations in a multitude of ways:

- "I love you no matter what."

- "There's always a Plan B. Nothing is absolutely necessary for you to have a successful life."

- "All I want is for you to develop yourself so that you can provide useful service to this world."

- "I have confidence that you can handle the challenges in your life [rather than "I have confidence you will always be successful"]."

- "I don't have a script for your life, because I don't know who you're going to want to be as an adult."

- "When I say that I expect you to do well, what I really mean is that I think you can do well and that I'm confident in you as a student—and as a person."

- "I think about the big picture. The world is full of successful people who weren't top students. So if you're not an academic superstar, it doesn't bother me. I know you're smart enough to get an education and learn skills that are helpful to people."

- "You're a great kid whether you work hard in school or not."

- "I'm looking forward to seeing who you decide to become."

You might be rolling your eyes as you read this. *My kid isn't pushing himself at all*, you might be thinking. *So I'm just supposed to tell him, no big deal?* We get that this advice seems like a record-scratch moment. But naturally, we have a few rebuttals.

If you're pushing your kid, is it working?

Also, do your efforts emphasize the unconditional love most parents say they want to convey above all else?

Bear in mind, we're not suggesting that whatever your kid says goes, and that unconditional love means that you accommodate his lack of effort. Stop paying for his car insurance if he's not doing his part to earn that privilege. Don't pay for a private school if he's not expending any effort to do well there. But you can set these boundaries and also convey, "I love you, and I think you're a great kid."

Finally, our advice is predicated on an assumption that all kids want their lives to work out. They want to be successful. They want to be happy. Without fully buying in to this belief, you might think that our advice doesn't make sense. If you're struggling with it, go back and read Chapter 2. Then read it again.

A Rule of Thumb: Take Your Thumb Out of It Completely

In the last chapter, we talked about the importance of pulling back when kids are working through their ambivalence. The same is true when it comes to expectations. The best way to ensure the healthy kind of expectations is to encourage kids to set *their own* expectations of themselves— without being burdened by crippling perfectionism, fear of failure, and fear of disappointing other people.

A large part of this work includes encouraging them to set their own goals. Goal-setting is not as simple as their announcing, "I want to make the varsity basketball team," or "I want to star in the next school musical," or "I want to get a 3.6 GPA this year." These are perfectly fine long-term goals, but to achieve them, we need smaller, but readily attainable goals. We should teach them about what are called SMART goals— goals that are Specific, Measurable, Attainable, Realistic, and Time-Bound. Making the varsity basketball team might not be attainable. But it might be attainable to make four out of five free throw shots five days in a row. It might not be realistic to get a 3.6 GPA if they are starting with a 2.0. But it might be realistic to commit to doing homework for an hour a night for four weeks.

There's an important prerequisite to setting goals, though: the child's belief that they can attain whatever goal they set. Support goal-setting by encouraging positive self-talk—which is an important tool of cognitive behavioral therapy—or verbal affirmations, which has been a staple of self-help psychology for almost a century.

For Gen Xers, this advice might bring to mind the character Stuart Smalley. Anyone who watched *Saturday Night Live* in the 1990s will remember Smalley, played by comedian and former senator Al Franken. Smalley was a self-help guru with no official training, whose most memorable line was "I'm good enough, I'm smart enough, and doggone it, people like me!" Throughout his appearances, Franken poked fun at a self-help industry rife with psychobabble. We were big fans of the sketch—Franken is hilarious, and some of his satire hit the nail right on the head.

And yet.

It turns out, just because self-talk like this is easy to make fun of doesn't mean it's not helpful. We all have a basic need to feel competent— remember, this is part of the three-legged stool of self-determination theory we talked about in Chapter 4. We've focused so much in this book on the two other legs—the needs for autonomy and relatedness— but the stool will still collapse if due focus is not paid to the need for a sense of competency. When a kid's need for competency is threatened— such as when they suffer a disappointment, or get into an argument, or are a victim of bullying—their natural tendency is to feel defensive. Self-protection kicks in, and they're not likely to react in ways that are particularly useful or to set healthy goals. Kids and teens are particularly prone to hyperbolic spirals of "I'll never [fill in the blank]." Positive self-talk provides kids a buffer to these negative responses. A good self-talk practice reduces defensiveness, like the inclination to blame others, and offers a layer of soft cotton between kids and the threat. It includes phrases you can share with your kid, like:

- "I'm good at a lot of different things."

- "I can handle this."

- "I can be successful if I apply myself."

- "I have some good ideas that are worth sharing."

- "I don't have to be the best, but I'm good enough."

- "Good things come my way."

- "I expect myself to be successful this semester."

Research shows these phrases work even better when you talk to yourself using the third person: "Bill, you can handle this!" or "Ned, you can be successful if you apply yourself."[6]

You can also talk with kids about training their brains to expect success. Early in his career, Bill left a job at a university hospital on poor terms. He started his own clinical practice right afterward—a risky venture at a time when his self-confidence had taken a bit of a beating. He didn't know if he could be successful in private practice or not, but he wanted to convince his brain to expect that he could be. So he combined his interest in the psychology of achievement with what he knew about the brain, and he wrote a list of everything he'd been successful at going back to first grade. Seriously—first grade! (Bill was an excellent first grader, you should know.) The list built his confidence, and he was able to set high expectations for himself and the future of his practice. The same technique works with kids. When Bill did therapy, he'd ask kids if they'd like to see themselves as more competent and train their brains to expect them to do well. If they said yes, he'd ask them to write down everything they could think of since they were little that they did well or got positive feedback about. He'd enlist the parents to help fill in things the kid had forgotten, and he'd ask the kid to review the list regularly. Often this simple exercise was all it took to help a kid move in a more positive direction.

We want kids to feel competent, but we also want them to know that they are more than their competence. This is where something called *self-affirmation theory* comes in—it builds on positive self-talk, but puts the emphasis on values.[7] So, for instance, when you write down a few sentences about one of your highest values (honesty, family, service, spirituality, friendship, loyalty) before going in to take a test or do something that feels threatening, the practice improves your performance because it keeps your amygdala at bay and the prefrontal cortex in the driver's seat.[8] You're not as afraid of failure because you know you are so much more than how you do on a test. So when you ask kids questions like, "What would your friends say are the best things about you?" or "What are some of the qualities you most like about yourself?," you are encouraging self-affirmation that helps put setbacks in context and provides kids with some distance. As a result, they're less likely to ruminate about past failures and are more open to setting healthy expectations for themselves.[9]

Modeling Expectations

William H. Jeynes, who has studied parental expectations for decades, says that the healthiest expectations don't come via edicts nor are they voiced as demands like, "You'd better make the cross-country team next year, because you're going to need it for college applications!" Healthy expectations are more often unspoken and communicated by modeling a strong work ethic, a strong faith in the future, and "a pleasantly steadfast spirit."[10]

One of the best ways parents can communicate the healthy kind of expectations is by verbalizing how they walk the line between healthy and toxic themselves. Reminisce, tell stories of expectations your own parents had (or still have!) of you, and how you dealt with them. Or perhaps you share a goal you've set for yourself, something that's important to you, and how you are pushing yourself to meet that goal. If you model a commitment to service or to helping family members or friends when they are in need, you are showing your kids the expectations you have for how you want to show up in the world.

Mastermind groups—a group of people who share goals, problem-solve, and hold one another accountable—are already popular with business groups and entrepreneurs.[11] They work for families, too. Families can meet each week to share goals they've set for themselves around their health, or school, or work. Even if your family's group lasts for only a few months, it's okay—even a little bit helps kids see that the entire family is goal-directed, and supportive of one another setting their own goals.

If you make a mistake, telling your kids about it, and asking for their advice, normalizes mistakes and guards against perfectionism. Practice using positive self-talk when you're speaking about yourself or other people. "I've got a presentation today," you might say; "I'm pretty well prepared, so I think it should go well." Or "I can do the work necessary to learn this piece on the piano."

When Kids' Expectations of Themselves Are Too High: The Problem of Perfectionism

After weeks of hard work and lots of practice, Ned's student Alice got her SAT scores: 1590 out of a possible 1600. She burst into tears, though not tears of joy. She had made a huge jump in her scores, one that most could only dream of and that positioned her for every one of the most selective colleges she had in mind. Ned looked at her, incredulous, and finally said, "You're an addict."

"What do you mean?"

"You've had, like, 437 consecutive As, and if you got a C, you'd burst into tears."

She stopped, thought, and then burst out, with all the fury her slight frame could muster, "I would NEVER get a C!"

When Ned shares that story with other kids, they laugh. But Alice's rebuttal wasn't delivered with swagger, or confidence, or to imply, "Please, Tutor Boy, you have NO idea who you are dealing with." Rather, her tone was pretty close to abject fear. So Ned told her, "Successful people work hard and have high goals, but sometimes fall short, and that's part of the process and has to be okay. Sometimes things are out of their control."

"What do you mean?"

"Imagine you were on your way to school and got stuck in a terrible traffic jam and showed up late for a test. Your teacher, unsympathetic, will only allow you the half of the class period that remains, and you can only finish two-thirds of the test."

"I would have left earlier," Alice insisted.

"What if you got a flat tire? Or a tree fell in front of you?"

"I'd back up and go around!"

"Okay"—Ned could see she'd be a tough one—"let's say a tree falls in front and then behind you. It's, like, a tree conspiracy."

She sat there, mind reeling. Just the thought of that lack of control was paralyzing, and yet it was something likely to come up again and again in her life. Not the tree conspiracy, but the lack of control.

Ned gently stated again his confidence in her abilities and commended her commitment to excellence, but suggested she try on a different perspective, one that didn't require so much fear. There's a difference, he explained, between striving for excellence (good) and feeling you can't make mistakes (bad). Excellence seekers adapt well when things do not turn out as planned and adjustments need to be made. Most successful people set very high standards for themselves, and they do not need the excessive fear that motivates perfectionists.[12]

In contrast, perfectionists strive for perfection to avoid negative judgment and appearing flawed to others. They feel that they have to be right every time and that they cannot make mistakes. Children and teens with maladaptive, obsessive perfectionism feel crushed if they get a 98 on a test, do everything they can to avoid or cover up mistakes, and are hyperalert to signs that they are not the best. Perfectionism often comes with other signs of mental inflexibility, like concern about orderliness, rule following, fastidiousness, and hypercriticality. Perfectionism in older adolescents and young adults has increased significantly since the 1980s. Recent generations are more demanding of themselves, have more excessive expectations of others, and perceive that others are more demanding of them.

This is worrisome, as perfectionism is related to numerous psychological disorders, including anxiety, depression, obsessive-compulsive disorder, and anorexia.[13]

As Brené Brown has pointed out, perfectionism is not self-improvement, it's about trying to gain approval and avoid negative judgment. She notes that children who are praised for their achievement and performance adopt a belief that "I am what I accomplish and how well I accomplish." The formula for these children is, "Please. Perform. Perfect."[14]

Alice certainly fit Brené Brown's description, and she was convinced her well-meaning if clueless tutor just didn't get it. After the debacle of the not-perfect SAT, Ned didn't see Alice until a few years later, when he ran into her at the grocery store. She was home from her sophomore year in college and reported that things were going really well. "And," she volunteered, "I thought you might like to know that I finally learned how to relax."

"That's fantastic," Ned replied. "How?"

"Pot."

Oh heaven help us. To be clear, this is *not* the outcome Ned wanted for Alice. Rather than self-medicating during a time when her brilliant brain was still developing, Ned would much rather have seen her address her perfectionism head on.

One of the cruel ironies of perfectionism is that it actually holds people back. Pot usage made this clear with Alice, but drugs aren't the only culprit. In school and in the workplace, excellence seekers outperform individuals with a rigid perfectionism. They're happier, and they enjoy the process of working hard to perform well, whereas perfectionists' obsession with mistakes often causes them to procrastinate, to expend too much time trying to achieve perfection, and to avoid challenges due to fear of failure. They also try to hide their mistakes, which keeps them from getting the constructive feedback they need to grow and improve.

It's tricky to root out the causes of perfectionism in kids. Research suggests there's a genetic component, which makes sense, because there's a genetic component to virtually everything about us. Perfectionist parents also tend to model perfectionist behavior, which doesn't much help matters. (So if you must make your bed perfectly, it's better for your child not to see that.) And then there are the messages parents convey, wittingly or not. If parental approval is contingent on a child's performance, the child feels this, even when parents try to hide it.[15] Overemphasizing a child's accomplishments can also easily lead to a kid thinking that their accomplishments are more important than they are.[16]

So what to do? What to say? When a child's perfectionism feels truly obsessive, and especially when it is associated with very high levels of anxiety and other obsessive tendencies, seek professional help. But if it hasn't gotten to this level, share your own mistakes and explain what you've learned from them, albeit in an offhand way that avoids sounding like a sermon. For example, "Life is weird. I said something in a meeting last week that I realized was kind of stupid. But in realizing how I screwed up, I ended up coming up with some really good ideas."

For younger kids who show signs of perfectionism, teachers can require a certain number of mistakes—and give extra credit for finding mistakes and correcting them as a way of helping to change the meaning of making mistakes. Parents can easily replicate this at home when their child is working on a task and feeling stress around it. For older kids and teenagers, it's more difficult. Telling them repeatedly that it's okay to make mistakes is not likely to land, nor is trying to get them to see that they'd be much less anxious—and would perform better—if they weren't so perfectionistic. Some perfectionistic kids aren't ready to make a change—it's not impacting their life enough for them to want to try something different. For these kids, pick your moments carefully. Don't begin a discussion about perfectionism right after their too-high expectations have left them disappointed. Wait until they've recovered some, and then use reflective listening and affirmation to help them feel heard:

- "It's really frustrating to put so much effort into something and not get the grade you were hoping for."

- "You worry that if you aren't the best at this, other kids will think less of you."

- "It hurts to think that kids who didn't work as hard as you did would get a higher grade."

- "It sounds like you felt really embarrassed when you played the wrong note."

Validate their effort by letting them know how much you value their work ethic: "I'm so grateful that you're not a slacker—or one of those kids whose parents have to be on them all the time to get them to do anything. I completely admire your determination and your desire to perform at a high level."

Once they feel heard and accepted, you can use strategies from motivational interviewing, and ask questions that get to the core of what they want for themselves:

- "I know that trying to achieve perfection can work for some kids—at least for a while. I'm wondering how you see it working for you."

- "I'm wondering how it affects someone's performance if they feel worthless if they get a B—or feel that they're an inferior person if somebody is better at algebra or writing or tennis than they are."

- "What do you think might be some advantages of looking at things differently?"

- "I know that you don't really like to try new things or sports you don't already know that you're really good at. Why do you think that is?"

If kids are open to considering both sides of their ambivalence, psychologist Sheila Josephs suggests that, as part of the process of considering the pros and cons of perfectionistic attitudes, you ask kids questions about perfectionism such as:

- "Does it make it harder to finish school assignments on time?"

- "Does it always trigger test anxiety and make it harder to perform well on tests?"

- "Does it cause you to avoid situations from which you might grow due to fear of mistakes?"

- "Does it prevent you from trying new challenges to avoid the risk of failure?"[17]

Depending on how open they seem, you can explain that there is an alternative way of achieving at a high level that is more effective and more sustainable: the pursuit of excellence rather than perfection. To these kids you might say, "This would mean setting high standards for yourself, but over time, changing your attitude toward making mistakes and what you now see as imperfection."

You can also encourage them to focus on their *personal* best, as focusing on personal improvement can help take the focus off comparison with others. Help them broaden their circle of contacts, to include those outside of where the competition is the hottest. Encourage them to volunteer for service opportunities outside of their social circle. Dr. Alicia Nortje, a research fellow in Cape Town, recommends a practice of gratitude, and, interestingly, changing the comparison from a person to a time period.[18] So instead of comparing themselves unfavorably with other kids, they can compare how well they are doing in the moment versus a harder period in their life. So they might say something like,

"Things aren't awesome, but I'm doing a lot better now than I was in seventh grade."

Inside the Brain

What we worry about with perfectionists is the development of anxiety and depression, which adolescent females are more vulnerable to than children or male teens. It's never one thing that causes kids to develop an anxiety disorder or depression. Rather, think of stress flowing in and flowing out. When the stress flows in faster than it goes out, it can corrode and eventually overload the system. Kids are often not aware of the effects on their brains of not getting enough sleep, of excessive caffeine, or of turning to things like drugs and alcohol for relief. Ned had a student who was impossibly driven. He took a survey of her sleep (which averaged five hours a night) and then asked how she stayed awake. It turns out she had a large latte on the way to school, one at lunch, and another after school. She was easily consuming more than 700 mg of caffeine daily, which because she was a small person made her utterly bonkers.

Kids like her may know that too much caffeine isn't good for them, or that they shouldn't drink as much alcohol or smoke as much pot as they do, or that they should sleep more. But they don't see the big picture of how these things can affect their level of happiness drip by drip (no pun intended!).[19] Because even just one depressive episode as an adolescent can make the brain more vulnerable to depression later in life, we really want to help perfectionistic kids keep stress well-managed.

Many perfectionists also have stomach issues, which isn't surprising, as the brain is intimately connected with the gut. In fact, 95 percent of all the neurotransmitter serotonin is in the gut, affecting both mood and gastrointestinal functioning.[20] Scientists have called the stomach the "second brain" or the "belly brain." This close connection is why the foods we eat can affect the way we think and feel, and why we can get a stomachache or indigestion when we're stressed or anxious. Bill moved from Seattle to Bellevue, Washington, in the spring of fifth grade, and went home early due to stomachaches four days a week for the first month—until he made friends. Now, it's pretty clear that symptom was a result of a stressful adjustment.

Although kids can inherit vulnerability to anxiety and/or depression, these are much less genetic than other conditions like ADHD and autism.[21] Which is all to say, there's a lot of opportunity to mitigate risk factors. It's thus so important for adolescent girls to get enough rest, to exercise, to spend time with people who aren't stressed, and to do all the self-care they can to develop strong connections between the PFC and amygdala.

But What About . . . ?

My wife and I both went to an elite college, which has given us a better life than we would have had otherwise. And it's not just about money—we've had choices that other people haven't had. We would not have gotten accepted at that school if we hadn't worked as hard as we did in high school. How do we make that clear to our kids without creating toxic expectations?

There's nothing wrong with going to an elite school. They clearly can offer some advantages—they can open doors and expose you to really talented people. We're not suggesting that you hide those advantages from your kids. But do you really know you've had a better life because of it? How do you know that?

We also believe you don't *have* to go to an elite school to have a great life. Remember to express confidence but minimize motivation through fear. Let them know that they can aim as high as they feel is reasonable, but that if they don't get into a 2 percent acceptance-rate school, there is absolutely no reason they can't get an excellent education and have an equally wonderful life. Further, while elite schools do open doors, if high schoolers are losing sleep and experiencing chronic stress or anxiety in an effort to open those doors, they are more likely to develop a brain that is susceptible to chronic anxiety, depression, and chemical dependency. And that vulnerability is something they will always have, open doors or not. Remember, we want kids to be sure to sculpt brains that are capable of *enjoying* their success.

I've always felt my parents didn't have high enough expectations of me, and that if they had, I would be further in my life right now.

We got this question—we kid you not—from a popular doctor, who was also a mother of two. How much further, exactly, had she wanted to go? Granted, research shows that having *low* expectations of kids leads to low performance. But this woman's parents had conveyed confidence in her—they just didn't expect her to be a concert pianist or an Olympic athlete. We encouraged her—and we encourage anyone for whom this comes up—to honestly answer the question: *What if* your parents had pushed you more? Would you have said, "Sure! Great, thanks for the push!" Or would you have rebelled? More likely, as this doctor conceded, the latter.

I don't put any pressure on my kid, but still he feels these enormous expectations. I swear, it's in the air, it's in his school and peer environment. What am I supposed to do?

It's great that you're not setting toxic expectations, but as you suggest, that's probably not enough. There's a proactive piece required, too—you can nurture your son's ability to set healthy expectations for himself and show him—through your own modeling—how to fight off the toxic ones. Stay in dialogue: Does he see his school environment as toxic? If so, would he like to either (a) look at alternative schools, or (b) consider ways to reframe his experience if he does want to stay?

Also, make sure that, even though you don't feel you put excess pressure on your son, he sees it that way, too. We've had dozens of conversations with parents who are sure they don't pressure their kids, while their kids insist they do. Both perceptions can be true—it's the communication that needs to be improved. So why not just ask, "Do you feel these enormous expectations coming from me?" What a great opportunity to clear the air if his answer is yes.

I'm trying to help my daughter set healthy expectations for herself, but no matter what, she always ends up comparing herself to her sister. I figure it's normal for her to feel this way, and in time, she'll get over it. But is there something more I can be doing?

Max Ehrmann wrote in *Desiderata: A Poem for a Way of Life*, "If you compare yourself with others, you may become vain and bitter; for always there will be greater and lesser persons than yourself."[22] And yet since Cain and Abel, siblings have measured themselves against the other. Though in time, most grow out of sibling rivalry, it can also harm kids' ability to set healthy expectations of themselves independently of anyone or anything else. As your daughter sets personal goals, you can use some motivational interviewing techniques. Ask, "What is it about your sister's accomplishments that you see as taking away from yours? Why is that?" Reflect her feelings back to her, validate her search for a unique identity as completely normal. Then, if you have sufficient buy-in, ask, "Is the way you feel about this now making you happy?" and "Is this the only possible way you could feel about this?" Work with her to understand what it is she finds threatening, then help her focus on what she has control over—which isn't what her sibling does or doesn't do, but her own ability to meet her goals. Note this is not a onetime conversation that suddenly eliminates sibling rivalry. Rather, it's a conversation likely to have many iterations as your child grows up and learns to be comfortable in her own skin and gets better at setting healthy expectations.

Putting It All Together

Sydney was an extremely bright and talented fourteen-year-old girl whose parents worried about her self-esteem and perfectionistic tendencies. They constantly told her to ease up on herself. She was on track to make a national gymnastics team and was a very strong student in an elite independent school. She came home upset one day because she'd gotten As in all her classes on her most recent report card, except for a B in English.

SYDNEY: I feel so stupid.

MOM: Why on earth would you feel stupid? You pretty much got straight As! You're a rock star!

SYDNEY: Yeah, but not in English. I'm just not a good writer. There are, like, at least five other kids in my class who are better writers than me. I can see them judging my stuff when they see it.

MOM: Hmm. I get it—I can see how that would feel crummy. What if you sought out a tutor? Doesn't your school have a tutoring program, where seniors teach freshmen? Or if not, we could look into hiring one for you.

SYDNEY: Yes! Great idea!

Sydney's mom's handling of the situation seems fine, right? She's trying to build her daughter up, and she's not setting expectations of Sydney—Sydney's setting them for *herself*. But implicitly, she's acknowledging that Sydney could feel happy with herself only if she was a straight-A student at one of the most challenging schools in the area. By offering to pay for a tutor, the mom is also accommodating Sydney's perfectionism.

What if it had gone like this instead?

SYDNEY: I'm just not a good writer. There are, like, at least five other kids in my class who are better writers than me. I can tell they're judging my stuff when they see it.

MOM: That feels pretty crappy, huh? I get that. You really like to put out strong assignments.

SYDNEY: Yes, and I'm sick of feeling stupid. Will you hire me a tutor?

MOM: You are so committed to excellence, which is wonderful. But I wonder, would you like to feel better about yourself, without needing to worry so much about always getting straight As?

SYDNEY: *Mom!* Getting As matters. I just need a tutor. I can fit it into my schedule. Maybe Saturday mornings?

MOM: I'd love to keep talking about this, but let's set aside some time this weekend, once the sting of the grade has passed.

[A few days later . . .]

MOM: I don't mean to suggest As don't matter, Sydney, and I know they're important to you. Wanting to do a good job is wonderful and healthy. But if you're feeling tortured by not getting an A in every subject, that's not.

SYDNEY: You just don't understand.

MOM: That's probably true. And I can't talk you out of the way you feel. I also can't stop you from finding free resources that can help you get your grade up. But I won't contribute financially to something I don't think is healthy for you, because that wouldn't feel right. What I would love to do is talk with you from time to time about whether there's anything I can do that would help you relax a little bit, because I worry your level of stress isn't sustainable.

As they talked more, Sydney's mom asked if she would like to be less perfectionistic. When Sydney acknowledged that she'd be open to it, her mom said, "One thing that's helpful to me when I'm feeling really worried about performing at work is that I think about how I am more than just my job. I'm a mom, I'm a daughter, I'm a wife. I help people in lots of different ways, not just in my work life. Would it be helpful to you to think about all the parts of you that make you pretty great?"

Sydney said yes, and the two wrote a list—of both the qualities Sydney liked in herself, and the qualities that her family and friends saw in her. Sydney continued to push her mom to get her a tutor, but let it go after it became clear her mom wouldn't budge, though they did agree that if her teacher felt she needed extra help in writing, her mom would reconsider. It wasn't a onetime conversation, but an important beginning to an ongoing dialogue between mother and daughter.

Remember What It's All About

We've written a lot in this chapter about words to say, questions to ask, and ideals to model. But we want to leave you with the idea that so often, the best way to convey the right kind of expectations is simply to trust your kids.

One mom we spoke with told us she wanted to show her middle school son how much she believed in him. One day he cooked something in the microwave, and after realizing that fifty seconds hadn't been long enough, he put it back in for three minutes. Whoops! The fire alarm went off, messes were made, the works. But the very next night, the mom had to go on an errand and asked her son to put the lasagna for dinner in the oven and to take it out when it were done. "You're responsible for dinner," she said.

The degree of trust he felt from this simple act, coming right after a night when he'd screwed up, was palpably impactful. "He felt so good," his mom said. "We went to back-to-school night after dinner, and the whole way there he wanted to chat with me. I cherished that whole conversation with my son—to get him for a whole hour. This kid doesn't talk. He was so happy. It was wonderful, a great feeling."

Remember, it all comes back to relationships—and is much less about saying exactly the right words—whether about expectations or anything else—and more about how we make our kids feel.

Chapter 7

Talking to Kids about the Pursuit of Happiness

When we ask parents what they want for their kids' futures, you can probably guess what most answer: "I want them to be happy." They also say that they want them to possess qualities like kindness, honesty, courage, responsibility, and compassion. They don't say, "I want them to be outrageously wealthy," or "I want them to have lots of power over other people," or "I want them to have as much status as possible."

But if you ask most kids what they think their parents want for their future, the answer is usually something like, "To get into a good college" or "To go to medical school." Or they shrug and offer, "To stop playing video games?"

We talked with a group of student leaders about wellness at an elite independent high school in the Southwest, and one of our questions was how many of them wanted to be happy as adults. They all raised their hands and gave us a sort of unanimous "duh" expression. Of course students want to be happy; they know intuitively what science tells us—that being happy can result in better relationships, better health, a longer life.[1] Happiness is so important that the U.S. Constitution protects our right to the "pursuit of happiness," and the fourteenth Dalai Lama even asserts that the "purpose of our lives is to be happy." And here's the thing: happiness begets success. So by focusing on happiness, you're actually making it *more* likely that your kid achieves, well, whatever they want.[2]

Satisfied that we were on the same page as these students that happiness is a good thing, we shifted the conversation to the *how*. What, we asked them, have adults told you about what it takes to be happy in adulthood? One boy answered, "The message we get is that if we get into a good enough college, everything will be set." The other students nodded their agreement. Where did they get this strikingly inaccurate idea? And what can we do to communicate to kids a healthier—and much more accurate—view of what it takes to be happy?

We believe part of the problem is that many parents don't explicitly talk to their kids about happiness at all. It just doesn't come up as a subject of conversation, and so kids form their impressions about it from listening to their parents emphasize the importance of grades and building a résumé for college. They supplement this with messages from their peers, teachers, or the culture around them, which, by and large, promotes materialism and photographic evidence that *Hey! Look! My life is great!* Kids get the message that money really matters, that happiness requires wealth and great career success, and that others' perception of your wealth and status is crucial.

Many parents we meet share the view that the key to a good life *is* getting into a good college, no matter what, because that good college will lead to a good job, financial security, and happiness ad infinitum. And many kids get this message surprisingly early in life. Bill recently asked a second-grade girl what kinds of things she worries about. She answered, "I worry about my grades because I know they're important for my college." Bill was somewhat relieved when she then explained, "I want to go to a good college like American University because they have an Elevation Burger and I love their fries!"

The problem is that we tend to be very poor predictors of what actually makes us happy. We think that having more money, getting a big promotion, or buying new stuff will make us happy when, in fact, we're happier if we prioritize having time more than things, giving more than getting, and appreciating what we have more than trying to get what we don't.[3] So when we equate academic achievement and career success with happiness, we do so potentially at the cost of our kids' well-being. Considering the marked increase over the last several years in the incidence of suicide among high-achieving kids and young adults, it appears that depression and hopelessness have no respect for accomplishment.[4]

Sure, achievement and success are important—we're not encouraging people to underachieve. But if we want kids to be happy and healthy *and to enjoy their successes*, that limited vision of achievement is part of the issue. Some parents think that if their child is miserable in high school in order to get the coveted admission spot, well, that's just the cost of being happy as an adult. But we have two concerns. One, young brains that are stressed, tired, and unhappy all the time can get used to that state and remain that way even when they achieve the successes they have sacrificed happiness to achieve. And two, what do we miss out on if we look at our kids' formative years as a time to push hard in order to get to the future? Education advocate Jonathan Kozol talks about viewing childhood as having "present value as a perishable piece of life itself," and we'd be wise to adopt that perspective.[5] After all, don't we want our children to be happy as kids and adolescents, and not just as adults?

In this chapter, we're going to take a hard look at the messages we send kids about the pursuit of happiness, and ways that we can effectively communicate to them how to find contentment in their lives. And we're talking about true, lasting contentment here. We're not trying to get kids to walk around with superficial smiles all the time (that would be terrifying!). We want kids to experience—and accept—the full range of human emotions, which is crucial for mental health.[6] So let's push for deeper conversations on happiness. We can't delve into any of that, though, until we get clear on what happiness actually *is*, and what it takes to achieve it.

A Formula for Happiness

There are scores of books about the science of happiness, the pursuit of happiness, the Tao and art of happiness. There are researchers, lecturers, writers, and thinkers who have dedicated the better part of their lives to answering the questions of what it takes to be happy. There's even a wildly popular class at Yale about it, Psychology and the Good Life—by far the most popular course in the school's three-hundred-plus-year history. At Harvard, too, Dr. Tal Ben-Shahar's Positive Psychology course was so popular from 2004 to 2008 that many schools like Stanford, MIT, and University of Michigan began offering happiness-oriented classes. The demand for these courses tells us that high-achieving kids are desperate to understand how to be happy. Why should they have to wait until college to figure it out? We want to help start those conversations about happiness much, much earlier. But in lieu of writing another book on the subject, we're cutting right to the highlights.

The first thing to understand about happiness is that it's different from pleasure. Pleasure is more about gratification—the thrill you get from eating a piece of chocolate cake, winning a game, doing well on a test, getting an award, buying something you really want, or even opening an acceptance letter to a college. Pleasure is great, but it's not long-lasting. If a teen buys a new jacket or gets invited to a party with the cool kids for the first time, the rush doesn't last, and they will return to their baseline level of happiness. This is called hedonic adaptation, and it's completely normal. Happiness, in contrast, is more ethereal. It's a sense of well-being that stays with you. It involves others as opposed to just you and is more about giving than getting.[7]

Also, the neurochemistry of pleasure and happiness are very different, as pleasure always involves the neurotransmitter dopamine, while happiness depends on serotonin, the neurotransmitter that's most important for contentment. The challenge is that while pleasure obviously isn't a bad thing, too much pleasure-induced dopamine actually depletes serotonin. This can lead to repeated seeking of pleasure, which can be addicting. In contrast, happiness isn't addictive because the serotonin it relies on isn't addictive.[8] This distinction matters—a lot—when you consider the strikingly high rates of substance use disorders in affluent teens and young adults from high-achieving schools, who apparently learned to pursue pleasure as a replacement for happiness.[9]

There *is* a formula for happiness, of sorts, according to those who study it, including Sonja Lyubomirsky, professor of psychology and the author of *The How of Happiness*.[10] Part of the formula involves genetics. If you see the glass half empty, it might be because a negative perspective is in your chemical makeup. Which doesn't mean there's nothing that you can do about it—just that there's a bit of an uphill climb. (We see it this way because we're both genetic optimists.) Lyubomirsky has suggested that approximately 50 percent of your mood—positive or negative—is genetically determined (although recent studies have found that the genetic factor may be more like 33 percent[11]). Lyubomirsky estimates that about 40 percent of happiness comes from intentional activity. This is actually great news. Learning the ukulele, taking a nap, meditating, doing something nice for someone else, cooking because you want to, spending time with a loved one, playing with your dog—they can all make you happier, and these intentional activities are ones you have control over. We'll get much more into this 40 percent (probably 40+ percent) in this chapter, as it's where parents can make the most difference.

The final 10 percent is made up of your life circumstances. This category includes what happens *to* you—so getting into a choice college or not, getting a girlfriend, winning an award, losing a job, losing a loved one. Just 10 percent! This is also the category where it's tempting (for both us, as parents, and our kids) to compare ourselves. Whether it's college acceptances, job titles, or anything else, comparing life circumstances means that we're comparing our experiences to the *perceived* experiences of others. The reality is life events don't matter nearly as much as most people think. And dozens of studies have shown that the impact of those life events stabilizes in time, which is consistent with what we know about hedonic adaptation. People who have something happen to them on either extreme will usually return to their baseline level of happiness after a period of either great elation (in the case of something like winning the lottery) or great loss (in the case of a paralyzing injury).[12]

When you look at this formula logically, all the pressure we feel, and often pass to our kids, to secure that coveted spot on the dais, in the college, or on the roster—it just doesn't matter nearly as much as we tend to think. Not if what we really and truly want is for them to be happy humans. When children get the message to channel their effort into the life circumstances category, which accounts for only 10 percent of happiness, they lose out on putting effort into that 40+ percent of "intentional activity" that's easier to control—where kids don't have to compete. There's no GPA involved in going to the beach, no valedictorian title for hanging out with friends, no team captain spot to vie for while baking cookies with Grandma.

There are many great voices about what steps to take to be happier—from the Dalai Lama, the Maharishi, and Eckhart Tolle to Sonja Lyubomirsky and Daniel Gilbert. One of our favorite thinkers on the subject of happiness, though, is Martin Seligman, who founded positive psychology in the late 1990s. Seligman emphasized that the primary focus of psychology for decades had been on how not to be completely miserable, but that we can, and should, focus on the creation of well-being. He's identified five elements toward this end, PERMA:

Positive emotion

Engagement

Relationships

Meaning and purpose

Accomplishment[13]

Most of these elements fall in the "intentional activity" bucket of the happiness formula. Your capacity for experiencing **Positive emotion** has some genetically imposed limits, although even here you can increase positive emotion through things like exercise, sleep, and meditation. Also, you can increase **Engagement** any time you're in a flow state, where time passes quickly and your attention is completely engaged. (Ned can get totally swept up in yard work, spending hours pruning trees or rebuilding stone walls, but it would be a much different experience if he was made to do it.) You can invest in the quality of your **Relationships**. You can pursue what gives you a sense of **Meaning and purpose** in your life. And yes, **Accomplishment** *does* matter. But accomplishment isn't necessarily all As or material success—rather, it's a sense of mastery, of competence, and it's only one-fifth of the happiness formula.

All too often, when we look at the average kid's or adolescent's life, there's not a lot of PERMA. For instance, Ned worked with a sixteen-year-old student who was intent on spending her summer doing test prep so she could take the ACT offered the first week of her junior year. Ned was puzzled about why she wanted to test so early, especially since school could teach her much of what she needed to know for the math sections—she didn't need Ned for that.

"I really need to do this now," she said when he pressed. "I just don't have time during the school year."

"Well, that seems like forward thinking. Out of curiosity, what about weekends? No time to squeeze in an hour of this work?"

"Oh, no. My weekends are completely spoken for."

Ned imagined the typical litany of travel soccer, robotics, and the like. Or, more likely, Saturday mornings committed to the service projects her Catholic school was known for and Sundays to church services. Instead, she told him that she woke up relatively early Saturday to do ten hours of homework. She said she did the same on Sundays. Where was the meaning and purpose? Where was the investment in relationship? Or the engagement, leading to that coveted experience of flow?

"Gosh, that is a *busy* weekend!" Ned said, surprised. "Is it pretty much like that every weekend?"

"Oh, yeah."

"Might it be possible to sometimes do only eight hours of work so you can have a couple hours with your friends, family, dog?" It's a sad state of affairs, by the way, when the SAT tutor sounds like the voice of reason when it comes to fun.

"No," she insisted. "That's just not what I do."

Now, there's always the possibility that this amount of studying made her happy. Some people are very academic and thrive this way. (Bill often gets teased for reading about the brain during his vacations—but he loves it. And Ned fondly remembers the packed schedules of his youth and all he "got to do.") But that wasn't the case here. She was stressed.

Then there's the possibility that she was exaggerating. And indeed, Laurie Santos, who started the Good Life course at Yale, has commented that lack of sleep and amount of studying time are often held up as a badge of honor by high-achieving high school and college students. So even if Ned's student was exaggerating, that's just as significant a problem as if she actually did spend twenty hours of her weekend studying. She is signaling that achievement is her greatest value—but remember, that falls into the 10 percent of what comprises happiness, the "what happens *to* you" part.

If her parents' goal for her future is a happy life and if she shares that goal, her car is speeding in the wrong direction. Has anyone told her? How can we help her turn her car around? But there are reams of articles with titles that suggest it's not our place: "The misguided desire of wanting kids to be happy," "Parents, it's not your job to make your children happy," and "Our obsession with happiness is making our kids miserable." We understand what drives this backlash, as we're obviously supporters of separating your kid's life from your own. And our default to shield our kids from the hard parts of engagement, like failure, to pick them up and place them on the other side of challenge, can deprive them of learning how to cope. So we can't and shouldn't prevent kids from ever experiencing upset, stress, sadness, or disappointment—those are all useful emotions that will help them develop high stress tolerance and resilience and learn to make good choices. We don't want to give kids the message that they're supposed to be happy all the time. But *some* upset, stress, and disappointment are very different from chronic stress, unhappiness, and exhaustion.

The consequences of chronic stress like that experienced by Ned's student can be profound. Being chronically stressed places kids at high risk for developing anxiety, mood, and/or substance use disorders, and for experiencing recurrent anxiety or bouts of depression as adults. As the neuroscientists say, teenagers are "sculpting" their adult brains, and we don't want them sculpting brains that are used to being stressed, tired, and unhappy most of the time—or workaholic brains that don't feel safe unless they're working. We think of Laurie Santos's observations from her time living in a residential college with Yale students: most of the students said they couldn't benefit from the school's incredible opportunities because they were so stressed, busy, and pressured. These will be the members of our workforce in five years, and many of them will become leaders in our society. These aren't brains that will know how to be happy, and that matters for all of us. Preventing mental health problems in children and teens is *the* single best way to pave their way to experience happiness as adults.[14] And coaching happiness, versus pleasure, is one of the best things we can do to ensure our kids' future wellness.

How Do We Talk to Kids about Success and Happiness?

The first rule for talking to kids about happiness is to *Talk about happiness.*
Pretty straightforward, right? But again, these conversations aren't explicit
nearly as often as you would think. Here are some questions to start with:

- When are some times when you feel really happy?

- What does it feel like when you're really happy? How long does it last?

- On a scale from 1 to 10, if 10 is really happy, where are you usually?
  How high do you get? How low? When you feel down, how long does
  it last?

- They say that happiness is different from pleasure. Does that make
  sense to you?

- What do you think it takes to be a happy person in this world?

- Do you see me as a happy person?

Also, share some of your own thoughts and experiences about happiness. Let your kids know about times when you feel really happy. Also
tell them about times when something pleasurable you thought would
increase your happiness permanently didn't last that long.

Talk about Engagement

Ned always tries to get to know what gives a bounce to his students'
steps. So he talks frequently with them about passion, and about when
they feel in a state of flow. Ned's student Maria loved playing soccer, but
her father thought it was a waste of time. He once said, "It's not like she's

going to get recruited. And all that time spent with her friends . . . how does *that* get her ahead?" Oy, this worries us. Maria had a lot of stress in her life, and the more stress she took in, the more stress she needed to blow off—be it by kicking around a soccer ball or being with her friends. Fortunately, Maria's intrinsic motivation pushed through her father's disapproval, and she kept playing, intuitively seeking what supported her happiness and stress release. This was reassuring, because while teens know what activities make them happy, when they talk about engagement, they so often bookend what they say with worries that echo their parents'. The dialogue goes something like this:

NED: Wow, Riley, that's great that you love baking so much. Is that something you think you'll continue to pursue?

RILEY: (shrugs) Can you make any money at it?

This is when Ned's face falls. Worse yet, though Riley's parents may be supportive of her passion for baking, it's only to a point. If it interferes with her studies or with her résumé-building extracurricular activities, then, like Maria's dad, they discourage time spent on it. Their worry is similar to Riley's—can she make any money at it?

We can't talk about engagement, then, without talking about materialism—its primary obstacle. Individuals living in most of the Western industrialized world are exposed frequently to messages that equate money, status, popularity, looks, and possessions with happiness, and this thinking has only intensified over the years.[15] It's not that any of these things are inherently bad, but we do know that placing a very high value on them is strongly associated with increases in anxiety and depression and decreases in life satisfaction.[16] At the very least, this focus prioritizes the superficial over a feeling of engagement.

We know one teen, for instance, who enjoyed playing golf. She liked that it brought her outside and that she could play with her friends and family. But eventually, she wanted to quit because she thought her golfer tan "looked stupid" when "everyone else" on Instagram had "gorgeous tans." Even if parents don't promote materialism, it seems to seep in, anyway—from peers, media, and our culture at large. It's not like we live in the 1800s, when if we'd spent our days slogging through the rain harvesting potatoes, we'd be none the wiser that someone else was relaxing on a beach eating coconuts. We know too much now. *Lifestyles of the Rich and Famous* is no longer a show you watch an hour a week—instead kids see those lifestyles every time they open Instagram. That's why it's not enough as a parent to simply not promote materialism—you have to actively fight it.

Talking about materialism and its shortfalls is one way to do that. Encouraging engagement in what kids are passionate about is another. Both ways require giving kids an accurate model of reality, a reality that does not always include prestige. For instance, we may talk a lot about William, who was the golden boy of his prestigious university and went on to a fancy law firm and a second home in the Hamptons, but we should talk as much about people like A.J. Shapiro—an audio engineer at Technicolor who struggled for three years in college before dropping out and going to technical school. A.J. says that if he'd paid attention to his love for the technical aspects of music and gone straight to studying sound engineering in vocational school right out of college, he'd have saved his family tens of thousands of dollars and been even further ahead in his career. Still, he won an Emmy in 2020 for his work on the critically acclaimed HBO series *Watchmen*, so we guess he's done all right. You probably know plenty of people like A.J. who pursued slightly more circuitous or unorthodox paths in their careers. Elevate their stories.

A recent college graduate, Kira, recollected for us how her dad approached this subject with her when she was still in high school. She listed all the things she thought would be great to do after she'd gone to college and had achieved in her career. He responded by telling her the John Lane parable of a contented fisherman who meets a businessman while fishing one day. The businessman tells the fisherman of all that he can do to improve his fishing business, so that he becomes rich and has everything he could possibly want, so that he'd be able to spend his days doing whatever it is he wants. But what the fisherman wants is to be doing exactly what he is already doing. "So," Kira's dad said, "don't do those things after you've had a career. Do them now. Make them your career." It was advice that helped guide her choices in high school and her journey through college.

We have visited countless schools over the decades and have seen many hoist banners that say things like, "Preparing kids for extraordinary lives." Unsurprisingly, we worry about this message, because it is impossible for these students to overachieve (if the expectation is extraordinary) and very likely that they will underachieve. In contrast, we love the mission of the Archer School for Girls in Los Angeles, in which they espouse, "Raising joyful girls." Along with a rigorous academic curriculum, the school offers six-week courses dedicated to pursuing a passion, ranging from neuroscience to dog training. When worried parents say that dog training is a waste of time, the administrators say, "Come see what your daughter can do after six weeks, and then say if it's a waste of time." At the end of the session, when students have learned to get recalcitrant dogs to run through an obstacle course, they have such a high level of self-confidence, it's no wonder that the Archer School has had its best college admissions successes since implementing this passion-driven program.

The truth is that there are many ways to contribute in this world, and many ways to be happy that do not involve making a lot of money or being the best. Bill learned this lesson years ago, in graduate school. He initially felt intimidated by his professors, who were clearly smarter and had much more talent for research than he did. While he felt inferior to them for many months, as he got to know them better, he realized his life was actually happier than theirs, and he concluded *I want my life. I don't want their life.*

Some ways to talk to your kids about engagement are:

- "Have you ever been doing something that makes you feel in the zone? Have you heard that scientists call that flow? It's that feeling when you do something that requires your full energy and effort and attention. You can be doing it for an hour and it feels like only fifteen minutes have gone by. When do you feel that way?" (Lots of kids will say "when playing video games." We'll talk about that in the next chapter.)

- "I value the things you become deeply engaged in because being passionately engaged in life is one of the things that makes people happy."

- "How much of the time do you feel like you're really into what you're doing?"

- "When do you feel like you're just going through the motions, and how often are you trying to do two or more things at once?"

- Talk to them about your own engagement—things that inspire you or that allow you to experience flow. "Man, I learned a new song on the guitar last night. I thought that I was at it for about forty-five minutes, but it was actually two and a half hours. I love that experience of being completely into what I'm doing." Also, tell them about times when you don't feel very engaged and how you handle them.

- "What do you love to do? How do you love to use your mind?"

- "When do you feel the happiest?"

- "Some people feel happiest and do best when they are a big fish in a little pond, while others are energized and motivated by being a relatively little fish. Some kids might make the travel basketball team but choose to play rec ball instead because they're playing with their friends

and it's more fun. Which do you think you like? Or does it change depending on what you're doing?"

- Talk about materialistic values and goals as part of a "values and goals"
  pie. (This comes courtesy of psychologist Tim Kasser, who has studied
  the negative effects of materialism for twenty-five years.) If the materialistic piece is too big, it leaves less room for the things that actually
  make you happy.

- Kasser also suggests that, as a way to offset the lure of materialism, we
  explain to kids that advertisers don't care about them. Say something
  like, "Although advertisers aren't bad people, they are not trying to
  make your life better, they're trying to sell as many of their dolls or
  games or apps as possible. We have to think about whether these things
  will actually make your life better."[17]

Talk about Purpose (Meaning)

It's actually fairly easy to talk about meaning and purpose with kids and
teens, because most of them want to talk about it. There is no "you
should care about this or that" in purpose conversations; there's only
what they *do* care about. Useful conversations about purpose and meaning begin with the acknowledgment that what's meaningful to the parent might not be meaningful to the child, and vice versa.

Toward that end, a parent's role is to help their child identify what
matters to them, and why, and also how to use their strengths toward
achieving what they think is important. One of the exercises parents can
do with their kids comes out of motivational interviewing (which we
talked about in Chapter 5). William Miller and colleagues came up with
"Personal Values" cards. Each card has a value and definition on it—like

"Adventure" or "Solitude" or "Tradition." You sort them into one of three categories: "Important to Me," "Very Important to Me," or "Not Important to Me." For the qualities that are Very Important, you can rank them, and then explain to others why they matter to you.[18] We see this as a great place to start, as it's free, and all you need are an internet connection and access to a printer.

While not every child will be a social justice warrior, impacting others in a positive way is important to everyone's sense of purpose. Finnish philosopher Frank Martela studies and gives frequent speeches about the meaning of life—which he describes as "doing things that are meaningful to you that make you meaningful to other people," which is consistent with findings that acts of kindness are strongly linked to a sense of well-being.[19] Simply put, helping others helps *us*. In one intervention, people on the street were given $5 or $20. Half were told they could spend the money on themselves, half were told they needed to spend it on others. In general, regardless of how they were told to spend the money, they *predicted* they would be happier spending the money on themselves, and that spending $20 would make them happier than spending $5. But a week later, those who spent the money on others reported a significant increase in happiness, and it turned out the amount of money—$5 or $20—didn't make a difference.[20] The same intervention was replicated in other places, including rural Uganda, where spending even a small amount of money can make an enormous difference in someone else's life. Researchers came back with the same results.

We can also help our children see that what they do doesn't have to be meaningful to *everyone*. While many kids find tremendous meaning through involvement in bigger movements like environmental or social activism (think of the March for Our Lives movement and its momentum among young people), many find meaning in smaller communities like their church or school clubs. Or to think even smaller, for most kids meaning is tied to a few people—their friends, or in volunteering at an animal shelter or helping their elderly grandparents. A kid raised in a multigenerational military family might relish order and find a strong sense of purpose in community service, whereas an artistic kid might thrive in chaos and find purpose in making spaces beautiful or in making others light up when she sings.

Dialogues about purpose can also include prompts like:

- "If you're on this planet for a purpose, what do you think it might be?"

- "What gives you a sense of meaning?"

- "How would you like people to remember you? What would you like to be remembered for?"

- Share your experiences, too. "I don't know if you have the same experience, but I really feel alive when I do something nice for someone for no reason. It makes me feel good about myself and the world."

- "When I play music with other people, I feel connected and inspired. Along with my family and my work, it's one of the things that makes my life meaningful."

- "My involvement in our synagogue is really important to me. It makes me feel connected to my parents and grandparents and to our community. Also, I love the fact that everyone there is committed to being a better person and improving the world."

Talk about Relationships

A friend of ours spoke on a panel offering career advice to undergraduates. Along with others on the panel, she talked about the trajectory of her career and explained some of the forks along the way. As the panel wrapped up, the moderator asked the speakers to give advice to their younger self. Our friend's heart rate raced, because she knew what she wanted to say, and she also knew it could come off badly, that it might not be welcomed.

In her early twenties, she had decided to apply for jobs where she could be near her boyfriend, who is now her husband of almost twenty years. When it was her turn, she went for it and said, "I'd tell my younger self I was right to make career decisions based on my relationship. Because the truth is that nothing has mattered as much to my happiness as the person I chose to go through life with." Something has gone awry in our world when a statement like this feels risky. Our friend Kathleen O'Connor, a highly respected college admissions counselor, has said for decades that who you marry (if you decide to marry) is more important than where you go to college. And that applies for both good partnerships and bad. Imagine your level of happiness if you're quarantined (an eventuality we probably need to plan for from here on out!) with a partner you can't stand, versus someone whose company you continue to enjoy. Spouses provide secure bases, leading individuals to seek out more challenges and growth opportunities.[21] Just think of how many successful people credit their spouse for support along their journey. We're not suggesting everyone needs to get married, or even that all relationships will turn into marriages, or that all marriages will work out. But it is a problem if we so prioritize career and the success trajectory that we leave the people part out of our intentions altogether, when people contribute so much to our sense of well-being and happiness in the world.[22]

It's not like you need to sit your kid down and say, "Son, let's talk about what you should look for in a mate." Rather, emphasize that relationships of any sort—friendships, romantic connections, family—*do* matter. Happy people prioritize social connections and spend more time with others.[23] Even talking to a stranger increases well-being.[24] Heck, even playing with a dog you know increases endorphins, oxytocin, and dopamine, which may be why a well-loved *Peanuts* strip shows Lucy snuggling with Snoopy, then saying, "Happiness is a warm puppy."[25]

Parents emphasize—or de-emphasize—these values all the time. Bill worked with one student who wanted to go to Butler University in Indiana because he thought the people there were really nice. His mother said with disbelief, "He's smart enough to go to Notre Dame—and he wants to go to Butler! Both my husband and I went to good colleges, and we want him to, too." Bill sees this all the time with his younger clients who don't want to transfer to a more elite school because they don't want to leave their friends—as if that represents completely skewed values.

Don't misunderstand: academic rigor, finances, and enrichment opportunities matter. Some kids are so terrified of leaving friends, they'll refuse to even look at a school that might better suit their learning needs, for instance. If your kid isn't making an informed decision that considers all the important factors, then you've got to help them make it. But in guiding our kids toward happiness, we should teach them that relationships *do* matter.

Talk to your kids about the relationships in your life that have contributed to your happiness, and how you've made decisions around those relationships—even if it's something as simple as calling in sick one day to be with a friend in need. And talk to your kids about how they feel around others—how their relationships contribute to their happiness. Some suggestions:

- "Who do you feel most close to on this planet?"

- "Who do you feel like you can be yourself the most with? Who do you feel you can really relax with and not worry you're going to say something wrong? Who do you feel safe with?"

- "Would you like to have more friends that you really feel safe with?"

- "What would happen if you put more time and energy into these relationships that make you feel good?"

- "Do you feel more connected to your friends when you text or talk face-to-face?"

- "It's not crazy to prioritize your friends over your grades, especially when they really need you. I'd feel hurt if my closest friends clearly cared more about their work than about me."

- "I sent an email to a friend from work yesterday, and I think he took it the wrong way. I'm going to meet with him in the office today and make sure he knows that although I had a different idea about the project, he's a great friend and colleague."

Let your kids know how important your relationships are to you, including your relationship with them. Tell them about what you get from having trusting friendships and why maintaining close connections is important for your happiness: "Doing a good job at work is great, but it's different from having friends who really care about me."

Talk about Learned Optimism

One of Bill's first therapy clients, Lila, was a depressed and pessimistic twelve-year-old who was having trouble connecting with other seventh-grade girls—and insisted that nothing good happened in her life. Bill had been reading a lot at the time about the psychology of success, which emphasizes the importance of focusing our attention on what we want, rather than on what we don't want. So he asked Lila to keep track of three things a day that went well. (Seligman has a term for the exercise: "WWW" or "What Went Well?") Bill quickly realized that they initially needed to lower the bar, so he asked her to track three things the first *week* that weren't terrible. Lila built up slowly, but after about six weeks, she was recording twelve positive things a day, and her depression had abated. To her shock, other kids started to want to be around her once her energy wasn't so negative. Not every case will be this easy to crack, but what the turnaround points to is the extent to which we can train our minds to think positive thoughts.[26] Seligman also coined the term "learned optimism," which suggests exactly that: optimism can be learned; a talent for looking on the bright side can be cultivated. And when it is, optimism can cut teenage depression in half.[27]

Another learned optimism strategy is practicing gratitude; committing to counting your blessings on a regular basis has been shown to help with overall well-being.[28] Many families have a gratitude practice, either within their faith community or simply at family dinners. (But families shouldn't overdo it—studies on counting your blessings have found that you feel more grateful and happy if you count your blessings once a week rather than three times a week.[29]) Even better, encourage your child to share their gratitude for others with them, by telling them straight out, sending them a text, or writing (then reading) them a letter. The latter are called "gratitude letters," and one study found that even though those who deliver the letter expect the encounter to be awkward, the recipients are typically very moved, and the people who write the letters experience a surge of well-being that can last for up to a month.[30]

Another important component of learned optimism involves talking back to negative thoughts and reframing negative incidents. Your mind has a lot more control than you think. To help her elementary schooler understand this concept, our friend Elizabeth compared negative thoughts to a boggart in *Harry Potter*. A boggart takes on whatever form the person it faces fears the most, and to fight it, witches and wizards use the power of their minds to make the creature comical. So if what a young wizard most fears are snakes, he might imagine them all trying to put on lipstick. This is not to say that you can make upsetting incidences funny, but it does point to the power your mind has to take something awful and recast it into something more controllable. We do this all the time as a society. We recast funerals as celebrations of life, we tell nervous public speakers to imagine the audience in their underwear. As we mentioned in Chapter 3, cognitive behavioral therapy is built around the principle of challenging distorted beliefs like all-or-nothing thinking and jumping to conclusions. Greek philosophers made that point, too—that it's not what happens to you but how you think about it that counts.

Universities are catching on, and trying to help stressed-out students recast their failures as (1) normal and (2) opportunities for growth, to retrain the mind to see the word *fail* as "First Attempt In Learning."[31] Smith College students are invited to write and share "failure résumés,"[32] and the Penn Faces Project at University of Pennsylvania boasts a Wall of Rejection and aspires to deconstruct the idea "that one must always appear busy, happy, and successful at everything all the time."[33] And Harvard's Bureau of Study Counsel offers five steps for successful failure, including feeling bad, but also learning and being willing to fail again.[34]

When we look beyond "failure" in education, we can reframe real-world difficulties as opportunities to teach kids about resilience. With the COVID-19 pandemic and the tragedies that it brought, many parents were wondering if the national turmoil would psychologically damage kids. In the turbulent summer of 2020, a mom who attended one of our virtual talks pointed out that despite the huge losses many families experienced, we may not have to worry that kids are going to be forever damaged by the pandemic. We call people who went through the Great Depression and World War II the Greatest Generation precisely because of the sacrifices and hardships they endured.

Some questions for talking to kids about learned optimism include:

- "What went well today?"

- "When was a time you did something really hard? What did you tell yourself when you were working through it? How did that self-talk affect what you did?"

- "When a friend messes up at something, what would you say to them?"

- "Do you think there's any other way to look at that? A way that maybe wouldn't make you feel so bad about yourself?"

- "Would you like to focus more on the positive things that happen to you? What would it be like if we all kept track of a few positive things that happen during the week and share some of the highlights at dinner on Friday nights?"

Tell your kids that you're committing yourself to practicing optimism, even if it doesn't come naturally to you. You can do this by noticing (and, ideally, writing down) positive things that happen and reframing perceived setbacks or failures as steps on the path of your development. The same is true for practicing gratitude, and you might say something like, "I've been noticing that I'm happier and less worried about life if I take a few minutes to remember the things I have to be thankful for. The shift can be pretty dramatic."

Talk about Lifestyle

Healthy practices matter. Doing half an hour of cardio per day has the same mood-enhancing effect as 75 mg of Zoloft. In fact, doing cardio in the morning bumps up your mood for more than twenty-four hours.[35] Sleep, which we'll get much more into in the next chapter, also has a huge impact on happiness. Administrators in elite public high schools told Laurie Santos that their students typically sleep four to five hours a night, which she noted was the same for her Yale undergraduate students. We could solve most of the mental health crisis on college campuses, Santos said, if we could get students to sleep.[36]

And then there's what we think of as brain hygiene. The great mindfulness teachers emphasize the benefit of being in the present moment. Similarly, Maharishi Mahesh Yogi, who introduced Transcendental Meditation to the world, used to say, simply, "Don't divide the mind," meaning be focused on the one thing you're doing. In reality, we pay attention to what we're doing about half the time.[37] Our perpetually "logged in" way of existence certainly doesn't make presence easier, and yet studies show that we are happier when we are paying attention than when our mind is wandering—even when it's wandering to positive thoughts.[38] Ned had this realization very vividly when recording a play his son performed in. *Would my level of happiness be greater*, he thought, *if I were fully here watching it instead of recording it for the future?*

Positive psychology has consistently emphasized the important contribution that meditation makes to happiness. Mindfulness meditation helps by training our minds to be aware—and accepting—of the present. Transcendental Meditation (TM) works because it makes it easy to experience the deepest levels of our mind, which are quiet, peaceful, and happy. We have both practiced TM for years, which involves silently repeating a mantra or a meaningless word. Repeating the mantra leads you to those deeper levels of your mind, so that you are fully alert but peaceful and calm. Over forty years of research has shown that when people experience these quiet levels of the mind regularly, they bring more peace and happiness into their daily lives, as evidenced by lower levels of stress, anxiety, and depression, as well as greater happiness, higher self-esteem, and a stronger sense of control.[39]

A few years ago, Bill tested Milton, a bright sixth grader with mild learning disabilities who was very depressed. A few months later, Bill was asked to meet with Milton and remind him of how capable he is because Milton was extremely discouraged and down on himself. So Bill met for an hour with Milton and his excellent psychotherapist. Milton cried most of the hour, as he focused on the ways he felt that he'd let his parents and teachers down. After the session, Milton's mother asked what else she could do to help, given that therapy and medication were clearly not enough. Bill said that she could see if Milton would learn TM.

Bill called Milton's mother about nine months later and asked how he was doing. She said that he was having a great seventh-grade year. He was doing well in school and in sports, had friends, and was happier than he'd been in years. Bill asked if Milton ever learned TM, and his mom said that, in fact, he did—and had been practicing it twice a day all year. Then a lightbulb went off in her head: "Oh my goodness, it's the TM that's made him happy!"

In our experience, when kids meditate, they get the same benefits that adults do. While it's not always easy to get them to do it, and while we don't want meditation to be something parents and kids fight over, we can encourage kids to learn and then decide for themselves. We can also meditate ourselves and model the benefits. The two of us are working to support schools in making meditation available to students, based on the marked improvement in students' mental health and academic achievement shown by numerous studies.[40]

A healthy lifestyle and good brain hygiene take work. And we should know because we work at them constantly. People often remark that Bill is one of the happiest people they've met, and it's true; most conversations begin with Bill reporting that he's "terrific." He was an anxious kid and a pretty cynical young man, but for over forty years, he has committed himself to his meditation practice (as well as prioritizing relationships, doing yoga and work that is meaningful to him, and actively talking back to negative thoughts). Ned, too, consistently works at it. With a brain that is vulnerable to depression, Ned not only meditates regularly but exercises almost every day, and has learned to be really disciplined about sleep. He has a calendar event of "bedtime" set at 10:15 p.m., daily, no end date. Most stresses in his life, he's found, can be managed if he gets at least eight hours of sleep. If he doesn't, the world looks very different indeed. In these ways, he works on his mental health every single day.

Prompts for talking to kids about lifestyle include:

- "Meditation seems to be something that's good for almost everything and everybody, kind of like sleep and exercise. I'm thinking of learning myself. I'd love for you to learn, too, to see if it could be a useful tool for you. I wouldn't try to make you meditate, but I'd want you to give it a good shot if I invest the money to learn—like doing it regularly for three months."

- "Do you notice a difference in your mood after swim practice—or after a workout? What kind of exercise seems to make the most difference in the way you feel?"

- "I've found that I feel happier, and I'm more successful, if I sleep for eight hours rather than six. Do you notice a difference in me when I sleep more?"

- "My mind is so much clearer after I meditate for a few minutes—and I can work so much more efficiently."

Modeling Healthy Self-Talk

Showing your kids how you pursue happiness is probably the single best thing you can do to influence them. Talk about what you're grateful for. Verbalize when you have a sense of contentment—ideally not when doing something that falls into the "pleasure" category, like taking an exciting boat ride, but when taking a walk around the neighborhood or doing something nice for someone else.

Also verbalize the way you try to train your own mind to look for the positive. Bill did this all the time with his kids. He remembers telling them one day, when they were young teenagers, "I felt bad today—I was late in getting a report to a client, and I feel like I let them down. I think I can see a way to make it up to my client. But I also realize that I can't expect myself to be perfect. I may not do everything as well as I want to, but that doesn't stop me from trying. And why add more suffering to the world by torturing myself for hours?" His daughter, Jora, then groaned, "I'm sick of this psychological crap." Fair enough, and Bill toned it down for a while after that. But over the following weeks and months, Bill occasionally overheard Jora talking to a friend who was having a problem, using the exact same language. Modeling matters.

But What About . . . ?

I would love my son to be happier, but come on—he's in middle school! There are so many hormonal and social changes. Being moody is just part of the deal. It seems unrealistic to expect much more.

You're right that a lot of changes are going on. On average, the baseline level of happiness is lower in middle school than at any other point in a kid's life.[41] It's also not realistic to expect anyone—no matter their age— to be happy all the time. But we've lowered the bar considerably when it comes to the adolescent and teen years, thinking of them as merely a time to endure and get through safely, rather than a time to enjoy.

We're not highly concerned about middle school kids' moods or moodiness, unless the negative moods are extreme or last longer than usual. But at a time when their brains are developing extremely rapidly, we want to encourage thoughts and experiences that can help them to be as happy as possible (which in some cases means less miserable!). Even middle school kids feel happiness when they act kind, get enough sleep, are physically active, do things for others, focus on the positive things in their lives, and spend time in nature (for many middle school kids, out-door summer camp is the happiest time of their lives).

Angst can exist alongside moments of great contentment, and middle schoolers should experience both. G. K. Chesterton wrote: "Virtue is not the absence of vices" but its own "vivid and separate thing." When we approach happiness and unhappiness not in an "either/or" situation, but as "vivid and separate things," we open up possibilities: for kids to learn to accept some dissatisfaction and disappointment, *and* to thrive.

I struggle with depression myself. How can I model happiness for my kids?

We're all doing the best we can. If you have depression, there's a good chance that you've got at least some genetically based vulnerability to things like negative mood, pessimism, and sleep difficulty, and have to work harder than most people to keep your head above water. It's okay to let your kids know you experience depression and that it seems to run in your family. Your mood-related challenges give you a good opportunity to *model* the process of working at it—at minimizing your suffering and elevating your own mood. For example, you can choose to practice optimism and gratitude to the extent that it is helpful. You can also model being consistent with sleep and exercise, learn to meditate, and find ways of helping others (and, if they're old enough, bring your kids along with you).

My daughter gets thrown off by the smallest things, and when I try to remind her how lucky she is, how much we have, she gets really angry with me. How can I instill a sense of optimism when she's intent on wallowing?

Talking about optimism and gratitude is important, but so is acknowledging feelings of disappointment. This relates back to what we covered in Chapter 2, about the importance of communicating as a consultant. Listen, ask questions, validate her feelings. Then and only then you might say something like, "Would you like to hear another way you might think about this?" If she says no, respect it. You can cultivate gratitude another time, like every Sunday over dinner, or nightly if you instill a routine of talking about "What Went Well." If, however, her wallowing carries on and on, you can say, "I don't find this conversation useful. I'd love to talk to you about solutions when you're ready, but I don't think it's helping your brain to go over and over the problem."

I come from a very wealthy family. Should my kids feel guilty about the considerable material comforts they have?

We don't want kids who grow up in a wealthy family to feel guilty about their financial advantages. We want them to be happy! However, because kids from wealthy families who attend high-achieving schools are at higher risk for anxiety, depression, and substance abuse than middle-class kids, you may have to pay particular attention to promoting healthy perspectives, values, and experiences in order to help them experience real happiness (along with the pleasures that affluence can afford). Focus strongly on the importance of giving and helping others. Support your kids in developing relationships with peers that don't center on having the coolest stuff. As always, maintain a strong and supportive emotional connection with your kids, and don't overemphasize the importance of high achievement for happiness and well-being.

My kid's depressed—you really think I'm going to be able to make him happy?

You absolutely cannot make your child be happy, any more than you can make them do homework, or eat their broccoli, or fall asleep. What you *can* do is facilitate conditions where they can attend to the 40 percent of their happiness that involves intentional activity.

You also have to start where your child is. If your child is depressed, then the first thing to do is to address the depression. Take them to see a therapist, and if necessary, talk to their doctor about medication options. Bill evaluated a girl named Rose who, when she was four, was walking on an ocean beach at sunset with her parents and her younger brother when she stopped, squatted down, and told her parents that she did not want to live anymore. Rose's parents weren't entirely shocked, as they both had suffered from depression much of their lives, as had their parents and their siblings. In this family, the genetic predisposition to negative mood was clearly very high. Rose started working with a therapist and, like her parents, she was then placed on Prozac to increase the availability of serotonin in her brain. When Bill tested Rose, she was six—and was upbeat, funny, and a complete delight to be with. She had needed a boost, though, to address the genetically based deficits she faced.

At the same time, with all children—whether there is need for medication or not—we should continue to talk about what happiness is, what it looks like, and the many routes possible to get to a happy life.

How am I supposed to give my kid time to pursue the 40 percent of intentional activity when 100 percent of his time is taken up by things he's expected to do?

We hear you and we're not suggesting it's easy. Pursuing happiness requires some tough choices. Let's say a kid is on a competitive soccer team that travels every weekend and practices every night. He's also in an academically challenging school where he has a ton of homework and resultant stress. The first question to ask is, What is it all in pursuit of? Is he playing soccer because he loves it and it gives him a feeling of flow, of total engagement? If so, great—keep it up, and maybe he can let his grades go somewhat, or choose a school that's less rigorous. Or perhaps he wants to stay at his school and keep up more easily with his academics. Can he play on a soccer team that demands less of his time, but still allows him the joy of playing? A huge lesson of life is learning to make these choices—we've met plenty of adults who are so busy doing everything that they enjoy nothing. Is that what we want for our kids, too? People who prioritize time—who are focused on "time affluence"—are happier than people who prioritize money.[42]

Putting It All Together

Javier's dad woke up at 2 a.m. one night because he could hear Javier pacing in the living room. He asked Javier, a high school senior, if he wanted to talk about what was on his mind, and though Javier typically held his feelings close, this time he said yes.

> JAVIER: I just feel like a nervous wreck. Nothing's settled for next year. I still don't understand why I didn't get into my top-choice school. And I might not hear back from the others for weeks or months. I know I won't be living here, but what will I do? What if no school accepts me?

> DAD: I get it, Javier. You're in a tough place right now. This time of your life is really stressful. There's still time to apply to one of your third-tier schools. Maybe you didn't apply to enough schools. You can always start there and then transfer to one of your first-tier schools later.

> JAVIER: What are you talking about? I applied to every school I would feel proud of attending. And, Dad, you don't know what it's like. All anyone ever asks me is where I've applied and whether or not I've gotten in. It's humiliating.

> DAD: You could just say you're still waiting to hear. You don't have to tell them about every rejection.

JAVIER: But then I'm lying. Dad, you just don't understand how stressful this is.

Javier's dad meant well, but the worldview he was communicating to Javier likely increased his anxiety. By jumping into advice and problem-solving (suggesting Javier apply to more schools, then transfer), he signaled that he was anxious about Javier's prospects, too. He also communicated a path that had a pretty narrow outcome: a degree from a sought-after college. He was playing into the happiness myth that "I'll be happy when. . . ." And his suggestion that Javier lie or dodge others' questions about his applications process suggested that he, too, was embarrassed that Javier hadn't been admitted. Likely neither of these messages sat well with Javier or did much to calm him down.

What if it had gone like this instead?

JAVIER: I just feel like a nervous wreck. Nothing's settled for next year. I still can't believe I didn't get into my top-choice school. And I might not hear back from the others for weeks or months. I know I won't be living here, but what will I do? What if no school accepts me?

DAD: That's a lot. No wonder you can't sleep.

JAVIER: Yes, it just sucks. It's all I can think about. And it's all anyone ever talks about or asks me about. *Where did you apply? Where did you get in?* It's just humiliating. It's why I can't sleep.

DAD: Wow, you're feeling pretty discouraged, huh? That must be hard, when it's also mixed with a feeling of everything being so unsettled. Can I tell you what's going through my mind right now, though?

JAVIER: I guess.

DAD: I just feel so certain that you are going to find your place in this world. And finding your place isn't just about where you go to college, or what you study, or how prestigious your résumé is. You have so much to offer, Javier. You're so outgoing and creative. People gravitate to you because you're so much fun to be around. You're the kind of person who is always looking out for others, and you have such a strong sense of fairness, of social justice. There are so many ways to use those gifts you have in pursuit of a happy life. This whole college admission thing feels really big and decisive, I know, but the truth is, it won't be the thing that makes you achieve in your life, or that holds you back.

JAVIER: Yeah, but what do I say if people keep asking me about it?

DAD: Well, you can check in with yourself and see if you want to share your feelings about it. So if it's a good friend you feel safe with, that's one thing. But if it's another kid's parents, and you don't want to tell them, just be honest and say something like, "Thanks a lot for your interest. But it's so all-encompassing, I'm just really trying to focus on other things and would rather not talk about it." Then change the subject.

Remember What It's All About

We have a lot of work to do to align our cultural norms with what we know about the science of happiness. But in our optimistic framing, the two of us feel hopeful. The coronavirus pandemic shook those norms, and while we were heartbroken by the pain and sickness it caused, we also saw a silver lining: with immediate gratifications and pleasures un-available, many people found happiness of the more ethereal kind—the kind that comes from eating dinner together every night, sleeping enough, slowing down, and, in the face of a crisis, focusing on what gives their lives meaning. Writer and poet Sonya Renee Taylor put it so well when she said: "We will not go back to normal. Normal never was. Our pre-corona existence was not normal other than we normalized greed, inequity, exhaustion, depletion, extraction, disconnection, confusion, rage, hoarding, hate and lack. We should not long to return, my friends. We are being given the opportunity to stitch a new garment. One that fits all of humanity and nature."[43] Maybe now we are on an accelerated course to find real happiness.

Chapter 8

The Hard Ones: Talking with Kids about Sleep and Technology

After a grandfather accompanied his daughter to one of our lectures, he turned to her—a mother of elementary schoolers—and said, "Oh my god, parenting was so much easier in the eighties." It sure seems true. It used to be that the hardest thing for parents to talk to kids about was sex ("the talk"), and there was always an after-school special or a Judy Blume book to help. Now when we ask parents what conversations with their kids feel the most fraught, they say, "How do I make him stop gaming/checking his phone all the time?" or "How do I get him to get more sleep?" (They also ask how to talk to kids about race, questions that we defer to those with more expertise—see page 82.) Technology and sleep are thorny, intertwined issues that have certainly complicated the parenting terrain. Kids who can be reasonable about most things will fight ferociously in defense of the idea that social media doesn't make them more jealous or anxious, or that they do fine on five and a half hours of sleep. And yet the principles of communicating effectively with kids actually haven't changed since the 1980s (or the 1880s). Listening carefully and respectfully, understanding, offering advice, not trying to ram our perspective down kids' throats, working problems out respectfully: these apply to every parenting challenge in every generation. We just need to remember to apply them to the new frontier.

While we offer plenty of language in this chapter for talking about these issues, our guidance starts and ends with asking, What is your job as a parent? Is it to control your child's tech use? Is it to enforce the amount of sleep your child gets? Hopefully not, because you can't. You can make life unpleasant enough that they will eventually comply, but even that won't work for very long. **Your job is not to control your kids, but to help them learn to control themselves.**

Because this is much harder to do than to read in bold lettering, let's start with a visualization. Imagine your kid in the future, and let's say they're in college, living in a dormitory. It's a costly time for you, because tuition is pretty outrageous, plus there are living expenses and books to budget for. You want this time to be meaningful and fun for your kid, but you also want them to be taking it seriously so that they can finish in four years and be on their way to self-sufficiency. It's 3 a.m. and your kid is playing Xbox. Which might be okay if they didn't have classes the next day, but they actually have a 9 a.m. exam. There's no resident assistant around to say, "Lights out!" or even, "Come on, man, shouldn't you get some rest?" because that's not their job. You're not around, either—and if you were, your kid would probably just say, "I'm nineteen! Lay off!" or "Don't worry. I've got this."

Your job, then, is to prepare your child for this situation. As tempting as it is throughout their childhood and adolescence to say, "Get off your screen right now and go to bed!" we encourage you to return again and again to this visualization of life away from home. And to remember your goal: a kid who knows when they're getting out of balance, how to get themselves back, and how to run their own life before they leave home.

The Futility of Forcing Sleep

If there's one thing parents learn, and quickly, it's that you can't make your child sleep. Toddlers or young children are known to insist "I'm not tired!" even as their eyes are half closed and they begin to cry at every little thing. If we are convinced their decision to stay up is not going to go well, we're invested in their failure. And if we fight them, they're more apt to be insistent that they don't need any part of our solution. Discussions about sleep become about who's right and who's wrong. The objective, then, is to talk with your kids in a way that generates their own interest to change, to convey your trust in them, and to encourage their self-reflection.

With very young kids, we're clearly in charge of helping them develop healthy sleep routines, but even with infants, we have to consider their rhythms. We can shift their rhythms somewhat over time, but we are severely limited in our ability to make kids fall and stay asleep. With elementary schoolers, we want to explain that our goal is to find a bedtime for them that allows them to not feel tired during the day. We can talk with them about night owls and larks (morning people). Whether you feel energized as midnight approaches or ready to go to bed by nine is genetically determined, and we need to be especially sensitive to kids who have night owl "wiring." As they get older and older, we want to play a consultant role, helping them find the best way to be as well rested as possible.

Citing empirical evidence about how important sleep is probably isn't going to be very useful to the discussion. Most parents and kids know that sleep is critical for physical, emotional, and mental health, and for learning (although many are not aware that it's also critical for optimal athletic performance). There's new, mind-blowing research being reported every year that clarifies its important functions, and the evidence is already overwhelming that if we as a society made staying well-rested the highest priority, many (if not most) of the problems that we—and our children—experience would be resolved. If you do want to geek out about the latest science, though, check out the endnotes.[1]

If denial of sleep's importance isn't the main reason kids don't get enough of it, the first step is to figure out—well, what *is* the problem? The most common is insomnia—which is difficulty falling and/or staying asleep—but sometimes kids just don't want to go to sleep. Here are the most common issues we come across:

- **Restlessness.** "I can't turn my brain off." When Bill used to do therapy with anxious kids, many of whom had trouble sleeping, he would always begin by reminding them that we *fall* asleep. We don't march toward sleep, and we can't force ourselves to go to sleep—we wind down, let go, and *fall* asleep. But for many kids, that's easier said than done, and they experience this form of insomnia.

- **Anxiety about not being able to fall asleep.** Many adults can relate to this form of insomnia. It can be harder for kids and teens to name it, as we might. Instead, they will procrastinate at bedtime. If they're little, they might ask for one more story, for a glass of milk, for a special blanket, for their stuffed animals to be arranged just so. They might insist that Mom or Dad (or both) lie down with them or at least sit in their room until they fall asleep, which sleep experts call behavioral insomnia. If they're older, they may try to disappear into a video game or an interactive app of some sort—that "one more level" becomes the new version of "one more story." They'll stay up until they're so exhausted that they crash.

- **Considering sleep deprivation a badge of honor.** Ned sees this cultural pressure all the time, particularly in perfectionistic teenage girls who make a point of telling him how little sleep they've gotten. (And sometimes their parents are no better.) When they say something like, *I was up until 2 a.m. studying,* what they are really trying to signal is, *Look* *how much harder than other people I am willing to work!* They also use it to preemptively exculpate themselves, thinking, *I studied until 2 a.m. What more could I have done?*

- **Anxiety about the safety of rest.** This is a particularly common problem with perfectionists, who think, *There's always more to study. How do I know I'm really ready for that test? Someone else will take my space at USC if I go to sleep instead of studying.*

- **Fear of missing out/FOMO.** Again, we see this at every age. The five-year-old doesn't want to go to bed until Mom and Dad do, because they don't want to miss any of the fun. We've known parents who will habitually pretend to be going to bed to alleviate this fear of their kids. Older kids and college students don't want to miss out on the group chat or the late-night party, because what if something truly epic happens? Or what if they are left out of future gatherings because they miss this one?

- **Difficulty prioritizing and managing time.** We touched on this in earlier chapters, but the overscheduled kid/teen/college student/adult is a much more common sighting than the individual who says, "You know, I said no to this opportunity and that opportunity because I really value sleep." A huge part of a healthy life involves making choices about what *not* to do. Also, many kids (boys especially) struggle to know how long things will take. Firmly in the grasp of hope over experience, they repeatedly think an assignment that ultimately takes four hours will only take two. Only experience (hard-earned and painful for parents to watch) corrects these misperceptions. (We personally each claim to be getting better at this as we get older.)

- **Difficulty with self-assessment.** Most kids, and teenagers in particular, are not very good judges of how tired they are. This is because among the important functions of the prefrontal cortex are self-awareness and self-evaluation, and a tired PFC is simply unable to assess its own alertness. Bill was struck by how commonly his own children, in their late teenage years and early twenties, would insist that they weren't tired (despite the fact that they were really irritable). He then watched them lie on the couch to watch television in the early afternoon and fall sound asleep within five minutes, which represents pretty severe sleep deprivation.

- **Other sleep disorders.** Many of our clients have breathing-related sleep problems, which are typically treated initially by removal of tonsils and/or adenoids. Also, many teenagers develop a phase-delay sleep disorder, where they don't feel tired until the early morning hours and have great difficulty waking up. Kids with ADHD, autism, anxiety, and mood disorders are all at higher risk for sleep problems.

So What Do You Say?

With any serious sleep problems, start by talking to your pediatrician. They may recommend melatonin for insomnia, which roughly half of Bill's clients take to help them fall asleep or to regulate their sleep cycles. You might also consult books such as V. Mark Durand's *Sleep Better!* and Colleen Carney's *Goodnight Mind for Teens.* But some sleep issues you can help problem-solve with your child merely through changing the conversation.

When Bill's daughter, Jora, was ten, she announced very clearly one night, "I don't feel like going to bed. I'm not tired." Bill momentarily considered lecturing her about the importance of sleep or insisting that she needed to go to bed but decided otherwise. He said, "I know that you know what it feels like when you don't get enough sleep, and I have a lot of confidence in you to make good decisions. I'm going to bed, and

I trust that you will go to bed when you need to." Bill never had another discussion about bedtime with Jora, who was in bed by 10:30 p.m. virtually every school night as a high school student. This won't work (at least the first time) with every kid, especially those who have weak self-regulation skills. But for more kids than you would expect, this solves the issue. It takes sleep away from being a battleground issue, and when kids feel they are in control of their sleep, they take measures to be well rested. Think about it: the very last thing anyone should do at bedtime, a time for quieting the mind and winding down, is engage in an argument—let alone one *about* bedtime. Finally, for many kids, the best thing you can do is to go to bed yourself. It's like a silver bullet because many kids will feel anxious if they're the only one awake.

But for other kids, they will continue a pattern of not getting enough sleep, and the problems associated with being tired will only build. It's safe to say you can't have a productive conversation about sleep until you've unearthed what's keeping them from going to bed. What's keeping them awake—is it a restless body, a restless mind, or anxious emotions?[2] How would they describe it? Many kids say that they can't turn their mind off. So the first thing parents should do is show curiosity. Ask questions that narrow in on what's going on with them, such as:

- "Do you feel tired at your usual bedtime?"

- "What do you think keeps you up when you do feel tired?"

- "Would you like to get more sleep?"

- "What in your life do you think keeps you from getting more sleep?"

- "When you hear your friends talk about how little sleep they get, what does that make you feel? Are you impressed? Worried you should be doing the same? Wondering why they are studying so much? Does everyone do that?"

Second, show empathy, not judgment. Use the active listening techniques from Chapter 1 to repeat back what you've heard them say, so
they feel listened to.

- (For a younger child) "I get that you feel left out. I still remember when
  I was a kid and my mom made me take a nap while my big sister got
  to play."

- "So you don't feel tired at bedtime, is that what you're saying? Should
  we try to find a bedtime that works better for you?"

- "That must be hard, to feel like you want to go to sleep but to feel worried that you won't be able to. I would hate that feeling, too."

- "You have so much work to do—it sounds like you feel like there aren't
  enough hours in the day."

The next step is using language from Chapter 2 to get buy-in to let
you help them problem-solve. The problem-solving phase will obviously
look really different depending on what the problem is. But it's almost
always a good idea to treat the way forward as an experiment, not a mandate.[3] For instance, you could say something like:

- "Let's find a solution that satisfies your need to figure this out for yourself and my need to feel like I'm doing everything I can to help you
  grow a healthy brain and a healthy body."

- "Is there a habit—or maybe more than one—that you could change to
  make it easier for you to get to bed? Is that something you'd like to
  change? I'm happy to support you if there is anything I can do."

- "What if you keep a sleep log? Write down the time you go to bed, the
  time you fall asleep, and how many times you wake up in the middle of
  the night and for roughly how long. It can be a good way to just get

some data about what your sleep is like. If it looks like something we don't know how to solve, we can talk to your pediatrician."

- "Obviously, I couldn't make you fall asleep, and I'm not going to try. And I know that you know what it feels like to feel tired during the day. I also know that you don't want to feel crummy and don't want to perform much worse in school than you could if you were well rested. I'm just here to help you figure out some solutions."

- "Let's set a family goal of not feeling tired during the day. To reach our goal, we need to fall asleep and stay asleep at night. It can help everyone in the family to figure out what we each need to do in order to have a calm body and a calm mind when we want to go to sleep."

- "You may disagree with me, but from my perspective you do better when you go to bed at 9 p.m. But if you don't see it that way, let's track when you go to bed and when you wake up each day, and how you feel, and how much you're fighting with others that day. We can create a rating scale to measure how alert you feel. Then at the end of two weeks, we can take a look at it and you can decide what works best for you."

- "If you knew that no one would text you or post something new on social media after 9 p.m., would it make it easier for you to sleep without your phone? If so, would it make sense to make an agreement with your friends about it? All the parents could sign on to the agreement, too, if you thought it would help."

- "If you could arrange your schedule any way you like, where would sleep fit in?"

- "What if you rate your level of alertness in school before lunch and after lunch, after school, and in the evening? It would be good to know when you feel the most alert and when you feel the most tired, and if necessary, make some changes. It may be that it will take you less time to do your homework if you get up just half an hour earlier in the morning, for instance, rather than staying up an extra hour at night."

- "I read that 95 percent of the problems kids get into on social media happen late at night when they're tired and not thinking clearly. Have you noticed that?"

- "Are there kids who seem to be doing well AND seem to get to sleep as much as they want to or as much as you'd want to? I wonder whether they are doing something you haven't tried yet."

- "I've been reading that a lot of high-achieving kids kind of brag about how little sleep they get. Have you noticed that with your friends? I'm reading that it's because kids want to show their friends—and their teachers, too—how hardworking they are. The problem is that getting five hours of sleep is terrible for their brains. Did you know that after you've been up for eighteen hours, your thinking is more impaired than if you're legally drunk?"[4]

- "Since your baseball games go so late and you're not getting enough sleep, what if you tried working a power nap into your schedule, right after school but before your game? What if you tried doing it just for a week and see if it makes you feel different?"

We've learned many great strategies for helping kids with sleep over the years, and one of our favorites comes from Eli Lebowitz, the developer of the SPACE program from Chapter 5, whose approach to helping anxious kids sleep in their own bed involves the kids and their parents putting on a make-believe show in which the child pretends to be asleep.[5] Whatever strategy you use, treat your child with respect instead of judgment. Ask them what ideas they have for testing their sleep and help them tune into their own bodies to ask what they need. To avoid lecturing kids about sleep over and over, write out what you really want them to know in a text, email, or better yet, a handwritten note.

Inside the Brain

The brain doesn't actually sleep—it's active all night. It is encoding and consolidating memories, strengthening important connections between the prefrontal cortex and the hippocampus (where new memories are formed), and replaying experiences. Let's say you're asked to do a simple motor task, like typing a sequence of five numbers as fast and accurately as possible. While additional practice may make your performance improve, you know what else does? Sleep, without any additional practice![6]

It's worth thinking through the value of rest, separately from sleep. And by rest we do not mean playing video games, but rather, the activation of the brain's default mode network (DMN). The DMN is a network in your brain that activates only when you aren't focusing on a task; it comes "on" when you're lying in bed before you fall asleep, or when you wake up but before you get out of bed, or when you're taking a shower. Lots of people call the DMN "the genius lounge" because it's when you aren't focused on a specific task that you get creative ideas and think of solutions to problems. This is also where self-reflection happens, and where the brain can analyze and compare ideas. The work of the DMN is essential for a healthy brain.

Ned constantly talks to kids about how they need to give their brains time to "think about nothing," because that's when they make connections. When a student who was prepping for the LSAT asked how he should spend his last couple of days before the test, Ned asked him what he had in mind. "Usually," the student said, "I'd do a bunch of tests."

"Well, a few thoughts," Ned said. "One, it's hard work, and time to reflect on that work, that allows your brain to see patterns. ('Oh yeah, that analogy problem was tricky in the same way as that one from last week.') So you won't see the test as a blizzard of different tricks that are so hard to prepare for, but as a test that has a few different plays with some wrinkles. So, yeah, do a section or two, but then go for a run or a walk (no phone!) so your brain can make those connections naturally."

The World Wide Web of Technology

There are a lot of interests and habits that we can just cut off altogether if they start to interfere with our life, though perhaps not easily. We might like to smoke, but we don't really need to smoke. We might like to drink alcohol, but we don't need to. We might like to gamble, but it can go. Technology is different. While there are some segments of it we can cut off if we have to, there are many more that if we want to live a productive life in much of the world in the twenty-first century, well, we need them. That's why our relationship with technology might best be compared to our relationship with food. Everyone needs to eat. What you eat and how much you eat requires judgment, restraint, self-knowledge, and good habits. The goal is to help our kids develop a healthy relationship with technology so that they make good choices about what to engage with and when. So a guiding question to use with kids is: **How do we make it so that technology's part of what you do and not all of what you do?**

Whereas with sleep the challenge is in figuring out what is blocking their ability to get enough of it, with technology the major challenges are that it changes so fast and that some of the smartest psychologists and behavioral scientists in the world are working to make it next to impossible for kids to stop playing, posting, or checking their phones. The use of science this way doesn't sit well with many in the profession. In 2018, the Children's Screen Time Action Network wrote a protest letter, signed by two hundred psychologists, to the president of the American Psychological Association.[7] The letter calls attention to what they see as unethical practices to get kids hooked by using "persuasive technology" (also called persuasive design or behavior design) to capitalize on children's developmental vulnerabilities, including their desire for social acceptance and fear of social rejection. As the psychologists are well aware, children—and especially preteens and teens—are particularly sensitive to being socially accepted or rejected. Also, psychologists and other behavioral scientists working in the video-game industry take advantage of the developmental drive in preteen and teenage boys to gain competence. They create video games with powerful rewards given on intermittent schedules that convince young players, especially teenage boys, that they are mastering important competencies through their game play.

It's quite a task to keep up with the latest from the field, or the new studies on technology, or the technologies themselves. Instead of pouring your energy into collecting information about tech, we recommend you seek to understand your kid. What need is technology filling for them? Is there another way to meet this need? The task at hand is to help them explore their own ambivalence about technology. Because even as it offers them something, almost all kids are aware it's got some problems, too.

Show You're in the Same Boat

Look, none of us is perfect. Most parents struggle with managing their own tech use. One study in the UK found that 60 percent of parents felt that their kids spent too much time on screens, while 70 percent of teens felt the same about their parents.[8] Many of the kids we work with repeatedly have the experience of needing to talk with a parent about something important but having to talk as the parent checks their phone while "trying" to listen. In many ways, we're all in the same boat. Whether we recognize it or not, we're remarkably adept at rationalizing our own screen time: "This is really for work." "I deserve some relaxation after working hard all day." "It's important to stay connected to my friends when it's so hard to get together given what busy lives we lead." "I am an adult. Screens don't really affect me like they do teens." Notwithstanding the accuracy of these statements, it's still possible to have an unhealthy relationship with your phone. Be conscious of your own habits. Communicate those habits to your kids, especially when you're struggling with keeping a balance. Be forthcoming about your mistakes, sharing things like, "I'm much too tired today—I really need to be better about binge-watching shows at night, because I've noticed it keeps me up too late" or "You know, I really screwed up today because I shot off an email to a colleague when I was worked up about something and looking at that email now makes me cringe. I wish I'd cooled off first."

What Not to Say and Do

Almost more than any other subject, parents have to watch their impulses around their kids' tech use. Most of us have been guilty of at least one of the following:

- Saying things like, "What good could possibly come out of being on social media ALL. THE. TIME!?!" or "How can you waste so much time on this stupid game?"

- Monitoring their tech use without telling them.

- Forcing them to get off a device right away, before they have a chance to close out a conversation or tell other players they're leaving. (It might lower our stress to make this pronouncement, as we feel we're doing our parental duty, but it increases theirs.)

- When they make a mistake on social media, scaring them with language like, "Do you want this to follow you your whole life?"

- Expressing snobbery about what they're following, by saying things like, "Ugh, this blog is ridiculous,"[9] or "This game is nothing but a time suck." If parents are dismissive of their kids' tech interest, they've lost the ability to help solve any tech-related problems.

- Oversimplifying by responding to kids' problems with social media by saying, "Then just don't use it," or "Just delete that app."

What all these responses have in common is that they're disrespectful—they don't communicate a belief that kids are intelligent and want their lives to work out, and for that matter, that they want their tech use to be balanced and healthy. And they do. Bill recently asked twenty-five ninth graders in Houston if they used their phones or computers more than is good for them. They all said yes. And many of Bill's clients who were gaming excessively in middle school stopped completely, or cut way back, in high school when they realized that it was hurting them academically and/or socially. Although there are kids who truly become addicted to gaming and need treatment for it, most can be helped to develop healthy patterns of use through the process of collaborative problem-solving.

First, Seek to Understand

Consider that you are a traveler to a strange new land. As you get your bearings, you're trying to sort out what the inhabitants like and dislike. What urges do they have and what drives them? What's the currency in their land? Know that after puberty, the drive for social connection spikes in a way few of us recall accurately. Adolescents get not only a huge rush of dopamine from being around other teens, but also serotonin and oxytocin (which promote a sense of well-being and social bonding).

Now, consider how these inhabitants interact with technology. Parts of their world might look familiar to you, but don't let that fool you. Their technology landscape is very different from what yours is, and the landscape of their childhood is very different from what yours was.

Teenagers, for instance, are so often on phones and computers because *other* teens are so often on phones and computers. Remember when you used to pass notes in class? Screens are now used for that. Remember when you used to go to the mall with your friends? Screens are used for that, too. Remember when you would hang out at the movie theater or video arcade all day? Screens again. Screens are the town hall, the central square, the *world* teenagers so often inhabit.

Teens are wired to protect their friendships and feel pressure to stay connected with their peers constantly, even when they don't want to. Emily Weinstein, who leads the Digital Dilemmas project at Harvard's "Zero to Three" program, points out that kids believe that not being available threatens their relationships. They worry that if they don't text a friend for a while, the friend will come up with an excuse to cut them off. Also, they don't want to hurt anyone's feelings by not staying in touch, and they feel a huge responsibility (and burden) to stay in touch with friends who are struggling. They worry that their friends might do something bad if they don't respond in time to stop them.[10] In short, you have to really comprehend why your kids are using these platforms—and what they use each one *for*—before you can engage in a discussion about setting boundaries around them.

Part of that involves using the platforms yourself. There's no time like the present to start a Pinterest board! Confused about the difference between Snapchat and Insta? Now's the time to sign up, and to "follow" your kids if they'll let you. The same is true for video-game platforms. Keep your mind open to understanding before you form an opinion or begin a conversation. Ask questions like:

- "Help me understand—I can see you love this game. Show me what you love about it."

- "Can I watch you play for a while?"

- "Can you teach me to play? You'll probably kick my butt, but I'd like to see what this is all about."

- "Who are some of the other guys you're playing with? What are they like?"

- "Which Pinterest boards do you like to follow? What's appealing about those?"

- "Why do you like Snapchat better than Instagram?"

- "Why is that YouTube star so popular, do you think?"

- "What do you love most about TikTok?"

- "What's the hardest part about *Fortnite*? Is there a pattern? Is there skill or luck in that final moment?"

For far too long, while justifying his own time on his phone or laptop, Ned silently (or not so silently) questioned or impugned his daughter's use. He asked questions like, "What are you watching?" or "How many hours will you be on there?," not in a spirit of inquisitiveness but of inquisitorialness. Over time, he made an effort to engage: "Collins Key? LUV that guy!" "How are the Norris Nuts folks today?" "You've seen all twenty-six seasons of *Criminal Minds*? Well, I suppose it offers more character development than I saw on *Gilligan's Island* or endless rewatching of *Three's Company*." It's not that Ned wanted his daughter to be spending as much time as she was on a device. But he had to understand what she was watching and what needs of hers were being met before he could hope to help her find some off-screen ways to also meet those needs.

Our understanding of what technology can offer deepens every day. Our friend Devorah Heitner, a writer who teaches and lectures widely about kids' tech use, points out there's a difference between using tech for consumption and using it for creativity. Many kids go online to explore their interests and expand the bounds of their creativity. If one of our goals as parents is to expose our kids to a wide array of possibilities about how to spend their time, technology is what makes so much of that possible. Your kid can look up how to build a computer, how to sew a garment, how to write music—all with the power of the web.[11] Kids are also more able to be civically active than we were when we were kids. They can create a website for a book drive or organize a protest. These are options that weren't available to us, and the opportunities are deeply valuable.

The bottom line in all this? It's complicated. Really smart social scientists say tech has destroyed a generation. Others think it's the salvation of humankind. We suspect the truth is somewhere in the middle, and that's what we need to explore with our kids.

What We Worry about, and What to Say

Foremost among our concerns about technology isn't the technology itself, but what it replaces. Research is very clear that kids need to sleep, and technology often cuts into their sleep time.[12] Research is also very clear that kids need to play in self-directed ways, and screen time too often replaces this process. Peter Gray, who has made his career studying play from a developmental and evolutionary point of view, has concluded that play is what children need most to develop into healthy and competent human beings. The young in all mammal species play, because it's through play that they learn how to become adults. Based on data from societies around the world, Gray says that children need less time in school and more time playing.[13] We take great risk with our children's development by short-circuiting their evolutionary drive to engage in creative, dramatic, and child-led play. That's why Bill loves watching his granddaughters—ages four and seven—act out elaborate scenarios of their own making; he knows they are learning to manage emotions, and that they are getting used to being a part of this planet in a way that doesn't overwhelm them.

We also want kids to have the experience of focusing on one task at a time, because it's much better for the brain. We really can't focus on two things at once, so when we try to, we're not really managing multiple tasks simultaneously; instead, we're quickly shifting our attention from task to task, which lowers the speed and accuracy of our performance and raises our stress hormone levels. We also know that exercise and time outside are good for the brain, the body, and the soul. And we know that nothing replaces the connection felt from in-person interactions. These are all important slices of the pie of a kid's day.

If your kid's pie is well-balanced, and they're still online a lot, it might be okay. Just as with food, there is no one-diet-fits-all. Some kids can consume a lot and be fine, while others will get a stomachache, and the inverse is also true. The best message, then, is "You know when you're full." While we're cheerleaders of this approach, there's also no denying that sometimes kids can't tell when they've had too much. Which brings us to another thing we worry about: tech addiction.

Although there's a lot of controversy about whether behavioral addictions (such as gambling, internet, and gaming addiction) are comparable to substance addiction, neurological imaging studies show similarities between the two in the dopamine system, particularly involving its regulation. Because dopamine levels rise most dramatically when we *anticipate* something positive happening, when we hear a buzz or a ding that tells us we have a new text, email, or notification, the fact that we don't know exactly what info is coming in piques our curiosity and lights up our motivation system. We can get to the point where it's hard to be motivated for anything *but* the ding.

Addiction is a risk for every technology we use, but particularly so for video games. Video-game addiction is such a serious problem that the World Health Organization included a gaming disorder addiction diagnosis in the International Classification of Diseases. We know that instant gratification is the route to addiction, and the shorter the duration between surges of dopamine, the bigger the rush. That's why you're more at risk for addiction playing a slot machine, where you anticipate a win or loss every thirty seconds, than you are playing an eight-minute poker game. As we said, psychologists employed by video-game companies focus their efforts and the knowledge they have about the brain to keep kids playing more.

While most kids who play video games don't become addicted, studies suggest that approximately 10 percent do.[14] Before you can tackle coming up with a solution, you have to determine what level of help your child needs—because if they are addicted, the rules of engagement change. Some of the criteria from experts who study video-game addiction include lying about how much time is spent playing, stealing games or money to buy games, spending increasing amounts of time and money to feel excited, and escaping problems through play.[15] (For more on what to do if your child is addicted, see page 248.)

We also worry about social media, the dangers of which many experts are already shouting from the rooftops. As the haunting Netflix documentary *The Social Dilemma* pointed out, the two industries that refer to consumers as "users" are the illegal drug trade and social media companies. Kara Bagot, a researcher who studies adolescent brain development, found that "Likes" activate the reward system in the same way that substances do.[16] If you don't get Likes, you'll feel sad; teens learn to post stuff in order to get Likes; and a negative cycle is born in which they will do things that are not good for them in order to gain approval.

A recent Pew Research Center study found that teens, on average, are neither positive nor negative about social media. Many (81 percent) report feeling more connected to their friends, and indeed there is truth to what researcher danah boyd says: "Teens aren't addicted to social media. They're addicted to each other."[17] Teens also point to social media's ability to enable them to use their creative side (71 percent). That said, a sizable minority report feeling overwhelmed by online dramas (45 percent) and feeling pressure to post only content that makes them look good (43 percent). What worries us about social media is its potential impact on a child's internal sense of control.[18] As Heitner writes, "We don't want kids to crowdsource their identity from this large and ever-present group of peers."[19] What we want for our kids is to dress, act, eat, and *be* in accordance with what they love and feel good about, independent of others' reactions. As this internal locus of control goes down, rates of depression, cutting behaviors, and suicide go up—and the most vulnerable group is middle-school-aged girls.[20]

We've never encountered a parent who is unaware of the danger areas of tech, but there are six that we find the most problematic:

- Excessive video gaming

- Pornography

- Exposing themselves on social media in ways that might be dangerous or objectionable

- Comparisons on social media that make them unhappy

- Unthoughtful consumption of anything on a screen/bingeing

- Using technology to meet needs unsolvable by tech

We've offered a sample dialogue for each of these danger areas—dialogues that bring together all that we've emphasized in the past seven chapters. While you will undoubtedly encounter different scenarios with your own kids, again, the principles of respectful engagement are the same.

Excessive Gaming

Wakiza was a twelve-year-old boy who played *Fortnite* hours a day. His parents didn't intervene too much at first, but then they realized Wakiza's grades had slipped and that he was always grumpy and tired. He would snap every time they told him to stop playing. It became a huge source of conflict between Wakiza and his mom. His parents began to worry that he was seriously addicted.

Their first step was to recognize that no, he wasn't. He wasn't lying about it or sneaking it at every opportunity, and while his grades had slipped, he was still keeping up in school. But they still worried that his level of play was on an unhealthy trajectory. At dinner one night, his mom began their dialogue by apologizing.

"I realize I've been trying to treat your video games as a problem to be solved, and that's wrong," she said. "I've read that you can develop some really positive skills from video games.[21] And if you were into baseball, I'd be fine with the amount of time you're spending. I'm starting to see video games differently. I want to understand what you love about them. Can you show me?"

Wakiza was surprised and a little mistrustful. What was her angle? But he taught her how to play the game, and she understood it a bit more when he played with others. He was actually really good at it—and got a lot of accolades from the other kids about how good he was.

He's getting a confidence boost out of this, she realized. He had never been especially good at sports, which she suspected had bothered him because it was such a social currency with the boys in their community. She had tried talking with Wakiza about that, but he was pretty closed off. She tried talking with him about it again when they were playing the game, and this time he was relaxed and admitted he loved that he was really good at it.

"I think I understand now why you love playing. I think you should keep playing, because it makes you happy, you've met some cool friends through it, and it gives you a lot of confidence. But it's also my guess that you don't want to play 24/7, and that if I 'let' you play for seven hours a day, your life probably wouldn't work the way you want it to work."

"But I'm not going to play seven hours a day, Mom."

"I know that, but you also used to play for just a couple of hours and now you play for four almost every day. The way that games like these work, they're actually designed to keep you wanting more and more."

"So what are you saying? You're going to cut me off?"

"I don't think that makes sense—I can't be here to monitor it all the time, and I don't want to. And you don't want me to."

"That's an understatement."

"I also don't want to be fighting about it. What I think we should do is talk about the amount of time you think it makes sense to play each day, where you still have time for other things, and then stick with that. That's the approach we would take if you were on the baseball team, right? But because this isn't baseball, because these tools are actually much more addictive than something like baseball, I think we need to be more proactive about it. If you find that you want to play more than the time we decide right now, and that it's hard not to, what could we do? Like, maybe you would actually ask me to take your Xbox for a while."

"What if I say I want to play for seven hours a day? Will you let me?"

"No, I wouldn't, because that doesn't feel reasonable, and it would keep you from doing other things that are important to your health, and as your mom, I wouldn't feel good about that. Plus, it's not going to make you any better at the game. I can show you some research on that if you want it."[22]

"So you're saying I can do what I want, but then you're saying I can't."

"Well, that's a good point. I'm not trying to talk you out of *wanting* to play all the time. I just want to talk about how, if you did, that would fit in with the life you want for yourself. But whatever number we come to an agreement about, it has to be something we both can live with."

Pornography

Dustin was an eleven-year-old boy whose dad saw via a browser history that he had been looking at pornography. Dustin's dad had covered the basics of puberty with him, and he'd had sex ed at school, but Dustin hadn't seemed overly curious. What his dad realized was that Dustin just really wasn't comfortable talking about it.

When they were alone one morning at breakfast, his dad said, "Hey, I was on the computer the other day and it looks from the browsing history like you were on a website that had some naked women on it. Don't worry that you're in trouble, because you're not. But I'm curious, is that something you're interested in, or that your friends are looking at?"

Dustin's face reddened. "No," he said.

"Look, Dustin, it's okay—it's really normal to be curious." He remembered—and told Dustin—about an incident when he was eleven where a nude magazine he had in his room had disappeared. He knew his mom had done it, that she must have found it when she was cleaning his room, but she never said anything to him about it. The silence made him feel really ashamed of what he'd done.

"I don't want there to be that weird silence between us, and I don't want you to feel shame about being curious. You'll probably only be even more so in the next months and years. The thing I need you to be aware of is that the things that are appropriate for you now, you can find on the internet. The things that won't be appropriate until later, you can find on the internet. The things that are never going to be appropriate, you can find that on the internet, too. The challenge is that you can't unsee those things."

Dustin watched his dad carefully, probably wondering *like what?* "I want you to explore things that are appropriate and meaningful," his dad said, "but try to make sure that you don't find yourself in places looking at things that are upsetting and not appropriate. And there are also people who are much older than you who use dark corners of the web to reach out to young people in ways that aren't okay. I can't watch everything you do on the internet, because you deserve privacy. But that means I also can't be there to protect you."

Dustin still didn't say much, but that was okay. His dad was confident that he was listening, and it might be a step too far to ask him to engage further. He reminded Dustin that he wouldn't police him, but that if Dustin got himself into a dark place, he should talk to a trusted adult about it—even if it wasn't his dad.

Exposing Themselves on Social Media in Ways That Might Be Dangerous or Objectionable

Cooper was a seventeen-year-old who, along with some friends, posted some pretty sexually graphic photos. His mom—a single parent—found out about it from one of the other kids' parents. She was afraid for his future. Would colleges find out about it? Would there be a record of this when he wanted to get a job?

Though she (understandably) wanted to rage at him—*How could you be so stupid? This will follow you your whole life! And why would you even be posing like that? That's so unlike you!*—she was careful to work through her feelings before talking with Cooper.

"Theo's mom called you," Cooper said, a statement—not a question—when he saw his mom's face.

"Yeah."

"It was just a stupid joke, Mom. I don't know why Theo's mom is making such a big deal out of it. We were just messing around."

"I know, Cooper."

"So what? Is this the part where you tell me I've ruined my whole life? That my future boss will see that photo and decide not to hire me?"

"No, but I have to be honest that initially I was worried. But now that I've calmed down, I don't think that's the case. All this just brings up how different your life is than mine was when I was seventeen. I didn't have to worry about this stuff. I could make stupid mistakes and no one would know who wasn't there."

"So you're saying you think this IS going to follow me?"

"I don't think so. But I think it's a good reminder that you start being known for what you put out into the world at an early age now. You have a pretty cool opportunity with social media to create a résumé, of sorts. You can practice being known for your work. People will look at your profile—and there's stuff that can't be taken down. Just know that, own it, and learn from the mistake. But also don't freak out too much about this one incident."

Comparisons on Social Media That Make Them Unhappy

Tiffany was really worried about her fourteen-year-old daughter, Li. It seemed to Tiffany that Li spent a lot of time prepping and posing for selfies that she would then photoshop and post. Tiffany didn't want to intrude, but she also didn't want Li to be so connected to her phone or dependent on what people thought of her.

One day Tiffany watched Li as she balanced her phone on different surfaces to capture the most flattering angle for a selfie. Tiffany cringed, but she knew Li would shut her out if she expressed any form of judgment. Instead, she said, "I love your outfit, Li. You have a really great fashion sense." Li smiled, and Tiffany asked if she wanted her to take a picture. Then she asked a bunch of questions to show she was genuinely curious about where Li was posting. Why did she choose to post when she did? What usually happened afterward?

"There's so much emphasis on appearance in high school, huh?" Tiffany said. Li had opened up a bit by this point and complained to her mom about how much pressure it was.

"I feel like I have to keep up my brand or something, you know?" Li said.

"What about looking at other people's photos? How does that make you feel?" Li shrugged, so Tiffany went on. "I know that looking at other people's lives makes me feel crappy sometimes," she said. "When that happens, I usually just quit social media for a while."

"Are you telling me to quit? Because I like it. And it's how I connect with my friends."

"No, not at all. But I do think you should check in with yourself periodically about how it makes you feel. I read somewhere that social media is fine to look at for a bit, but that after about half an hour, your mood tanks.[23] I wonder if you've noticed that. Or if it makes you feel good more often than bad?"

"I don't know," Li said.

"Maybe we could just check in with each other about it sometimes. Would that be okay?"

Li shrugged, so her mom went on. "Look, this is all stuff that can be helpful to talk about. Setting boundaries with your friends is hard enough *without* social media, but now you have this whole other world to navigate, too. I honestly don't know how you do it, and I just think it would be healthy for both of us to be in conversation about it. But it's not something I would ever want to come between us."

Thoughtless Consumption

Johann was a teenager who watched a lot of streamed shows. He was like a contemporary Mike Teavee from *Charlie and the Chocolate Factory*. He also checked his phone constantly and couldn't be without it, even at dinner. He didn't have just one source of obsession—he was happy to move between apps and technologies, but he was always, always plugged in to something. He was particularly caught up in "doomscrolling," encountering one disaster after another on his social media feed.

It made Johann's dad so angry every time he saw Johann mindlessly check his phone, he wanted to just throw the device out the window and tell Johann too bad.

But, after talking with Johann about what he loved to do on his phone, his dad asked, "Do you think you're on your device about the right amount of time?"

Johann shrugged. "I'm not on it that much."

"How much do you think would be about the right amount of time?"

"I don't know. Maybe three hours a day?"

"Okay. And do you think three hours a day would give you the amount of time you need to do other things that are important? Like, if you look at your day like a pie, with a chunk of time for school, some for exercise, some for family time, what would tech look like? Would three hours be enough?"

"Yeah, sure."

"I suggest we track it. All of us—not just you. I think three hours sounds good, too. So what if we use these trackers for our phones, and then see our tech use at the end of the week?"

Johann agreed, and much to his surprise (but not his dad's), his usage far exceeded three hours a day. Everyone's did. So they had a family meeting to discuss what to do. They ended up starting a practice on Sundays where they mapped out everyone's schedules—putting blocks in for nonscreen use. Each Sunday they printed out their tech use for the week and used it to guide their scheduling.

It worked pretty well, but Johann still struggled with the phone diet, even though he'd agreed to it. One day when his dad saw him studying and checking his phone, his dad told him that he was far more likely to remember the information he was studying if his brain wasn't engaged in multitasking. Then his dad said, "I know that it's important to you to do well on these exams. I also appreciate how important it is to stay connected to your friends to support each other. Is there a way I can help you manage your phone so you can accomplish both?"

Later, the whole family watched *The Social Dilemma* together, which educated them all about the nature of tech addiction, and how the content they love and social media they use are designed to keep them engaged, such that it's much harder to stop than continue. Nobody—least of all a teenaged boy—wants to feel like they're being played, and the more Johann understood *why* he kept reaching for his phone, the less inclined he was to do it.[24]

Looking to Tech to Offer What Tech Can't

Ten-year-old Violet was obsessed with YouTube. She had a slew of YouTube stars she followed, from those who just recorded their everyday activities to those who created imaginary worlds. Her parents were aware of everything she watched, and they tried to watch with her when they could to better understand her enthusiasm. They also helped her with balance—ensuring she had time for sleep, exercise, chores, focused work (usually on school), and times that were intentionally unscheduled, but where she couldn't use technology.

They felt her tech use was pretty well handled, but they worried because Violet didn't have many friends. She was a social kid who loved hanging out with her cousins during family gatherings, but she never asked to have friends over and wasn't often invited to go to friends' houses after school. When her parents suggested that she join a club or reach out to some other kids her age, she bristled. She preferred retreating to her room to watch her YouTube stars. Her parents became even more worried when her siblings would talk about something a friend did, and Violet started referring to how her YouTube icons did that, too.

Her mom asked her to go with her on a walk one day, and as they walked, she brought up some of the icons. "It's almost like you know them, personally," her mom said.

"I know!" Violet said. "I feel like I do."

"Does watching those shows make you feel like you're friends with them?"

"Yes, totally. I know everything about them."

"Violet, I think that's wonderful. It does make me wonder, though: What do they know about *you*?"

"Mom, don't be ridiculous. It's a *show*. Of course they don't know me."

"Right, I know that," her mom said. "It's just that I've been doing some reading lately about what really makes people connect to each other. And part of it is being in person together and knowing about each other. You know, having a more equal relationship. I think if you don't have that with people your age, it's easy to feel lonely. And if you feel lonely, it's easy to put on a YouTube show of familiar faces so that you don't feel that way anymore."

Violet was quiet for a long time. Then her mom asked, softly, "Honey, do you feel lonely?"

Violet admitted that sometimes she did. Violet had a lot of friends when she was younger, but as she got older, she became more worried about saying the wrong thing.

"Do you think part of the reason you like YouTube is that you don't have to worry about anyone judging you?" her mom asked.

"Yeah," Violet said. "It feels safe."

"Are you open to having somebody help you with feeling safe when you're around kids at school?"

Violet said she would like to have more friends, and that she was open to talking with her doctor about her worries. Together, they set about creating a plan to tackle Violet's social anxiety.

But What About . . . ?

When I tell my kid he needs to get more sleep, he objects and says he actually feels more tired on Saturdays, when he sleeps twelve hours instead of seven.

It's a fair question with two explanations. First, he is simulating the feeling of jet lag because his hours are so off. If you wake at noon rather than eight, you are groggy from waking up in a new time zone. And, by reducing his sleep debt, he's improved his ability to evaluate how tired he is. He's more aware that he feels terrible. Ned often jokes, "Do you think zombies know they're zombies? Imagine if they started to recover into their old, healthy selves. There would be a transition period where they'd be like, 'WOW. I feel like @#&$!'"

My kid insists that he can't go to bed because he has too much homework. What can I do?

As you can guess, we recommend engaging in collaborative problem-solving that starts out by empathizing with kids' perceived need to complete their homework and validating their desire to learn and do well in school. But if they actually do have way too much homework, it might be time for you to wear your advocate hat.

The National Education Association and the National PTA have, for many years, recommended ten minutes per grade as the maximum time spent on homework. Schools that far exceed this amount of homework do so with absolutely no scientific justification. If your child is at a school that claims to use evidenced-based practices and your child has excessive homework, ask where the evidence is that supports that amount of homework. It doesn't exist.

My son meets all the markers for gaming addiction. What do I do?

We strongly recommend bringing in a therapist who specializes in video-game addiction. Though there are different strategies you might expect an expert to use, we're fans of the approach taken by Dr. Clifford Sussman.[25] His approach respects kids while also giving strong guidance, and it includes three stages: (1) dopamine detox—going cold turkey, without any game-induced stimulation; (2) achieving balance, which is initially regulated heavily by parents, with kids earning trust and privileges back with parental supervision; and (3) self-regulation. Sussman points out that for kids to maintain healthy use of their games, they need a schedule that involves periods of high-dopamine and low-dopamine activities—the latter being things like shooting baskets, taking a walk, drawing, or reading a comic. In the same way that some teens with substance abuse issues need residential care, some kids with a severely addictive relationship to gaming will also need residential treatment.

My daughter has an eating disorder, though it's well managed right now. I worry about her exposure to social media and am not sure a collaborative approach would work with her.

You're right, and we recommend getting a professional involved. We do think it makes sense to have strict controls on sites like TikTok, Instagram, and Snapchat, until, with the help of her therapist, you can begin to lift those controls.

My daughter has a set amount of TV she's allowed to watch, but I caught her sneaking some on her iPad. What do I do?

Ideally, when you agree to the amount of TV time, you also agree to what happens if she breaks that agreement. If you haven't, we recommend talking with her about what she feels would be an appropriate consequence, and coming to a solution you can both live with.

There's more to this, of course. In fact, so much more that we decided to include a chapter on limits, consequences, and problem-solving . . . which is next up!

Remember What It's All About

As we vent that our parents never had to navigate such complicated terrain during our upbringing (like, how hard was it to figure out mixtapes?), it's worth considering the future. If our kids become parents, what parenting issues will they struggle with? What technologies will they need to have at least a rudimentary understanding of so that they can connect with their kids? Honestly, we might have gotten off easy. It's reassuring to know that when everything will surely look so different, much will also be the same—because at the end of the day, now or a hundred years from now, the end goal is a close and respectful relationship with our kids. And so far as we know, there's not an app for that.

Chapter 9

What about Consequences?

One Sunday morning when Ned's kids were still in elementary school, Ned was tired of nagging them to clean up after themselves. So he announced that the family was going out for brunch—a special treat—but if the kids didn't have their assigned areas clean in thirty minutes, they couldn't go. They agreed to the plan in a lukewarm way, but didn't make much of a move to actually pick up, even when Ned gave them countdown warnings.

After the thirty minutes had passed, the kids' spaces looked as messy as ever. You can imagine Ned's thought process: *Wow, do they not even listen to me at all?* And *I have to follow through on this, otherwise they'll never do what they're asked. They won't know I'm serious.*

The kids were *very* unhappy to be left out of brunch. Ned and Vanessa went anyway, but were irritable, and a little worried, too, because they didn't often leave the kids home alone. They raced through their meal, barely tasting the food, and were home not even an hour later. For the rest of the day, everyone was grumpy and short with one another. And the house still didn't get cleaned up.

Many would look at Ned's tactics that morning and say that it was good parenting. He was clear, consistent, and true to his word. You can't set limits, they would say, unless you're prepared to enforce them. You don't want kids who will walk all over you, and you don't want to raise kids thinking they don't have to take responsibility for their actions. We don't want an entitled generation!

We certainly don't take the position that it was *bad* parenting (Ned is half of the team writing this, after all!). But was it effective? Could Ned be confident that the next time he asked his kids to do something under threat, they would comply? And was he prepared to always have a threat built into the behaviors he wanted to nurture in his kids? No, no, and no.

With parenting decisions large and small, we always come back to the question of what it is we want for our kids long term. Obviously, we want them to learn from negative behavior; we want them to learn what works and what doesn't in life. We also want for them to learn to run their own lives. Punishment, it turns out, isn't an effective way to learn these things, as we talked about in Chapter 1. Neither is rewarding them for doing what we want them to do. And neither is having a toxic relationship with them, for it costs us the opportunity to lead by example.

Parent as consultant, positive parenting, authoritative parenting—these are all ways of describing the same philosophy: kids need limits to feel and be safe, but we also need to treat them respectfully and work out rules and limits collaboratively, using natural consequences and problem-solving as our most powerful teaching tools. Ultimately, parenting isn't about power, but about influence. That's why we take a literal interpretation of the word *discipline*, for which the Latin root means "pupil." Our job is that of a teacher, and teachers guide and motivate.

So what might Ned have done? It wasn't fair to him that their house was always a wreck, and he also wanted to teach his kids to take responsibility for their messes. He thought about this a lot in the days following the Great Brunch Debacle. He might have gathered everyone together that Sunday morning and expressed his need for a family cleanup hour. When the kids protested—as they surely would have—that they didn't care whether the house was clean or not, he could have used the strength of his relationship with his kids to say, "Look, I know this isn't important to you. But it is to me, and we share living space. The way families work, sometimes we all do things for the other that we don't necessarily want to." They could have decided collaboratively who would do which jobs, when the best time to clean up was, and what they might do afterward to reward themselves.

This chapter covers what to say to your kids about limits and consequences, but also incorporates dialogues around values differences. As Ned's story shows, the two are linked. Ned cared about cleanliness; his kids didn't. Let's say you're in a family meeting—which we highly recommend—and sorting out rules around your ten-year-old's desire to stay home instead of going on a family walk. Or your twelve-year-old's desire to wear makeup. Or your sixteen-year-old's desire to skip church in favor of band practice. If your child doesn't value what you do, chances are you want to *make* them. But you can't. And so you have to negotiate and persuade, which are much harder all around than just setting a rule.

If the work ahead feels daunting, know that—if you've made it to this part of the book—you're already most of the way there. The more autonomy you have granted your child, the less likely they are to fight you in order to maintain a sense of control. The more you have emphasized rest, the less likely they are to be overtired. The calmer you have been with them, the calmer they will be with you. And you are less likely to escalate arguments when you understand, as Ross Greene reminds us, that kids do well when they can. Tired, stressed, discouraged, angry kids misbehave. So what's making them tired, stressed, discouraged, or angry? Start there, and the rest is much easier than you might think.

What Not to Say

"You have to learn that you can't get away with this."

In *The Little Mermaid*, Sebastian wrung his, er, claws about the rebellious Ariel and pronounced: "Teenagers: You give them an inch, they swim all over the place." And we all know how well King Triton's authoritarian approach turned out. Well, what didn't work for headstrong mermaids doesn't work for kids, either. The problem with language like, "You have to learn you can't get away with this!," and with the punishment that results, is twofold: (1) it hurts your relationship with them, and (2) it doesn't work. The truth is, dispensing punishments increases our sense of control (at least we're doing *something*), but it's not an effective tool for changing behavior. Again, there is no evidence that punishment, including scolding, lecturing, yelling, sending a child to his room, or taking away privileges, is needed to achieve our goal of raising self-disciplined kids. Although a punishment may briefly stop a meltdown, it doesn't inspire positive behavior or teach kids what *to* do, and can even be counterproductive.[1] Jane Nelsen, author of the seminal *Positive Discipline*, points to the four "Rs" that follow punishment: Resentment, Revenge, Rebellion, and Retreat (sneaking).[2]

Many of the parents we work with say things like, "I've tried everything. I've grounded him, taken away his Xbox, turned off the internet, and made him quit the soccer team. I've got nothing left to take away." When a kid repeatedly misbehaves, the temptation is to think, *Well, they'll never learn with a five-foot wall. Better make it ten feet.* But Ross Greene, who is also a champion of collaborative problem-solving, points out that the kids who get the most negative consequences often learn the least from them. Years of research have shown that children can become self-disciplined, empathic, compassionate, and successful adults without painful punishment. So if they don't seem to learn after a mild consequence, give them time. They might have to crash into that five-foot wall more than you'd like them to. Be patient. Express confidence that they'll figure it out. They will.

"Say you're sorry."

While trying to make a child apologize can make us feel like we're being good parents, it rarely makes the child feel better, and it is usually not very satisfying for the person being apologized to. Of course, teaching a child to take ownership of their missteps, to make amends when they have wronged someone, and how to restore relationships, is important. But that's a quite different process than a mandate to say sorry. We can help kids learn emotional responsibility by modeling it ourselves. For instance, if we get mad at our child for making a mess, we can later apologize and explain that we overreacted—that the mess wasn't really that big a deal, but it felt like it during the moment because we were stressed.

Taking Ownership

The best way to teach taking ownership of mistakes is—drumroll—to take ownership of your mistakes. If you lose your temper, you can say, "I'm feeling a little bad because I think I overreacted and I'm sorry. I'd like to make it up to you." More than fifty years have passed since Bill's dad would come into his room at night and apologize for having gotten mad at him earlier in the day—and Bill still remembers how loved and respected that made him feel. When you show that you will walk the talk, then the next time your kid acts out and hurts someone, you are in a better position to say, "I've found that the best way to handle feeling sorry is to say you're sorry and then do something nice to make it up to the other person. Hopefully, you can make your conscience feel better and the other person feel better."

"That's it! You're grounded!"

When you're flooded with anger, avoid making threats or imposing consequences. You may find you want to, because it satisfies your need for a sense of control, and maybe your desire to retaliate (it is a fight-or-flight response, after all). But it's much better to calm down and brainstorm solutions when your prefrontal cortex is online. You don't have to react immediately, or even every time a child does something wrong.

"I told you so."

There is probably no better phrase for ensuring a kid won't learn from mistakes than saying, "I told you so." It turns learning opportunities into struggles of who's wrong and who's right, and there are no winners in that game. Many kids will repeatedly engage in self-defeating behavior to prevent their parents from being able to gloat.

"This behavior is unacceptable."

The problem with this phrase is, in part, that it puts you in the role of morality police and arbiter of etiquette. When you say that something is unacceptable and shut it down, you're blowing up the opportunity to have a larger, important conversation about values. When friends bemoan, "My daughter questions everything I say," we tell them, "Great!" We want kids to struggle with right and wrong, not just have a rule they follow without really understanding why.

"It's my job to keep you safe."

When children are little, of course it is a parent's job to keep them safe. But as they get older, one of the most dangerous things we can tell them—whether it's when we are enforcing a curfew or forbidding alcohol use—is that it's our job to keep them safe. It's a job we cannot by any measure do successfully. We're not with them all the time. We don't have trackers on them, nor should we. In our experience, when they think it's our job to keep them safe, and not theirs, they are more apt to behave recklessly, thinking there is a safety net when really, there is not.

So What Do You Say?

"Let's figure this out together."

Collaborative problem-solving is the backbone of any discussion of limits or consequences. Problem-solving is part of the long tradition of authoritative parenting, which has always emphasized discussing problems and respectfully brainstorming possible solutions in family meetings.[3] More recently, Ross Greene and Stuart Albon have refined the problem-solving process for use with resistant children, but it is effective no matter a child's age or disposition.[4] Let's say your child hasn't done a chore they agreed to or has misbehaved. When you talk about it, start with empathy. "Let's talk about what happened earlier tonight when you hit your cousin. You seemed pretty upset. What was going on for you?" Listen to their reasoning, reflect their feelings back to them, and leave judgment aside. Then you can say, "Well, I see that you were pretty frustrated. You felt like no one was listening to you. But hitting doesn't work as a way to get them to listen. You hurt your cousin. It made me feel upset to see you do that." Then you work with the child to find a solution, which may have to do with ways of making amends and brainstorming about alternative ways to manage frustration. "What do you think you could do next time you're with your cousins and you're feeling frustrated? What might work?"

You can get into more specifics with kids about why certain behaviors are important, and what logical consequences might follow if you come to an agreement and they don't keep their side of the bargain. For instance, Katherine Reynolds Lewis writes in her book *The Good News about Bad Behavior*, about an agreement in her family surrounding teeth brushing. After discussing why it's important to brush teeth at night, they made an agreement that if teeth are not brushed at night, there would be no sweets the next day. This consequence was both logical (since dental hygiene is connected to sugar) and something she could stick to, because she wasn't requiring her child to do anything; she was simply withholding something they agreed she would. This is important because the last thing you want to do is set yourself up to be either a monitor or an enforcer.[5]

A similar process can work when you reach an impasse over family decisions. Let's say you want to go on a family camping trip, but your fifteen-year-old daughter is dead set against it. It's frustrating, because "no way" is her default answer to any activity you enjoy. But begin with empathy and inquiry. State your own feelings without judgment or blame. Problem-solve approaches that you both can live with.

We recognize it's easier for us, as hired professionals and thus outsiders, to get kids to engage in problem-solving. But we often suggest that parents use a variation of the script below when managing the many impasses that come up in daily family life.

PARENT: I can see that you are not thrilled about camping
this weekend, and I clearly can't make you go. After all, you're
way too big to fit into that backpack carrier we had. But I really

like your company and have been looking forward to spending some time outdoors with you. Would you be willing to chat about how we can make this fun—or at least more bearable—for you?

CHILD: I just hate camping!

PARENT: Yeah, I get that it's not your favorite. Is there a particular site or campground that would motivate you? Or something we can do on the trip? And I'd love to talk about what activities *you'd* like to do next weekend—not camping, I realize—that maybe we haven't done enough of lately.

CHILD: Well, would it be okay if we . . .

Not all conversations will go smoothly, and collaborative problem-solving takes intention and practice. But it's also rare for kids to take a "screw you" attitude and refuse to negotiate altogether when their parents come at the subject collaboratively and respectfully.[6]

"I love you completely no matter how many rules you break."

What we love so much about this phrase is that it emphasizes that relationship is paramount. Prizing your relationship isn't about closing your eyes and covering your ears, nor is it about being your child's best friend. Rather, it's about being an effective teacher. A few years ago, Bill lectured about the adolescent brain to a group of experienced middle school and high school teachers and asked them, "What's the single most important factor in teaching adolescents successfully?" One attendee answered, "It's the three Rs of teaching: Relationship. Relationship. Relationship," with which the whole audience concurred. Remember that discipline means teaching, and that kids are much more likely to behave in ways that we approve of—and to learn from us—when they feel close to us. And they are much more likely to take their responsibilities seriously when we convey confidence that they will.

When Ned's son, Matthew, was a senior in high school, he was in a musical and came home from rehearsal fuming one night—a rarity for him. The choreographer had spent most of the evening yelling at the actors for talking. "Yeah, we were talking," he acknowledged, "but she doesn't have to keep yelling at us every five minutes. We weren't that bad." At one point she apparently said, "If you don't stop talking, I may cut you from the show!" Matthew, who is such a do-gooder, repeated this to Ned incredulously. "Really?!? She's going to cut us? Then what? Who will fill in for us? And she's not even the director. It's not her call. It was ridiculous." Ned was struck by how much Matthew's motivation was eviscerated by what he felt was disrespectful treatment. "I mean, I really like her," Matthew conceded, "but this is NOT how you motivate teens!"

"I'm not going to talk about this now. I need some time to think this through."

In the face of badgering, tantrums, or really undesirable behavior from your kid, one of the best things you can do is to put yourself in a timeout. Go listen to music, put on noise-canceling headphones if you have them. You do not have to respond to any request or any misbehavior in the moment. You will make better decisions when you can think from your prefrontal cortex and when they are thinking from theirs. Explain to your child why you're doing it: "I want to calm my mind down so I can think more clearly. I'll be better able to help find a solution if I'm calmer."

Kids can learn to take positive time-outs, too—or "time away." Instead of saying "Go to your room and think about what you did!" you can say, "Let's each go to a place where we can calm down, and then we can come back together. I think things will go better if we do."[7]

"I don't feel comfortable with this."

One of the biggest misconceptions people have about the parent-as-consultant philosophy is that they think parents give away all their power. That's not the case at all. This is not a battle between Father-Knows-Best and a model where your needs are consumed by your child's. Parents should not do things for their children if they'll feel resentful; that's not good for anyone. "I'm not leaving my workday to bring you your cleats again," you might say, "because I don't want to be mad and resentful." Or "I'm not cleaning up this mess you made because it would make me resentful, and neither of us wants that."

The same general principle applies when it comes to matters of negotiating acceptable risk. Some risks you obviously are not going to be okay with your kid taking—like driving too fast or not wearing a bike helmet. But others might fall into a gray area and require some problem-solving. One of our favorite stories involves a boy who was a confident daredevil but whose antics worried his parents constantly. He got an electric scooter for his birthday, and he was determined to use it one day even though it was raining. His parents weren't comfortable, but he got offended and implored them to trust him. So they relented. Almost immediately he fell off the scooter and broke his arm. On the way to the hospital, he grinned. "That was totally worth it!" he said.

You can imagine these poor parents as this kiddo grows older, right? "I've been thinking about this," they might say, post arm pain. "We've been fighting a lot about risks you want to take, and I don't want that. One of the things I love about you is that you push boundaries—we need people like that in the world, we need people to be fearless and bold. But let's figure out how to compromise a bit, so that it doesn't make me crazy. Because as it is, I'm not comfortable with some of the risks you're taking."

"I'm offering you amnesty."

A friend of ours described his daughter Cami as entering "the terrible twos" at eighteen months and not coming out of it until she was twenty-one. As a teenager, she constantly tested limits, broke family rules, and lied to her parents about what she was doing. Cami's mother felt her misbehavior needed to be met with firm consequences, which would prevent her from getting into trouble that could haunt her the rest of her life. It never worked. Cami and her parents became stuck in a vicious cycle of misbehavior and lying, scolding, lecturing, and grounding. Her parents knew their relationship with Cami was strained, and they worried about it. But they didn't know what to do. It's so easy to fall into the trap of thinking, *I'd be nicer to her/our relationship would be better if she would behave better or make good decisions.* The problem with this thinking is that it has the cause and effect backward.

One weekend when Cami was a high school junior, a neighbor called her parents—who were out—and told them Cami was having a party. Though evidence of the party had been cleared away by the time the parents got home, they told her about the neighbor's call. Cami calmly but firmly denied having anyone over. When her dad said, "But John saw you and the other kids; do you think he's lying?" she replied, "He must be. I didn't have a party."

Her parents were upset enough that they told her they needed to cool off, and that they would talk about it later. As her dad went to his bedroom, he was much more troubled by the lack of closeness and tension in their relationship than about the party—after all, he remembered going to plenty of parties in high school at homes where parents were out. After discussing it with his wife, he decided to give Cami amnesty as a way of breaking the cycle of acting out, punishment, and revenge. He knocked on Cami's door and asked if they could talk. He then said, "I don't believe that you're telling me the truth. I don't know about you, but if I lied straight to my parents' faces, it would really eat at me. I'm thinking that, if you're lying, you probably feel bad about it, and I don't want to pile on. I'm therefore offering you amnesty, which means that whatever happened tonight didn't happen. End of story."

Later that night, Cami admitted to her parents that she had been lying. This started their first open discussion in over a year. Rather than making the wall between them ten feet or higher, her dad had lowered it to zero, allowing Cami to make the brave trek across the demilitarized zone to make peace. Shortly thereafter, Cami made a dramatic change in her peer group. Ten years later she told her parents that the kids she hung around with in high school were a bad influence on her—and apologized for everything she put them through.

Jill and her ex-husband, Dave, faced a similar struggle with their son, Gavin. One weekend when Dave was out of town, Gavin had a party at his house, which Dave learned about because he found the party remnants in the trash. (Dumb move, Gavin!) Jill and Dave sat down together with Gavin and explained that they weren't stupid. They let him know they were upset, but they also treated him respectfully, and they didn't punish him. A few weeks later, Jill was the parent who was out of town and Gavin had a party at *her* house. It may seem that Jill and Dave's approach didn't work, that by not punishing Gavin after the first party, they made it easier for him to decide to have another. But here's the thing: when the party at Jill's got out of hand, which happened almost immediately, Gavin called Dave for help. It was a testament to their relationship that he felt he could call on his dad when he needed him most, and without the fear of repercussions. While naturally Jill and Dave weren't happy with Gavin about the second party, it was also pretty evident that Gavin had seen how quickly things could spiral out of control and had no desire to host a party again.

This isn't to say that Gavin's parents or Cami's parents—or any parent—should take a laissez-faire attitude toward teen drinking and partying. As we discussed in the Inside the Brain box on page 145, alcohol is clearly bad for the developing brain, and we should be talking with our teens about this. But these stories illustrate the power of focusing on our relationship with our kids, and they underscore the point that kids can learn from their experiences in many ways that don't involve administering consequences, especially consequences that don't really help them learn the lessons we'd like them to learn.

"I love you, but I don't like being around people when they're mean to me. I'll be back in a few minutes and maybe we can try talking again."

You've probably heard about "natural consequences" before. If a kid spills water on their iPad and breaks it, they go without until they can save enough money to buy a new one. If they stuff themselves on sweets, they feel sick. If they refuse to wear a coat, they will be cold. Natural consequences are a parent's great ally, because all the parent has to do is not rescue the child from letting events take their course. (There are exceptions, of course. If a child needed an iPad for school, the parent might work out some sort of payment plan and get them a new one. If a kid drank too much and couldn't drive home, obviously the parent wouldn't tell them too bad.) There are natural consequences to relationships, too. You can let your child know you love them unconditionally, and that it's okay if they're upset or not feeling cheerful. Even so, let them know that you don't like to be around them when they're rude or disrespectful. Saying so isn't manipulative or mean, so long as you make clear that you would never abandon them. What's more, it's the way most healthy relationships work, an important life lesson.

"What should we do if we make this agreement and you don't do your part? What if I don't do my part? Let's come up with some consequences that make sense and can help us both stick with our agreement."

Again, we take a page from Jane Nelsen's book in that we recommend favoring natural consequences and problem-solving, and using logical consequences—determined with your child's input—sparingly. For Nelsen, logical consequences, like punishment, follow a rule of four Rs: they are Respectful (they don't involve blame or humiliation); Reasonable (to the child and parent); Related (to the misbehavior); and Revealed (in advance). Let's say chores have been a source of contention between you and your teen. They don't want you "nagging" them, and they want to do what's required on their own time, not yours. But they're not doing them, and you're having to pick up the slack. So you might agree that if they forget to take out the trash in time for it to be picked up, then they need to take the trash to the dump so it won't pile up. Then make a plan for what if they don't do *that*. And if you nag them about the trash, breaking your end of the bargain, then you need to take it out for them that week. If neither one of you follows through, it's back to the drawing board.

But What About . . . ?

I'm a pretty open-minded parent, but the one thing I cannot stand is when my kid lies to me. I need him to know how important trust is to our relationship. How do I communicate that to him?

When Bill used to do therapy, parents would frequently seek his help because their child was lying to them. Bill first asked the parents to stop telling the child, "It's important to tell the truth so that people will trust you." While an entirely understandable response, it became part of a complex family dance because children felt judged and inclined to lie more, and parents became more distrustful, and on and on. Bill then met with the whole family and asked, "Who is the least honest person in your family?" It was fascinating to see how often the child in therapy for lying was not rated by anyone in the family as being the least honest, and it was not uncommon for children to rate their mother or father as being the least honest. Bill encouraged everyone in the family to talk about a time when they told at least a "white lie," which everyone would admit to. Taking lying out of the realm of moral judgment was much more effective than repeatedly imploring the child to be trustworthy and punishing them for not telling the truth. Bill then worked with the family to make being honest with one another a family goal.

There's another pretty simple tactic we recommend to decrease lying: avoid asking questions in response to which the child may lie. Don't set them up. "Have you done your homework?" is an open invitation for many children to lie and, because we want to be homework consultants, not homework police, it's counterproductive. It begs the question, too, of why we're asking. Are we asking because it makes us feel better? Ned struggled with this recently when Matthew, now a college freshman, was home during the winter holidays. He seemed to regress to the nocturnal habits he'd had as a high schooler, playing video games with friends online all night. When Ned saw him in the afternoon, his impulse was to ask him what time he'd gone to bed the night before. And he did ask this question a few times. But then he thought, *Why am I asking? To calm my own fears? If he admits he was up until four, we're going to have a variation of a conversation that's grown tired between us. So he'll probably lie, and what purpose would that serve? What is it I'm really wanting out of this dialogue, and is it for me or for him?* Bill and Starr talked to their kids about drugs and alcohol and kept an eye out for problems, but they never asked them as teenagers whether they used substances because Bill learned through his work that when kids use, they commonly lie.

It feels counterintuitive to most parents to imagine that the best solution to a child's lying is to stop asking them questions. But no one ever wins the lying debate—it just becomes their word against yours, with bad feelings spread all around. That's why we love the approach of a friend of ours, who, after a couple of years of feeling she was being lied to by her teenage sons and lecturing them ineffectively about the importance of trust, refused to get into any more truthfulness debates. Instead she told them, "I'm just going to assume that absolutely everything you're telling me is true. If you're telling me the truth, great. If not, it will be on your conscience." She's not sure if they actually never lied to her again. But she is sure that she had a lot more peace in her life and that within a couple of months, her relationship with her kids improved by 80 percent.

Another upside of our friend's approach may be that your kids may tell you when they're feeling pressured to lie. When Jenna was twelve, she had a new and quite popular friend spend the night who pressured her to sneak out so they could meet some boys who lived in the neighborhood. Jenna had a close relationship with her mom and didn't want to lie to her. So she woke her mom up and told her what was going on, essentially asking permission to sneak out. Jenna's mom, grateful her daughter had confided in her, said it was okay (and then likely watched the kids from the corner the whole time).

My high schooler is a walking pigsty. His appearance is messy, his room is messy. How do I implement logical consequences when he just doesn't care?

Few other topics will drive so many parents to the brink. For this reason, make sure that any conversations around cleanliness or orderliness happen when you're not frustrated. These moments may be few and far between, but trust us—you're wasting your breath if you're not communicating PFC to PFC. And remember that you can't make a kid want what he doesn't want. If he isn't bothered by a messy appearance, room, or car, you can't *make him* be bothered by it. The best you can do is to: (1) Tell him why *you* think it's important to care for belongings, something like, "Caring for objects is a way of showing respect." (2) Decline to purchase items for him that you don't think he will take good care of, or replace items that he hasn't treated well. You might say something like, "You don't need to care about this as much as I do. I'm not asking you to value the things that I value. But I want to feel that if I spend the money to give you something, you're going to take good care of it." And (3) Explain that if he doesn't contribute to the family (assuming that his mess is bothering others) by keeping his spaces clean, you won't feel like contributing to him as much. Then the issue isn't so much about personal standards of cleanliness, which vary, but about respecting those you live with.

People have different values and standards about cleanliness all the time. One parent we know determined two sets of standards with her messy teenager: There was "everyday clean" and there was "company clean." She agreed to let "everyday clean" be beneath her ideal standards, so long as the much more vigorous "company clean" was used whenever people were coming over. Bill and Starr's friends have repeatedly wondered how they can bear to leave dirty dishes overnight after a dinner party. But they know that if they do the dishes in the morning, when they're fresh and rested, the process will be much quicker than doing them at night.

My kids are constantly fighting and pulling me in. It drives me nuts, and it seems reasonable that if they can't play nicely together, I should just separate them. Is that fair, or is that punishment?

Adele Faber and Elaine Mazlish's classic book *Siblings Without Rivalry* recommends putting kids "in the same boat" and removing yourself as referee and judge. So while separation makes good sense, they should make this decision, not you. If your kids are fighting and one asks you to play referee, instead of accepting the job, become coach instead. "I'm not going to get involved because I didn't see what happened and I couldn't possibly figure out who started it. What I can do, though, is coach you in how to stand up to your brother if he's too rough. I mean, the thing he wants most in the world is to play with you—so you've got a lot of power in this situation. All you have to do is say, 'If you're too rough, I'm not going to play with you for half an hour.'" It's also okay to simply say, "You have two choices: get along inside, or fight outside."

There is so much pressure on me from my child's school to make sure he's completing his work. I don't want to get involved, I don't want to pin him into lying, and I don't want to be the homework police. But I feel like a lax parent if I don't get involved, and I worry the teachers are judging me.

If we could wave a magic wand and change the school's culture, believe me, we would. But stay strong. As much as possible, make the child's schoolwork an issue between him and the school. Especially with teenagers, if the school sends an email about missing work, simply forward it to your kid.

We found out our teenager raced cars with his friends one night. We were furious, obviously. He usually makes really good decisions, so this was dramatically out of character. How can we help him make better decisions with the sixteen-year-old brain he has?

You might say something like, "Leaving aside consequences for a moment, I want to talk to you about your brain. I have enormous respect for your brain and its ability to make good decisions. You've done so time and time again. It's also true that your brain is different from mine because of your age. Your brain is much more drawn to being impulsive and it is much more activated by being around your friends. It tends to focus more on how much fun it will be to do something kinda wild with your friends than on the potential dangers. It's as if you're an amazing, hypercompetitive receiver in a game of tackle football—you know you are athletic enough to catch that ball and it's going to feel so good. But you're also not wearing a helmet, so you have to be really careful. We all make decisions about what risks to take every day. You just have to weigh those risks, and be aware that you're also helmetless. If you're in a situation where you want to—and your friends want you to—do something risky and you're nervous about it, please come and talk to me—or call me or text me. And if you feel like you want a ready-made excuse for next time, to get you out of doing whatever it is, I'm happy to help you come up with one."[8]

Putting It All Together

Becca was an observant Jew whose twelve-year-old son, Noah, was refusing to have a bar mitzvah. The boy questioned his religious faith, and he felt that participating in the bar mitzvah ceremony would be hypocritical.

BECCA: I can't believe you would fight me on this, Noah. This is our faith. We've been going to synagogue and working up to this since you were a baby. I feel totally betrayed.

NOAH: Geez, Mom, don't be so dramatic. All that time was about you, not about me. You can't make me religious.

BECCA: But you're only twelve, and we are your parents. This is too big a deal for you to decide on your own. You *have* to do this. You might really regret it if you don't.

Becca's faith—and her religious community—was so much a part of who she was, it was excruciating to her that her son didn't share her beliefs. While we're not discounting her very understandable pain, the fact is, no one could make Noah read from the Torah or perform the other tasks required of him if he flat out refused. But they could problem-solve together—which meant discussing things respectfully and hearing the other's point of view, which neither of them was doing. What if it went this way instead?

BECCA: Your father and I are not going to force you to do a bar mitzvah; obviously that wouldn't work very well if we tried. I want you to understand, though, that a bar mitzvah is really important to us, and also to your extended family. We aren't asking you to believe every tenet of Judaism, and we *hugely* respect the integrity with which you are approaching this—it reflects a remarkable degree of maturity and concern about your authenticity and honesty. We are hoping that you can find a way to do the bar mitzvah that will not sacrifice your integrity but still will enable us to have the satisfaction of welcoming you into the Jewish community. It would mean the world to your grandparents, aunts, and uncles to welcome you in this way.

NOAH: I just don't want to feel like a hypocrite, Mom. But I'll think about it.

BECCA: Okay, thank you. Think about what we could do to make it more palatable for you. We can talk again in a couple of days.

[Two days later]

NOAH: I guess it would be okay if it was only family who attended.

BECCA: No friends from synagogue?

NOAH: No, no friends of mine, or of yours. I'm just doing it for the family, so they're the only ones who get to come.

BECCA: Okay. Do you want a party after?

NOAH: I'd be okay with dinner at a restaurant or something. But that's it. I really don't want to make a big deal of it.

Remember What It's All About

Perhaps one of the most comforting thoughts for parents is that you are not responsible for teaching your child everything. They will learn lessons from countless others that they couldn't possibly learn from you—or at least, not as well from you. Their algebra teacher can teach them study habits; the girl in fourth period can teach them with a scrunch of her nose that they should probably shower more often; their first job can teach them how to follow through on tasks. This isn't to say a parent's teaching doesn't matter; it's impossible to overstate a parent's influence on their child. But when you find yourself thinking *I need to do X or they'll never learn Y!*, know that that's simply not true. Kids learn in lots of ways, from lots of sources, so give yourself a break. So many of the kids Bill sees who avoid their responsibilities and fight with their parents at home are completely responsible and appropriately behaved in internships or their first summer jobs. They learned—even if it wasn't always obvious when they were at home.

Cutting yourself slack applies to much more than just limits and consequences. Know that there will be times when you say the wrong thing. There will be times when your amygdala gets the better of you and the words are out of your mouth before you can really think. It's okay. We all have buttons that get pushed, and kids—particularly teenagers—are quite good at finding them. There will be times when your words are driven not by anger but by fear: fear of your child getting hurt; fear of your child failing in some way; fear that you haven't done everything you're "supposed" to do. Offer yourself grace. Apologize, and use it as an opportunity to educate them about how the brain works—and that yours didn't work so well in that moment. Then move on.

Words matter—otherwise we wouldn't have written a book about them. (And we've used quite a lot of them in the process!) But words are not everything. Warmth, connection, and affection still remain the best gestures to offer your child, and they require no words at all.

Acknowledgments

We wish to acknowledge the many wonderful people whose contributions of powerful stories, insights, and sharp-eyed editing helped to shape this book.

First, we will be eternally grateful to our brilliant literary agent, Howard Yoon (and his team), for his confidence in our first book and for encouraging us to write a second. We are also hugely grateful to Howard for introducing us to the incredibly talented Jenna Land Free, our partner-in-scribe who helped us immeasurably with the writing of our two books (and helped to arrange focus groups with kids and parents before we started writing this book). In addition, a huge thanks to our gifted, supportive, and very funny editor at Viking, Laura Tisdel, whose close reads and insightful feedback so improved our book. Laura's assistant, Victoria Savanh, was also very helpful (and patient) in the parallel work of information gathering and coordinating publicity with the good folks at Viking. Yep, it takes a village. A special thanks to the talented Anne Harris, who, as she did on *The Self-Driven Child*, made the process of editing the text and compiling references for our endnotes easy and fun. She's a gem.

Our sincerest thanks also to Ross Yoon Agency's Dara Kaye, who made *The Self-Driven Child* available to people in ten countries (with all those fun, though unreadable to us, covers!), and has already assured *What Do You Say?* will be read (or at least available) in China. We also owe a huge debt of gratitude to Kathy Hedge, Patti Cancellier, Katherine Reynolds-Lewis, and Marlene Goldstein of the wonderful Parent Encouragement Program, who gave us helpful feedback, shared invaluable insights, and allowed us to share our ideas with their parent body during an important formative stage.

We further want to thank the many scientists, clinicians, and other professionals who were kind enough to share their time and ideas with us, including the following: Daniel Pine, Dan Shapiro, Sheila Ohlsson-Walker, Joshua Aronson, Danny Lewin, Bonnie Zucker, Eran Magen, Clifford Sussman, Sarah Wayland, Amy Killy, and Tim Kasser. Additionally, we are grateful to Devorah Heitner, Simon Kantner, and Phyllis Fagel, whose insights on talking to kids about the effects of technology were so very helpful.

We would further like to thank Kelly Christensen for her insights regarding the use of motivational interviewing with teenagers—and for arranging a focus group of students at her school. We are also indebted to Anne Henderson for her useful thoughts about parental expectations, and to Laurent Valosec, who generously brought us up to date on the most recent studies of students practicing Transcendental Meditation in schools. Additionally, we want to thank Brooke MacNamara for taking the time to discuss her research on Mindset Theory and practice with us. We are further grateful to Charlene Margot, the founder of the Parent Education Series in the San Francisco Bay Area, for her continual support of our work.

Last, we want to thank the many parents and students who met in our focus groups prior to writing the book, as well as the thousands of children and parents we've worked with over the decades. Without them, and their trust in us, many of the insights we stumbled upon may have lain undiscovered.

Bill would like to thank his wife, Starr, for her patience and support, and his children, Jora and Elliott, for their good-humored willingness to be talked about in this book. Bill also wants to thank Norman Rosenthal, Bob Roth, and Mario Orsatti for their continual support and for their inspiration in bringing meditation to young people and their parents. He's also grateful to his colleagues at The Stixrud Group, who have been very supportive of the ideas he and Ned write about.

Ned would like to thank his wife and partner in parenting, Vanessa, herself a teacher from whom Ned has begged, borrowed, or (only occasionally) stolen so many good ideas. He is incredibly grateful to her and to their children, Matthew and Katie, for being so open about their own thinking and being willing to have hard conversations about things that matter to them.

Ned also wants to give a quick shout-out to his colleagues at PrepMatters and the members of the "Bad Ass" Parenting Squad, whose collective wisdom and support helped him see this book through and kept him (relatively) sane during the oh-so-challenging year of 2020. Finally, Ned would like to thank Kathleen O'Connor, Brent Toleman, and Anne Wake, who have shared so generously their wisdom about how to talk with (and listen to) kids—his own and those of other loving parents.

NOTES

Introduction: Why Effective Communication with Kids Is So Important Now

1. Sally C. Curtain, M.A., and Melonie Heron, PhD, "Death Rates Due to Suicide and Homicide Among Persons Aged 10–24: United States, 2000–2017," NCHS Data Brief no. 352 (October 2019).

2. Laurie Santos, "Laurie Santos, Yale Happiness Professor, on 5 Things That Will Make You Happier," *Newsweek Magazine* (January 8, 2021), https://www.newsweek.com/2021/01/08/issue.html. Retrieved March 8, 2021.

Chapter 1: Communicating Empathy: A Recipe for Closeness and Connection

1. Numerous studies have shown that the foundation of emotional resilience in children and teens is having close personal relationships, particularly with parents, and especially with mothers. Relationships that are supportive and comforting during childhood are highly associated with better health outcomes in infancy, childhood, and adulthood. See Edith Chen, Gene H. Brody, and Gregory E. Miller, "Childhood Close Family Relationships and Health," *American Psychologist* 72, no. 6 (September 2017): 555–66. See also M. R. Gunnar et al., "Stress Reactivity and Attachment Security," *Developmental Psychobiology* 29, no. 3 (April 1996): 191–204. See also Valarie King, Lisa Boyd, and Brianne Pragg, "Parent-Adolescent Closeness, Family Belonging, and Adolescent Well-Being Across Family Structures," *Journal of Family Issues* 39,

no. 7 (November 2017): 2007–36. The power of close relationships with parents is also emphasized in Madeline Levine's excellent book *The Price of Privilege* (New York: HarperCollins, 2006), and by the relationship expert John Gottman in his book *Raising an Emotionally Intelligent Child* (New York: Simon & Schuster, 1998).

2. For a good discussion of the importance of secure attachment, see Lise Eliot's book *What's Going On in There? How the Brain & Mind Develop in the First Five Years of Life* (New York: Bantam Doubleday, 1999). See also L. Alan Sroufe, "Attachment and Development: A Prospective Longitudinal Study from Birth to Adulthood," *Attachment & Human Development* 7, no. 4 (December 2005): 349–67. Also see Michael J. Meaney, "Maternal Care, Gene Expression, and the Transmission of Individual Differences in Stress Reactivity Across Generations," *Annual Review of Neuroscience* 24, no. 1 (February 2001): 1161–92.

3. *The New York Times* Modern Love series investigated the effects of staring into someone's eyes for four minutes, which is described as part of a "formula" for falling in love with anyone. See Mandy Len Catron, "To Fall in Love with Anyone," *The New York Times*, January 15, 2015. This idea was based on research conducted over twenty years ago on the facilitation of emotional closeness through eye contact. See Arthur Aron et al., "The Experimental Generation of Interpersonal Closeness: A Procedure and Some Preliminary Findings," *Personality and Social Psychology Bulletin* 23, no. 4 (April 1997): 363–77.

4. Bill's own parenting was influenced by Dr. Ross Campbell's book *How to Really Love Your Child* (Colorado Springs: David C. Cook, 2015). Campbell similarly taught that unconditional love is the foundation of a healthy relationship with children. He taught that each child has an "emotional tank" that is filled by love—and that we fill a child's tank by making eye contact, using appropriate touch, giving our undivided attention, and employing discipline rooted in love and empathy.

5. Proximity is one of the recommendations made in Gordon Neufeld and Gabor Maté's book *Hold On to Your Kids: Why Parents Need to Matter More Than Peers* (New York: Ballantine, 2005). Neufeld and Maté emphasize the importance of maintaining a strong connection with kids, which is based on Neufeld's theory that attachment to parents continues to develop during childhood. Neufeld's model posits that this attachment progresses and deepens through six stages over the first six years of life. These stages are: (1) Proximity—Attachment begins through closeness, contact; (2) Sameness—The child wants to be like us, we recognize things we share in common; (3) Belonging or loyalty—Children start to feel possessive of and loyal to their parents; (4) Being known—If a child is securely attached, they'll share their emotional life with their parents; (5) Significance—Children start to grasp how important they are to their parents; (6) Love—Emotions deepen and feelings of love foster connection.

6. Suniya S. Luthar and Bronwyn E. Becker, "Privileged but Pressured? A Study of Affluent Youth," *Child Development* 73, no. 5 (September–October 2002): 1593–

1610. This early study found that depression and other internalizing disorders such as anxiety and substance use were associated with isolation from parents, especially low perceived closeness to mothers. See also Suniya S. Luthar and Shawn J. Latendresse, "Children of the Affluent: Challenges to Well-Being," *Current Directions in Psychological Science* 14, no. 1 (February 2005): 49–53.

7. A report by the Robert Wood Johnson Foundation found excessive pressure to excel to be one of the main factors contributing to mental health problems in adolescents, following poverty, discrimination, and trauma. https://www.rwjf.org/en/library/re search/2018/06/inspiring-and-powering-the-future--a-new-view-of-adolescence .html.

8. Luthar and her coauthor, Shawn Latendresse, write in "Children of the Affluent": "Among upper-middle class families, secondary school students are often left home alone for several hours each week, with many parents believing that this promotes self-sufficiency. Similarly, suburban children's needs for emotional closeness may often suffer as the demands of professional parents' careers erode relaxed 'family time' and youngsters are shuttled between various after-school activities." In *The Price of Privilege*, Madeline Levine reports that affluent parents tend to overestimate their closeness to their children. She adds that controlling and overinvolved parents commonly leave kids feeling alienated or angry.

9. The connection between empathy and children's emotional development was explored in a study by Eyal Abraham et al. Abraham and colleagues investigated two empathy networks in the brains of parents of infants. The study followed eighty-seven first-time parents across the first six years of family formation. It found that stronger connectivity within an empathy network for tuning into the child's feelings during infancy predicted lower child cortisol production in preschool and at age six. It also found that the strength of connection between this network and one for determining the baby's mental state was associated with more advanced emotional regulation skills in preschool and with fewer "internalizing" emotional problems, such as anxiety, at age six. The study concluded that the integrity of empathy-related networks in the parental brain shapes children's long-term stress reactivity and emotional regulation. See Eyal Abraham et al., "Empathy Networks in the Parental Brain and Their Long-Term Effects on Children's Stress Reactivity and Behavior Adaptation," *Neuropsychologia* 116, pt. A (July 31, 2018): 75–85.

10. See Gottman, *Raising an Emotionally Intelligent Child*.

11. See Jorge Barraza and Paul Zak, "Empathy Toward Strangers Triggers Oxytocin Release and Subsequent Generosity," *Annals of the New York Academy of Sciences* 1167, no. 1 (July 2009): 182–89. In subsequent studies, Paul Zak has also shown that oxytocin is the molecule of trust (and even morality) and that hugging is one of the most powerful ways of increasing oxytocin. Empathy induced by a short video clip about a father whose young son has brain cancer produced a 47 percent increase in

oxytocin levels (higher in women than in men). Higher empathy levels were associated with greater generosity toward strangers.

12. "Righting reflex" refers to the well-meaning attempt to solve another person's problem. It is a term from motivational interviewing, a therapeutic approach that we discuss in more detail in Chapter 4.

13. Ross Greene, *The Explosive Child* (New York: HarperCollins, 1998). Dr. Greene is also the author of *Raising Human Beings: Creating a Collaborative Partnership with Your Child* (New York: Scribner, 2016). See also Barry Neil Kaufman, *To Love Is to Be Happy With* (New York: Ballantine, 1977). Kaufman and his wife, Suzi, are the authors of a book that Bill credits with helping him learn how to stay in a positive mood most of the time. The title of the book means that when we love someone, we are happy with them the way they are—rather than how we think they should be or how we want them to be. We accept rather than judge. The Kaufmans also emphasize that believing that people (including ourselves) are always doing the best they can is very powerful for promoting happiness.

14. For children who are refusing school, requiring them to stay at school unless they are physically sick is important (assuming their school program is appropriate for their needs). See Andrew R. Eisen, Linda B. Engler, and Joshua Sparrow, *Helping Your Child Overcome Separation Anxiety or School Refusal* (Oakland, CA: New Harbinger, 2006). In this case, it was the only message Molly heard.

15. These include motivational interviewing, which we discuss in depth in Chapter 4; the collaborative problem-solving process popularized by Ross Greene and Stuart Albion (see Ross Greene, *Lost at School: Why Our Kids with Behavioral Challenges Are Falling Through the Cracks and How We Can Help Them* [New York: Scribner, 2014]); dialectical behavioral therapy, developed by Marsha Linehan; and Thomas Gordon's teacher effectiveness training.

16. See Karyn Hall and Melissa Cook's book *The Power of Validation* (Oakland, CA: New Harbinger, 2012), which is an excellent resource for ideas about careful listening and validating children's emotions and experiences.

17. This comes from Neuro-Linguistic Programming (NLP), a set of communication tools described in a book by Richard Bandler and John Grinder called *Reframing: Neuro-Linguistic Programming and the Transformation of Meaning* (Moab, UT: Real People Press, 1982).

18. Eran Magen, personal communication. Magen observes that we make deposits in our "relational accounts" with our children through expressions of care, trust, and/or respect. We can do this by keeping promises, listening closely, saying thank you, expressing faith in our kids, anticipating their needs, and respectfully helping them solve problems. We make withdrawals by asking our kids to inconvenience themselves. To keep our relationships positive, we need a dynamic flow. Ideally, we make deposits several times a day because lots of small deposits are better than one grand

gesture. Magen also makes the point that effective teachers make "deposits" in their "relational accounts" with their students on a daily basis. In our view, this is an excellent way of thinking about how to stay connected with our kids. (See Magen's YouTube workshop: Charlene Margot, "Managing Emotionally-Intense Conversations with Your Teen—Eran Magen, PhD," YouTube video, June 15, 2017, https://www.youtube.com/watch?v=DC3pdVG3-MI&t=345s.)

19. Dialectical behavioral therapy teaches the importance of validating children's actions, emotions, thoughts, and physiological responses—and not invalidating them ("How could you be tired? You slept until 10:00 a.m.!"). See Hall and Cook, *The Power of Validation*.

20. Anna Goldfarb, "Kick Dismissive Positivity to the Curb," *The New York Times*, December 22, 2019, https://www.nytimes.com/2019/12/22/smarter-living/9-delightful-tips-for-living-a-smarter-life-in-2020.html.

21. Gottman, *Raising an Emotionally Intelligent Child*.

22. See an article by a top expert in behavior management, Alan Kazdin, "Can You Discipline Your Child Without Using Punishment?" *Psychology Benefits Society*, American Psychological Association, February 15, 2017, https://psychologybenefits.org/2017/02/15/can-you-discipline-your-child-without-using-punishment/. Also see an article about Dr. Kazdin's approach that argues punishment is ineffective: Olga Khazan, "No Spanking, No Time-Out, No Problems," *The Atlantic*, March 28, 2016, https://www.theatlantic.com/health/archive/2016/03/no-spanking-no-time-out-no-problems/475440/. See also Eve Glicksman, "Physical Discipline Is Harmful and Ineffective," *APA Monitor on Psychology* 50, no. 5 (May 2019), https://www.apa.org/monitor/2019/05/physical-discipline.

23. Greene, *The Explosive Child*.

24. In a study of rats, Michael Meaney found that pups who were frequently licked and groomed by their mother following a stressful experience every day for their first two weeks of life turned into adult rats who were practically impervious to stress. They even earned the nickname, "California laid-back rats." Empathy is the human equivalent of licking and grooming. See Michael J. Meaney, "Maternal Care, Gene Expression, and the Transmission of Individual Differences in Stress Reactivity Across Generations," *Annual Review of Neuroscience* 24, no. 1 (February 2001): 1161–92. See also an article about Meaney's research by Carl Zimmer, "Brain Switches That Can Turn Mental Illness On and Off," *Discover Magazine*, June 15, 2010, https://www.discovermagazine.com/the-sciences/http-discovermagazine-com-2010-jun-15-brain-switches-that-can-turn-mental.

25. Peter Vermeulen, "Autism and Self-Determination Theory: The Path Towards Successful Citizenship," *Autism in Context* website, August 28, 2019, https://petervermeulen.be/2019/08/28/autism-and-self-determination-the-path-towards-successful-citizenship/.

26. Jacqueline Nadel et al., "Children with Autism Approach More Playful and Imitative Adults," *Early Child Development and Care* 178, no. 5 (May 22, 2008): 461–65. See also Tiffany Field, Jacqueline Nadel, and Shauna Ezell, "Imitation Therapy for Young Children with Autism," in *Autism Spectrum Disorders—From Genes to Environment*, ed. Tim Williams (London: InTechOpen, 2011), https://www.intechopen.com /books/autism-spectrum-disorders-from-genes-to-environment/imitation-therapy-for -young-children-with-autism. Barry and Suzi Kaufman made extensive use of imitation as a way to join the world of their young son with autism, which they describe in their book, *SonRise: The Miracle Continues* (Tiburon, CA: HJ Kramer, 1994).

Chapter 2: The Language of a Parent Consultant

1. Recounted in Jane Nelsen's classic parenting book *Positive Discipline* (New York: Ballantine, 2006).

2. Diana Baumrind, "Rearing Competent Children," in *Child Development Today and Tomorrow*, ed. William Damon (San Francisco: Jossey-Bass, 1988), 349–78.

3. Laurence Steinberg makes the case for authoritative parenting in his excellent book *Age of Opportunity: Lessons from the New Science of Adolescence* (Boston: Mariner, 2014). Also see Diana Baumrind, "The Influence of Parenting Style on Adolescent Competence and Substance Use," *Journal of Early Adolescence* 11, no. 1 (1991): 56–95. See also Koen Luyckx et al., "Parenting and Trajectories of Children's Maladaptive Behaviors: A 12-Year Prospective Community Study," *Journal of Clinical Child & Adolescent Psychology* 40, no. 3 (May 2011): 468–78.

4. John Gottman, *Raising an Emotionally Intelligent Child* (New York: Simon & Schuster, 1998).

5. Susan Stiffelman, in her excellent book *Parenting without Power Struggles* (New York: Atria, 2010), refers to this dynamic as parents being the captain of the ship and emphasizes our natural authority as parents.

6. Baumrind, "The Influence of Parenting Style." Also see Steinberg, *Age of Opportunity*, and Madeline Levine, *The Price of Privilege* (New York: HarperCollins, 2006).

7. Ironically, Finns say that the ideas for their world-leading education system came from studying the progressive education movement in America, which attempted to base education on a deep understanding of child development. We've abandoned most of these ideas, as we overemphasize standardization, testing, teaching kids academic skills at younger and younger ages, increased instructional time, and accountability.

8. A persuasive body of research documents the effectiveness of engaging families for promoting academic achievement and other positive outcomes. See William H. Jeynes, "Parental Involvement and Student Achievement: A Meta-Analysis," *Harvard Family Research Project* (2005), https://archive.globalfrp.org/publications-resources /publications-series/family-involvement-research-digests/parental-involvement-and

-student-achievement-a-meta-analysis. See also Anne T. Henderson et al., *Beyond the Bake Sale: The Essential Guide to Family/School Partnerships* (New York: New Press, 2007).

9. Susan M. Bögels and Margaret L. Brechman-Toussaint, "Family Issues in Child Anxiety: Attachment, Family Functioning, Parental Rearing and Beliefs," *Clinical Psychology Review* 26, no. 7 (2006): 834–56. The first study finding that overprotective and critical parenting styles are linked to higher risk for anxiety problems in children was published in 1931!

10. Jessica L. Borelli et al., "Children's and Mothers' Cardiovascular Reactivity to a Standardized Laboratory Stressor: Unique Relations with Maternal Anxiety and Overcontrol," *Emotion* 18, no. 3 (April 2018): 369–85. Children of highly anxious and more controlling mothers showed significantly greater physiological reactivity to a stressful situation. The data lend additional support to the notion that overcontrol may operate like behavioral avoidance in mothers with high anxiety. That is, being controlling may be a way in which higher-anxiety parents avoid fearful situations (e.g., viewing their children's distress) and avoid experiencing their own heightened reactivity.

11. Emily L. Loeb et al., "Perceived Psychological Control in Early Adolescence Predicts Lower Levels of Adaptation into Mid-Adulthood," *Child Development* 92, no. 2 (March/April 2021): e158–e172.

12. According to John Gottman, research has found that 75 percent of the dinner table fights between parents and kids are started by the parents. Global HR Forum, "Global HR Forum 2014 | D-1 | The Art of Emotion Coaching," YouTube video, January 6, 2015, https://www.youtube.com/watch?v=dUE0kaQnQoo.

13. Steven F. Maier, "Behavioral Control Blunts Reactions to Contemporaneous and Future Adverse Events: Medial Prefrontal Cortex Plasticity and a Corticostriatal Network," *Neurobiology of Stress* 1 (January 2015): 12–22. Interestingly, fifty years ago, Maier and Martin Seligman began research on what they called "learned helplessness," or the phenomenon of animals who repeatedly faced uncontrollable stress (e.g., mild electric shock) seeming to feel helpless when faced with additional stressors, for example, by making no attempt to avoid subsequent shocks. In a recent paper, Meier and Seligman concluded that these animals didn't learn helplessness—but rather failed to learn a sense of control. Steven F. Maier and Martin E. P. Seligman, "Learned Helplessness at Fifty: Insights from Neuroscience," *Psychological Review* 123, no. 4 (July 2016): 349–67.

14. Daniel Kahneman's peak-end rule was discussed in his book *Thinking, Fast and Slow* (New York: Farrar, Straus and Giroux, 2011).

15. This was given to us by teachers of the Parent Encouragement Program, an outstanding parent education program based in Maryland.

16. Ross Greene, *The Explosive Child* (New York: HarperCollins, 1998).

17. This is Julie Lythcott-Haims's point in *How to Raise an Adult: Break Free of the Over-parenting Trap and Prepare Your Kid for Success* (New York: St. Martin's Press, 2015). The point was also made to Bill and Ned in Houston, where they mentioned an extremely elite independent school in Washington, D.C., during their lecture. After the talk, a woman introduced herself as a psychotherapist at the Menninger Clinic in Houston—a highly respected mental health establishment. She mentioned that she and her fellow therapists at Menninger were very familiar with this school in D.C. because many of its graduates get into the most elite colleges—and then have emotional breakdowns and come to the Menninger Clinic for treatment. She added that almost all these kids who come from college to Menninger have had very little experience managing their lives on their own prior to starting college.

18. Amy Chua, *Battle Hymn of the Tiger Mother* (New York: Penguin Books, 2011), 101.

19. Steinberg, *Age of Opportunity*.

20. Daniel Siegel, *Brainstorm: The Power and Purpose of the Teenage Brain* (New York: TarcherPerigee, 2015).

Chapter 3: Communicating a Nonanxious Presence

1. Jeanne Marie Laskas, "The Mister Rogers No One Saw," *The New York Times Magazine*, November 19, 2019, https://www.nytimes.com/2019/11/19/magazine/mr-rogers.html.

2. Nonanxious presence is a term we learned from Edwin Friedman, a rabbi, family therapist, and organizational consultant and the author of *A Failure of Nerve: Leadership in the Age of the Quick Fix*, rev. ed. (New York: Church Publishing, 2017). Friedman taught that organizations, ranging from families to corporations, function best when the leaders are not highly anxious and emotionally reactive—and thus serve as a nonanxious presence.

3. Richard J. Davidson and Sharon Begley, *The Emotional Life of Your Brain* (New York: Plume, 2012). Also, a recent study of older adolescent girls at risk for major depression similarly identified connections between the prefrontal cortex and the amygdala as an important marker of resilience. Brain imaging showed that the resilient girls (who did not develop depression) had greater connectivity between the amygdala and the orbitofrontal prefrontal cortex. They also had stronger connections between the dorsolateral prefrontal cortex and the fronto-temporal regions. The study concluded that resilient girls had compensatory functional connectivity patterns in brain networks specialized for emotional regulation. Adina S. Fischer et al., "Neural Markers of Resilience in Adolescent Females at Familial Risk for Major Depressive Disorder," *JAMA Psychiatry* 75, no. 5 (2018): 493–502, https://doi.org/10.1001/jamapsychiatry.2017.4516.

4. Andrew Newberg and Mark Robert Waldman, *Words Can Change Your Brain* (New York: Plume, 2013).

5. Nelly Alia-Klein et al., "What Is in a Word? No Versus Yes Differentially Engage the Lateral Orbitofrontal Cortex," *Emotion* 7, no. 3 (August 2007): 649–59.

6. Suniya S. Luthar, Samuel H. Barkin, and Elizabeth J. Crossman, "'I can, therefore I must': Fragility in the Upper-Middle Classes," *Development and Psychopathology* 25, no. 4, pt. 2 (November 2013): 1529–49.

7. In longitudinal research, John Gottman and Robert Levenson found that this ratio could predict marriage longevity with 90 percent accuracy. See John M. Gottman and Robert W. Levenson, "Marital Processes Predictive of Later Dissolution: Behavior, Physiology, and Health," *Journal of Personality and Social Psychology* 63, no. 2 (August 1992): 221–33. Gottman has identified the kinds of positive interactions used by couples in healthy relationships—that also help in our relationships with our kids. These include (1) showing interest and listening attentively; (2) demonstrating affection; (3) showing that the other person matters; (4) focusing on the things about your partner you appreciate; (5) finding opportunities for agreement; (6) empathizing and apologizing; (7) accepting your partner's perspective; and (8) using humor. See also Kyle Benson, "The Magic Relationship Ratio, According to Science," *The Gottman Institute Blog*, October 4, 2017, https://www.gottman.com/blog/the-magic-relationship-ratio-according-science/.

8. Bonnie Zucker, personal communication. Dr. Zucker is the author of an outstanding book for parents and kids called *Anxiety-Free Kids* (Waco, TX: Prufrock Press, 2017), as well as an excellent book for children with obsessive-compulsive disorder called *Take Control of OCD: The Ultimate Guide for Kids with OCD* (Waco, TX: Prufrock Press, 2010).

9. Sara F. Waters, Tessa V. West, and Wendy Berry Mendes, "Stress Contagion: Physiological Covariation Between Mothers and Infants," *Psychological Science* 25, no. 4 (April 2014): 934–42.

10. John M. Gottman and Lynn Fainsilber Katz, "Effects of Marital Discord on Young Children's Peer Interaction and Health," *Developmental Psychology* 25, no. 3 (1989): 373–81.

11. See Patricia Pendry and Emma K. Adam, "Associations Between Parents' Marital Functioning, Maternal Parenting Quality, Maternal Emotion, and Child Cortisol Levels," *International Journal of Behavioral Development* 31, no. 3 (2007): 218–31. We discuss various neurological mechanisms of stress contagion in *The Self-Driven Child*, including the child's amygdala sensing and reacting to stress in the environment and the role of mirror neurons in "picking up" emotional distress in the faces and body language of others.

12. Golda S. Ginsberg et al., "Preventing Onset of Anxiety Disorders in Offspring of Anxious Parents: A Randomized Controlled Trial of a Family-Based Intervention," *American Journal of Psychiatry* 172, no. 12 (December 2015): 1207–14.

13. We know from multiple studies that warmth and affection help kids feel safe and protected and more willing to "get back out there" and take some risks. See N. Tottenham et al., "Parental Presence Switches Avoidance to Attraction Learning in Children," *Nature Human Behaviour* 3 (July 2019): 1070–77.

14. Michael J. Meaney, "Maternal Care, Gene Expression, and the Transmission of Individual Differences in Stress Reactivity Across Generations," *Annual Review of Neuroscience* 24, no. 1 (February 2001): 1161–92. Meaney and his colleagues separated rat pups from their mothers, who were low licking and grooming—and easily stressed—and put them in the "foster" care of high licking and grooming mothers. These fostered rats grew up to be extremely difficult to stress, even though they were genetically programmed to be anxious. The extra nurturing affected the young rats' stress systems by making changes in the way genes were expressed—changes that can be passed on to future generations. This was a powerful demonstration that calm is contagious.

15. McLean School, "Anxiety in Children and Adolescents with Dr. Jonathan Dalton," YouTube video, November 8, 2018, https://www.youtube.com/watch?v=wmIs7x34Esc.

16. An excellent book by Mary Karapetian Alvord and Anne McGrath called *Conquer Negative Thinking for Teens* (Oakland, CA: Instant Help Books, 2017) discusses these and six other negative-thinking habits—and teaches kids how to talk back to negative thinking and substitute more positive, realistic thoughts.

17. We get this term from Albert Ellis. Ellis founded rational emotive therapy, which developed contemporaneously with cognitive behavioral therapy.

18. Meaney, "Maternal Care, Gene Expression, and the Transmission of Individual Differences in Stress Reactivity Across Generations."

19. Sarah E. Fiarman, "Unconscious Bias. When Good Intentions Aren't Enough," *Educational Leadership* 74, no. 3 (November 2016): 10–15, https://www.responsive classroom.org/wp-content/uploads/2017/10/Unconscious-Bias_Ed-Leadership.pdf.

20. Abiola Keller et al., "Does the Perception That Stress Affects Health Matter? The Association with Health and Mortality," *Health Psychology* 31, no. 5 (September 2012): 677–84.

21. Alicia H. Clark, "How to Harness Your Anxiety," *The New York Times*, October 16, 2018, https://www.nytimes.com/2018/10/16/well/mind/how-to-harness-your-anxiety .html. For a more detailed discussion, see Dr. Clark's book *Hack Your Anxiety: How to Make Anxiety Work for You in Life, Love, and All That You Do* (Naperville, IL: Sourcebooks, 2018).

22. Laura E. Kurtz and Sara B. Algoe, "When Sharing a Laugh Means Sharing More: Testing the Role of Shared Laughter on Short-Term Interpersonal Consequences," *Journal of Nonverbal Behavior* 41, no. 1 (2017): 45–65. Also see Larry Cohen, *Playful Parenting* (New York: Ballantine Books, 2001).

23. Ginsberg et al., "Preventing Onset of Anxiety Disorders in Offspring of Anxious Parents."

24. That the calm produced when a person meditates can affect his family—and even his community—has been well documented. To date, there are twenty-three published studies of the environmental effects of individuals practicing Transcendental Meditation (TM) and people practicing the more advanced TM Sidhi program in large groups. These studies have consistently provided support for what is called the "Maharishi Effect" (named after Maharishi Mahesh Yogi, who predicted it), which refers to the ability of meditation to positively affect the larger environment. Research has shown that meditation can lower crime rates, reduce accidents and hospital admissions, improve classroom behavior and workplace environments, and even have a positive effect on the economy. It would likely have a calming effect on your family, too! See also David W. Orme-Johnson, "Preventing Crime Through the Maharishi Effect," *Journal of Offender Rehabilitation* 36, nos. 1–4 (2003): 251–81. See also studies of the effects of meditation on improving school environments such as Betsy L. Wisner, Barbara Jones, and David Gwin, "School-Based Meditation Practices for Adolescents: A Resource for Strengthening Self-Regulation, Emotional Coping, and Self-Esteem," *Children & Schools* 32, no. 3 (2010): 150–59. See also Michael C. Dillbeck and Kenneth L. Cavanaugh, "Societal Violence and Collective Consciousness: Reduction of U.S. Homicide and Urban Violent Crime Rates," *SAGE Open*, April 14, 2016, https://doi.org/10.1177/215824401 6637891. For a readable book-length discussion on the effects of meditation on the larger environment, see a new book by Barry Spivack and Patricia Saunders called *An Antidote to Violence: Evaluating the Evidence* (Alresford, UK: John Hunt Publishing, 2018).

25. Although it may not be entirely surprising, when the mom is happy, kids tend to be happier, feel closer to their parents, and experience stronger connections in the family. Harry Benson and Steven McKay, "Happy Wife, Happy Life: Millenium Cohort Study," Marriage Foundation (UK) website, September 2019, https://marriagefounda tion.org.uk/wp-content/uploads/2019/09/MF-Happy-Wife-Happy-Life-FINAL.pdf.

26. Barry Neil Kaufman, *To Love Is to Be Happy With* (New York: Ballantine, 1977).

27. U.S. Department of Health and Human Services, Centers for Disease Control and Prevention, *Crisis + Emergency Risk Communication (CERC): Introduction* (2018), 3, https://emergency.cdc.gov/cerc/ppt/CERC_Introduction.pdf.

28. A. A. Milne, *The House at Pooh Corner* (New York: Dutton Children's Books, 1928), 133.

29. William James, *The Principles of Psychology, Volume 1* (New York: Cosimo, 2007), 402.

Chapter 4: Pep Talks: Talking to Help Kids Find Their Own Motivation

1. It is possible to offer rewards in ways that support autonomy, that is, by avoiding the use of controlling language, providing a clear rationale, acknowledging that a given

task is boring, and emphasizing choice. Fostering relatedness also helps, as children are more likely to choose to do what we request and to value it if they feel close to us, even if the task is not appealing. See Edward L. Deci and Richard M. Ryan, "The Paradox of Achievement: The Harder You Push the Worse It Gets," in *Improving Academic Achievement: Impact of Psychological Factors on Education*, ed. Joshua Aronson (Cambridge, MA: Academic Press, 2002), 61–87.

2. Deci and Ryan, "The Paradox of Achievement." Intrinsic motivation is also associated with increased attention to the quality of one's performance, as well as with improved self-regulation (which is presumably why kids with ADHD can work carefully on their own projects but not on projects that are assigned to them).

3. Stefano Di Domenico and Richard M. Ryan, "The Emerging Neuroscience of Intrinsic Motivation: A New Frontier in Self-Determination Research," *Frontiers in Human Neuroscience* 11 (March 2017): 145. Also see Lisa Legault and Michael Inzlicht, "Self-Determination, Self-Regulation, and the Brain: Autonomy Improves Performance by Enhancing Neuroaffective Responsiveness to Self-Regulation Failure," *Journal of Personality and Social Psychology* 105, no. 1 (2013): 123–38.

4. Studies by a number of scientists have found intrinsic motivation to be associated with ERN (error-related negativity wave), which is a feature of brain activity that occurs almost immediately after making an error on a task. The ERN reflects an error detection system that monitors performance and detects incongruity between intended and actual responses. See Legault and Inzlicht, "Self-Determination, Self-Regulation, and the Brain." See also Betsy Ng, "The Neuroscience of Growth Mindset and Intrinsic Motivation," *Brain Sciences* 8, no. 2 (February 2018): 20.

5. For further reading on these ideas, we suggest Diane Tavenner's book *Prepared* (New York: Currency, 2019).

6. A study of parental autonomy support during the COVID-19 pandemic showed its usefulness in helping children adjust. A. Neubauer et al., "A Little Autonomy Support Goes a Long Way," *Child Development* 19 (January 2021), https://doi.org/10.1111/cdev.13515/.

7. Mel Levine, *The Myth of Laziness* (New York: Simon & Schuster, 2003).

8. Carol S. Dweck, *Mindset* (New York: Ballantine, 2007).

9. Ng, "The Neuroscience of Growth Mindset and Intrinsic Motivation."

10. David Scott Yeager et al., "The Far-Reaching Effects of Believing People Can Change: Implicit Theories of Personality Shape Stress, Health, and Achievement During Adolescence," *Journal of Personality and Social Psychology* 106, no. 6 (June 2014): 867–84.

11. A recent study found little support for several of the premises of mindset theory, for example, that people with a growth mindset have "learning goals" (are primarily motivated to learn rather than to get good grades), or that people with a fixed

mindset believe that success can be achieved without effort. See Alexander P. Burgoyne, David Z. Hambrick, and Brooke N. Macnamara, "How Firm Are the Foundations of Mind-Set Theory?" *Psychological Science* 31, no. 3 (February 2020): 258–67. Also, a number of studies have found little evidence that school-based interventions for promoting a growth mindset produce significant improvements in cognitive ability, academic performance, students' responses to challenges, or academic progress. See Yu Li and Timothy C. Bates, "Does Growth Mindset Improve Children's IQ, Educational Attainment or Response to Setbacks? Active-Control Interventions and Data on Children's Own Mindsets," *SocArXiv* (July 7, 2017): 1–27, https://www.re search.ed.ac.uk/portal/files/53884982/Li_and_Bates_2017_SocArXiv_Dweck _Replication.pdf. See also Victoria F. Sisk et al., "To What Extent and Under Which Circumstances Are Growth Mind-Sets Important to Academic Achievement? Two Meta-Analyses," *Psychological Science* 29, no. 4 (2018): 549–71. See also David Moreau, Brooke Macnamara, and David Z. Hambrick, "Overstating the Role of Environmental Factors in Success: A Cautionary Note," *Current Directions in Psychological Science* 28, no. 1 (2019): 28–33.

12. Research has shown that the hippocampus, the major memory center in the brain, is much larger in London taxicab drivers who have to remember all the streets and various routes in London. See Eleanor A. Maguire et al., "Navigation-Related Structural Change in the Hippocampi of Taxi Drivers," *PNAS* 97, no. 8 (April 11, 2000): 4398–403. Similarly, the parts of the brain that control skilled finger movements are larger in professional piano players. See Bernhard Haslinger et al., "Reduced Recruitment of Motor Association Areas During Bimanual Coordination in Concert Pianists," *Human Brain Mapping* 22, no. 3 (July 2004): 206–15, https://doi.org/10 .1002/hbm.20028.

13. Carol S. Dweck, "Brainology," National Association of Independent Schools website, Winter 2008, https://www.nais.org/magazine/independent-school/winter-2008 /brainology/.

14. Research has found a significant correlation between the amount of time musicians reported practicing piano as teenagers and the volume of white matter in the corpus callosum (which connects the right and left cerebral hemispheres). See Adrian Imfeld et al., "White Matter Plasticity in the Corticospinal Tract of Musicians: A Diffusion Tensor Imaging Study," *NeuroImage* 46, no. 3 (July 1, 2009): 600–607. Also see Thomas A. Forbes and Vittorio Gallo, "All Wrapped Up: Environmental Effects on Myelination," *Trends in Neurosciences* 40, no. 9 (September 2017): 572–87.

15. See the discussion of praise in Jane Nelsen, *Positive Discipline* (Ballantine, 2006).

16. Others have challenged the wisdom of simply praising effort. As Alfie Kohn has pointed out, praising effort can communicate to students that they are not very capable—and thereby cause them to think that they are unlikely to succeed at future tasks ("If you're complimenting me for just trying hard, I must really be a loser"). Kohn has also made the point that Dweck's recommendation to *praise* effort is

problematic, as praise is a verbal reward or extrinsic inducement that can be construed by children as manipulative. Kohn notes that praise is more about control than encouragement and that praise can communicate that acceptance is conditional on a child's continuing to impress us. Kohn notes that research has found that nonevaluative feedback—simply providing information about how someone performs without judgment—is preferable to praise. In Kohn's view, praise is just "a different kind of carrot." In the same way that providing rewards for children to do what they enjoy doing reduces their interest in doing it, praising children for their effort may actually backfire, especially if they work hard at something they enjoy. Alfie Kohn, "The Perils of 'Growth Mindset' Education," *Salon*, August 16, 2015, https://www.salon.com /2015/08/16/the_education_fad_thats_hurting_our_kids_what_you_need_to _know_about_growth_mindset_theory_and_the_harmful_lessons_it_imparts/.

17. Luke Wood, an expert on educational issues facing Black boys and men, argues that growth mindset theory is not wrong but is simply incomplete. He asserts that there is a false dichotomy between affirming effort and ability that can hurt boys and men of color. In Wood's view, we should affirm both. He notes that many boys and men of color have never been told that they have the ability to perform well, and that expressing belief in their ability to do so is one of the most important ways of supporting them. Adriel A. Hilton, "Prominent Scholar Called Growth Mindset a 'Cancerous' Idea in Isolation," *Huffington Post*, November 12, 2017, https://www.huffpost .com/entry/prominent-scholar-calls-growth-mindset-a-cancerous_b _5a07f046e4b0f1dc729a6bc3. In a recent telephone call with Brooke Macnamara, who has conducted several studies evaluating growth mindset theory and interventions, Macnamara said that even when studies show a shift in mindset, they have not demonstrated that this shift has "downstream" effects on academic performance. She also emphasized that it's not helpful to tell kids that they can become as smart as they want, as there are limits on the extent to which abilities can be developed purely through effort. Additionally, she noted that some people with a fixed mindset actually perform better on tasks, as believing that they are naturally good at something gives them confidence. Brooke Macnamara, personal communication.

18. Sally Shaywitz, M.D., *Overcoming Dyslexia*, 2nd ed. (New York: Knopf, 2020).

19. Matthew H. Schneps, "The Advantages of Dyslexia," *Scientific American*, August 19, 2014, https://www.scientificamerican.com/article/the-advantages-of-dyslexia/.

20. Jean Nakamura and Mihaly Csikszentmihalyi, "The Concept of Flow," in *Flow and the Foundations of Positive Psychology: The Collected Works of Mihaly Csikszentmihalyi* (New York: Springer, 2014), 239–63.

21. Mihaly Csikszentmihalyi, *Flow: The Psychology of Optimal Experience* (New York: HarperCollins, 1991).

22. Reed Larson and Natalie Rusk, "Intrinsic Motivation and Positive Development," *Advances in Child Development and Behavior* 41 (2011): 89–130.

23. Marian Diamond and Janet Hopson, *Magic Trees of the Mind* (New York: Plume, 1999).

24. Laurence Steinberg, *Age of Opportunity* (New York: Houghton Mifflin Harcourt, 2014).

25. Nora D. Volkow et al., "Evaluating Dopamine Reward Pathway in ADHD," *JAMA* 302, no. 10 (September 9, 2009): 1084–91.

26. P. Shaw et al., "Attention-Deficit/Hyperactivity Disorder Is Characterized by a Delay in Cortical Maturation," *PNAS* 104, no. 49 (December 4, 2007): 19649–54.

27. Deborah Yurgelun-Todd, "Emotional and Cognitive Changes During Adolescence," *Current Opinion in Neurobiology* 17, no. 2 (April 2007): 251–57.

Chapter 5: The Language—and Silence—of Change: Understanding Ambivalence

1. Sarah J. Erickson, Melissa Gerstle, and Sarah W. Feldstein, "Brief Interventions and Motivational Interviewing with Children, Adolescents, and Their Parents in Pediatric Health Care Settings: A Review," *Archives of Pediatric and Adolescent Medicine* 159, no. 12 (December 2005): 1173–80.

2. Stephen Rollnick, Sebastian G. Kaplan, Richard Rutschman, *Motivational Interviewing in Schools: Conversations to Improve Behavior and Learning* (New York: Guilford Press, 2016).

3. Kathleen Ries Merikangas et al., "Lifetime Prevalence of Mental Disorders in U.S. Adolescents: Results from the National Comorbidity Survey Replication—Adolescent Supplement (NCS-A)," *Journal of the American Academy of Child and Adolescent Psychiatry* 49, no. 10 (October 2010): 980–89. Jean Twenge recently reported a dramatic increase in anxiety, depression, and loneliness in teenagers from 2012 to 2017. See Jean Twenge, "Have Smartphones Destroyed a Generation?" *The Atlantic*, September 2017, https://www.theatlantic.com/magazine/archive/2017/09/has-the-smartphone-destroyed-a-generation/534198/. See also an excellent recent article by Kate Julian, "What Happened to American Childhood?" *The Atlantic*, May 2020, https://www.theatlantic.com/magazine/archive/2020/05/childhood-in-an-anxious-age/609079/; Eli Lebowitz et al., "Parent Training for Childhood Anxiety Disorders: The SPACE Program," *Cognitive and Behavioral Practice* 21, no. 4 (November 2014): 456–69.

4. Yaara Shimshoni et al., "Family Accommodation in Psychopathology: A Synthesized Review," *Indian Journal of Psychiatry* 61, Suppl. 1 (January 2019): S93–S103, https://doi.org/10.4103/psychiatry.IndianJPsychiatry_530_18. Also see Kristen G. Benito et al., "Development of the Pediatric Accommodation Scale," *Journal of Anxiety Disorders* 29 (January 2015): 14–24, https://doi.org/10.1016/j.janxdis.2014.10.004.

5. An excellent new book presents the tools from the SPACE program to parents who want to help their children with anxiety and/or OCD. Eli Lebowitz, *Breaking Free of*

Child Anxiety and OCD: A Scientifically Proven Program for Parents (New York: Oxford University Press, 2021).

6. A recent study documented the effectiveness of the SPACE program. Children aged seven to fourteen who had been diagnosed with an anxiety disorder were assigned to standard CBT or to the SPACE program. Each treatment program consisted of twelve weekly sixty-minute sessions with a therapist. Both treatments reduced the child's level of anxiety and anxiety-related emotional disorders to a similar degree. Parents of both groups experienced drops in parenting-related stress. The findings suggest that both approaches work equally well to reduce childhood anxiety. Eli R. Lebowitz et al., "Parent-Based Treatment as Efficacious as Cognitive-Behavioral Therapy for Childhood Anxiety: A Randomized Noninferiority Study of Supportive Parenting for Anxious Childhood Emotions," *Journal of American Academy of Child and Adolescent Psychiatry* 59, no. 3 (March 2020): 362–72.

7. Lebowitz et al., "Parent Training for Childhood Anxiety Disorders."

8. Haim Omer and Eli R. Lebowitz, "Nonviolent Resistance: Helping Caregivers Reduce Problematic Behaviors in Children and Adolescents," *Journal of Marital and Family Therapy* 42, no. 4 (October 2016): 688–700.

9. Thanks to Jonathan Dalton for pointing out this illustration of the power of staying calm and standing firm.

10. Jessica Lahey, *The Addiction Inoculation* (New York: Harper, 2021).

11. See Helen Shen, "Cannabis and the Adolescent Brain," *PNAS* 117, no. 1 (2020): 7–11.

12. For example, are kids with memory problems more likely to smoke pot, or does pot cause memory problems? Similarly, although there is a significant correlation between high-dose pot use and psychosis, it's unclear whether pot causes psychosis or young people who are vulnerable to psychotic breaks are more likely to smoke pot. See Louise Arseneau et al., "Cannabis Use in Adolescence and Risk for Adult Psychosis: Longitudinal Prospective Study," *BMJ* 325, no. 7374 (November 2002): 1212–13, https://doi.org/10.1136/bmj.325.7374.1212.

13. Marc Brackett, *Permission to Feel* (New York: Celadon Books, 2019).

14. Ken C. Winters and Amelia Arria, "Adolescent Brain Development and Drugs," *PMC* 18, no. 2 (2011): 21–24.

15. Daniel J. Siegel, M.D., *Brainstorm: The Power and Purpose of the Teenage Brain* (New York: TarcherPerigee, 2014).

16. According to the National Institute on Drug Abuse, approximately 10 percent of marijuana users become addicted. This number increases "among those who start young (to about 17%) and among daily users (to 25–50%). Thus, many of the nearly 7% of high school seniors who (according to annual survey data) report smoking marijuana daily or almost daily are well on their way to addiction, if not already addicted, and

may be functioning at a suboptimal level in their schoolwork and in other areas of their lives." NIDA, "Is It Possible for Teens to Become Addicted to Marijuana?" *National Institute on Drug Abuse,* June 2, 2020, https://www.drugabuse.gov/publications/princi ples-adolescent-substance-use-disorder-treatment-research-based-guide/frequently -asked-questions/it-possible-teens-to-become-addicted-to-marijuana.

17. Randi M. Schuster et al., "One Month of Cannabis Abstinence in Adolescents and Young Adults," *Journal of Clinical Psychiatry* 79, no. 6 (October 2018), https://doi .org/10.4088/JCP.17m11977.

18. Nora Volkow, "Marijuana Research Report." Revised July 2020. National Institute on Drug Abuse.

19. Volkow, "Marijuana Research Report."

20. Susan A. Stoner, "Effects of Marijuana on Mental Health: Anxiety Disorders," Alcohol and Drug Abuse Institute, University of Washington (2017): 1–6.

21. Stoner, "Effects of Marijuana on Mental Health: Anxiety Disorders."

22. Linda P. Spear, "Effects of Adolescent Alcohol Consumption on the Brain and Behaviour," *Nature Reviews Neuroscience* 19 (2018): 197–214.

23. Marisa M. Silveri, "Just How Does Drinking Affect the Teenage Brain?" https:// www.mcleanhospital.org/essential/what-you-need-know-about-alcohol-and -developing-teenage-brain.

24. Aaron M. White, PhD, "Keeping It Real—And Safe," *School Counselor Magazine,* November/December 2018.

25. Lahey, *The Addiction Inoculation.*

26. Laurence Steinberg, *Age of Opportunity* (New York: Houghton Mifflin Harcourt, 2014).

27. If parents want more information, see Cynthia Kuhn et al., *Buzzed,* 4th ed. (New York: Norton, 2014).

Chapter 6: "What if I don't want to live up to my potential?": Communicating Healthy Expectations

1. Xitao Fan and Michael Chen, "Parental Involvement and Students' Academic Achievement," *Educational Psychology Review* 13, no. 1 (2001): 1–22. Also, a meta-analysis of fifty-two studies of parental expectations conducted in 2005 by William Jeynes concluded that parents' expectations had nearly twice as strong an effect on students' achievement as parenting style. See William H. Jeynes, "Parental Involvement and Student Achievement: A Meta-Analysis," Harvard Family Research Project (2005), https://archive.globalfrp.org/publications-resources/publications-series/family-in volvement-research-digests/parental-involvement-and-student-achievement-a-meta -analysis.

2. Donald D. Price, Damien G. Finniss, and Fabrizio Benedetti, "A Comprehensive Review of the Placebo Effect: Recent Advances and Current Thought," *Annual Review of Psychology* 59 (2008): 565–90. Also, see a more recent meta-analytic review by Joël Coste and Sébastien Montel, "Placebo-Related Effects: A Meta-Narrative Review of Conceptualization, Mechanisms and Their Relevance in Rheumatology," *Rheumatology* (Oxford, UK) 56, no. 3 (March 1, 2017): 334–43.

3. Silke Gniß, Judith Kappesser, and Christiane Hermann, "Placebo Effect in Children: The Role of Expectation and Learning," *Pain* 161, no. 6 (June 2020): 1191–201.

4. Since the late 1980s educators who pay attention to brain research have characterized the optimal learning environment as "high challenge, low threat." (See Renate Nummela Caine and Geoffrey Caine, *Making Connections: Teaching and the Human Brain*, rev. ed. [Boston: Addison-Wesley, 1994].) Considerable research has supported the idea that students need to be sufficiently challenged to avoid boredom, which undermines learning (see Virginia Tze, Lia M. Daniels, and Robert Klassen, "Evaluating the Relationship Between Boredom and Academic Outcomes: A Meta-Analysis," *Educational Psychology Review* 28, no. 1 [March 2015]: 119–44). Extensive research has also demonstrated the negative effects on learning caused by perceived threat. See Susanne Vogal and Lars Schwabe, "Learning and Memory Under Stress: The Implications for the Classroom," *NPJ Science of Learning* (June 29, 2016), https://doi.org/10.1038/npjscilearn.2016.11. A well-received recent book by Mary Myatt called *High Challenge, Low Threat: How the Best Leaders Find the Balance* (Woodbridge, UK: John Catt Educational, 2016) offers educators and school administrators ideas for achieving school cultures that are challenging but not threatening.

5. Suniya Luthar, Phillip J. Small, and Lucia Ciciolla, "Adolescents from Upper Middle Class Communities: Substance Misuse and Addiction Across Early Adulthood," *Development and Psychopathology* 30, no. 1 (February 2018): 315–35. See also Mary B. Geisz and Mary Nakashian, "Adolescent Wellness: Current Perspectives and Future Opportunities in Research, Policy, and Practice," Robert Wood Johnson Foundation report, July 2018, https://www.rwjf.org/en/library/research/2018/06/inspiring-and-powering-the-future--a-new-view-of-adolescence.html.

6. See a study by Ethan Kross et al., "Self-Talk as a Regulatory Mechanism: How You Do It Matters," *Journal of Personality and Social Psychology* 106, no. 2 (February 2014): 304–24. A recent study has explained the brain mechanisms that account for this effect and found that third-person self-talk helps people to regulate their thoughts, feelings, and behavior under stress: Jason S. Moser et al., "Third-Person Self-Talk Facilitates Emotional Regulation Without Engaging Cognitive Control: Converging Evidence from ERP and fMRI," *Scientific Reports* 7, no. 1 (2017): 4519, https://doi.org/10.1038/s41598-017-04047-3.

7. Andrew J. Howell, "Self-Affirmation Theory and the Science of Well-Being," *Journal of Happiness Studies: An Interdisciplinary Forum on Subjective Well-Being* 18, no. 1 (2017): 293–311.

8. Christopher N. Cascio et al., "Self-Affirmation Activates Brain Systems Associated with Self-Related Processing and Reward and Is Reinforced by Future Orientation," *Social, Cognitive, and Affective Neuroscience* 11, no. 4 (April 2016): 621–29. See also Emily B. Falk et al., "Self-Affirmation Alters the Brain's Response to Health Messages and Subsequent Behavior Change," *PNAS* 112, no. 7 (February 17, 2015): 1977–82.

9. Geoffrey L. Cohen and David K. Sherman, "The Psychology of Change: Self-Affirmation and Social Psychological Intervention," *Annual Review of Psychology* 65 (2014): 333–71.

10. William Jeynes, "Aspiration and Expectations: Providing Pathways to Tomorrow," in *Handbook on Family and Community Engagement,* ed. Sam Redding, Marilyn Murphy, and Pam Sheley (Charlotte, NC: Information Age Publishing, 2011): 57–60. Jeynes also emphasizes that warm and loving lines of communication between parent and child are very important for the transmission of positive expectations. See also an article by Bryan Goodwin, "The Power of Parental Expectations," *Educational Leadership* 75, no. 1 (September 2017): 80–81.

11. To our knowledge, the idea of a mastermind group—or a group of peers who meet to share advice and support—was originally promoted by one of the early self-help writers, Napoleon Hill, in *The Law of Success in Sixteen Lessons* (reprint of the original rare 1925 edition) (Salem, MA: Orne, 2010) and later in *Think and Grow Rich* (Shippensburg, PA: Sound Wisdom, 2016). Mastermind groups continue to be promoted by writers in the success/self-help field.

12. Miriam Adderholdt and Jan Goldberg, *Perfectionism: What's Bad about Being Too Good?* (Minneapolis: Free Spirit, 1987).

13. Thomas Curran and Andrew P. Hill, "Perfectionism Is Increasing Over Time: A Meta-Analysis of Birth Cohort Differences from 1989 to 2016," *Psychological Bulletin*, 145, no. 4 (April 2019): 410–29.

14. Brené Brown, *Daring Greatly* (New York: Avery, 2012), 129. From Carol Dweck's perspective, excellence seekers have a growth mindset, whereas perfectionists have a fixed mindset. She notes that perfectionists endorse beliefs such as "People will think less of me if I make mistakes," "People will not respect me if I do not do well all the time," and "If I do poorly on something, it's as bad as complete failure." She also states that perfectionistic kids have to "shrink their world" to avoid situations in which they may not be the smartest or the best." (The School of Life, "Carol Dweck on Perfectionism," YouTube video, July 31, 2013, https://www.youtube.com/watch?v=XgUF5WalyDk.)

15. Kathleen Y. Kawamura, Randy O. Frost, and Morton G. Harmatz, "The Relationship of Perceived Parenting Styles to Perfectionism," *Personality and Individual Differences* 32, no. 2 (January 19, 2002): 317–27. See also Hara Estroff Marano, "Pitfalls of Perfectionism," *Psychology Today*, March 1, 2008, https://www.psychologytoday.com/us/articles/200803/pitfalls-perfectionism.

16. Suniya S. Luthar and Bronwyn E. Becker, "Privileged but Pressured? A Study of Affluent Youth," *Child Development* 73, no. 5 (September–October 2002): 1593–1610.

17. Sheila Achar Josephs, "Reducing Perfectionism in Teens," Anxiety and Depression Association of America website, April 25, 2017, https://adaa.org/learn-from-us/from -the-experts/blog-posts/consumer/reducing-perfectionism-teens.

18. Alicia Nortje, "Social Comparison: An Unavoidable Upward or Downward Spiral," PositivePsychology.com, January 9, 2020, https://positivepsychology.com/social -comparison/.

19. This point was made to us in an interview with Daniel Pine, the chief of the Section on Development and Affective Neuroscience at the National Institute of Mental Health and one of the world's experts on anxiety disorders and depression in children and teens.

20. See Michael Gershon's book, *The Second Brain: A Groundbreaking New Understanding of Nervous Disorders of the Stomach and Intestine* (New York: HarperCollins, 1998), vii. See also Siri Carpenter, "That Gut Feeling," *Monitor on Psychology* 43, no. 8 (September 2012): 50.

21. If an identical twin is diagnosed with either ADHD or autism, the other twin has an 80 percent chance of being diagnosed with it, too. Stephen V. Faraone and Henrik Larsson, "Genetics of Attention Deficit Hyperactivity Disorder," *Molecular Psychiatry* 24, no. 4 (April 2019): 562–75. Sven Sandin et al., "The Heritability of Autism Spectrum Disorder," *JAMA* 318, no. 12 (September 26, 2017): 1182–84. However, if a twin is diagnosed with anxiety or depression, the identical twin has only a 30 to 40 percent chance of being diagnosed. Kirstin Purves et al., "A Major Role for Common Genetic Variation in Anxiety Disorders," *Molecular Psychiatry* 25, no. 12 (December 2020): 3292–3303. See also Elizabeth C. Corfield et al., "A Continuum of Genetic Liability for Minor and Major Depression," *Translational Psychiatry* 7, no. 5 (May 16, 2017): e1131, https://doi.org/10.1038/tp.2017.99.

22. Max Ehrmann, *The Desiderata of Happiness: A Collection of Philosophical Poems* (New York: Crown, 1995). See also Chapter 7: "Talking to Kids about the Pursuit of Happiness."

Chapter 7: Talking to Kids about the Pursuit of Happiness

1. A study of the intensity of the smiles of major-league baseball players in the photographs on their rookie season baseball card predicted the players' longevity. Players who smiled broadly lived longer than those who did not smile or politely smiled for the camera. A later study failed to replicate this finding (Michael Dufner et al., "Does Smile Intensity in Photographs Really Predict Longevity? A Replication and Extension of Abel and Kruger [2010]," *Psychological Science* 29, no. 1 [September 2017]: 147–53). However, other studies have shown that smile intensity in childhood predicts successful marriage, as both men and women with low-intensity smiles in childhood photographs were more

likely to divorce. See Ernest L. Abel and Michael L. Kruger, "Smile Intensity in Photographs Predicts Longevity," *Psychological Science* 21, no. 4 (April 2010): 542–44, https://doi.org/10.1177/0956797610363775. Also see Matthew J. Hertenstein et al., "Smile Intensity in Photographs Predicts Divorce Later in Life," *Motivation and Emotion* 33, no. 2 (2009): 99–105, https://doi.org/10.1007/s11031-009-9124-6.

2. According to researchers, happy people "are more productive at work, make more money, and have superior jobs. They are also more creative and are better leaders and negotiators. They are more likely to marry and have fulfilling marriages, have more friends and more social support, are physically healthier, and even live longer; are more helpful and philanthropic; show more resilience to stress and trauma." Sonja Lyubomirsky, Laura King, and Ed Diener, "The Benefits of Frequent Positive Affect: Does Happiness Lead to Success?" *Psychological Bulletin* 131, no. 6 (November 2005): 803–55. See also Catherine A. Sanderson, *The Positive Shift* (Dallas, TX: BenBella Books, 2019).

3. Daniel Gilbert, *Stumbling on Happiness* (New York: Alfred A. Knopf, 2006). We were also struck by the findings of a 2015 study by Krieger and Sheldon called "What Makes Lawyers Happy? A Data-Driven Prescription to Redefine Professional Success." This study found that factors like autonomy, relatedness, and intrinsic motivation were much more highly correlated with happiness than the correlations with income, class rank, or making law review, which ranged from low to zero. Lawrence S. Krieger and Kennon M. Sheldon, "What Makes Lawyers Happy? A Data-Driven Prescription to Redefine Professional Success," *George Washington Law Review* 83 (2015): 554–627.

4. The rate of suicide in children and young adults aged ten to twenty-four increased nearly 60 percent between 2007 and 2018. U.S. Department of Health and Human Services, Centers for Disease Control and Prevention, "State Suicide Rates Among Adolescents and Young Adults Aged 10–24: United States, 2000–2018," by Sally C. Curtain, *National Vital Statistics Reports* 69, no. 11 (September 11, 2020), https://www.cdc.gov/nchs/data/nvsr/nvsr69/nvsr-69-11-508.pdf. Chandler, Arizona, recently reported thirty-five teen suicides in a twenty-two-month period, including numerous honors students. Jim Walsh, "2 More Young Lives Lost to Suicide," EastValley.com, May 26, 2019, https://www.eastvalleytribune.com/news/2-more-young-lives-lost-to-suicide/article_92525176-7e76-11e9-9764-2b0d7447b97e.html.

5. Jonathan Kozol, *The Shame of the Nation: The Restoration of Apartheid Schooling in America* (New York: Three Rivers Press, 2005), 95.

6. Marc Brackett, *Permission to Feel: Unlocking the Power of Emotions to Help Our Kids, Ourselves, and Our Society Thrive* (New York: Celadon Books, 2019).

7. Robert H. Lustig, *The Hacking of the American Mind: The Science Behind the Corporate Takeover of Our Bodies and Brains* (New York: Avery, 2018).

8. Lustig writes that all hedonic behaviors, in the extreme, lead to addiction, as every substance and behavior of addition goes through essentially the same neural pathways.

Dopamine excites neurons, and too much excitement causes reduction in dopamine receptors. Get a hit or a rush—and the number of dopamine receptors goes down. Next time you need a bigger hit to get the same rush (you develop tolerance). In contrast, serotonin inhibits and calms other neurons. Stress can decrease serotonin receptors, resulting in diminished happiness. But you can't overdose on too much serotonin—or too much happiness.

9. Suniya S. Luthar, Phillip J. Small, and Lucia Ciciolla, "Adolescents from Upper Middle Class Communities: Substance Misuse and Addiction across Early Adulthood," *Development and Psychopathology* 30, no. 1 (February 2018): 315–335.

10. Sonja Lyubomirsky, *The How of Happiness: A Scientific Approach to Getting the Life You Want* (New York: Penguin Press, 2007).

11. A recent meta-analytic study of the heritability of well-being, which analyzed the results from many twin studies that included more than fifty thousand participants, found that the heritability of overall well-being was 36 percent, while the heritability of life satisfaction was 32 percent. (Meike Bartels, "Genetics of Wellbeing and Its Components Satisfaction with Life, Happiness, and Quality of Life: A Review and Meta-Analysis of Heritability Studies," *Behavior Genetics* 45, no. 2 [March 2015]: 137–56.) This is similar to the heritability of generalized anxiety disorder (about 30 percent), whereas the heritability of major depressive disorder appears to be in the 40–50 percent range. (Michael G. Gottschalk and Katharina Domschke, "Genetics of Generalized Anxiety Disorder and Related Traits," *Dialogues in Clinical Neuroscience* 19, no. 2 [June 2017]: 159–68.)

12. Gilbert, *Stumbling on Happiness*. There is some recent evidence that, in our increasingly materialistic culture, the correlation between income and happiness has increased steadily over the last forty years. See Jean Twenge and A. Bell Cooper, "The Expanding Class Divide in Happiness in the United States, 1972–2016," *Emotion*, advance online publication (2020), https://doi.org/10.1037/emo0000774. However, other recent studies looking at countries around the world, including the United States, have found that the correlation drops off dramatically after a modest level of income. Andrew T. Jebb et al., "Happiness, Income Satiation, and Turning Points Around the World," *Nature Human Behaviour* 2, no. 1 (January 2018): 33–38.

13. Martin Seligman, "PERMA and the Building Blocks of Well-Being," *Journal of Positive Psychology* 13, no. 4 (February 2018): 1–3.

14. Dr. Daniel Pine, personal communication.

15. Jean M. Twenge and Tim Kasser, "Generational Changes in Materialism and Work Centrality, 1976–2007: Associations with Temporal Changes in Societal Insecurity and Materialistic Role Modeling," *Personality and Social Psychology Bulletin* 39, no. 7 (May 1, 2013): 883–97.

16. Tim Kasser, *The High Price of Materialism* (Toronto, ON: Bradford Books, 2003).

17. Tim Kasser, personal communication.

18. William R. Miller et al., "Personal Values Card Sort," University of New Mexico, www.motivationalinterviewing.org/sites/default/files/valuescardsort_0.pdf.

19. In a study of fourth, fifth, and sixth graders, those who were asked to perform three acts of kindness per week for four weeks became happier over time. Kristin Layous et al., "Kindness Counts: Prompting Prosocial Behavior in Preadolescents Boosts Peer Acceptance and Well-Being," *PLoS One* 7, no. 12 (2012): e51380, https://doi .org/10.1371/journal.pone.0051380.

20. Lara B. Aknin et al., "Pro-Social Spending and Well-Being: Cross-Cultural Evidence for a Psychological Universal," *Journal of Personality and Social Psychology* 104, no. 4 (April 2013): 635–52. See also Elizabeth W. Dunn, Lara B. Aknin, and Michael I. Norton, "Prosocial Spending and Happiness: Using Money to Benefit Others Pays Off," *Current Directions in Psychological Science* 23, no. 1 (2014): 41–47.

21. Brooke C. Feeney and Roxanne L. Thrush, "Relationship Influences on Exploration in Adulthood: The Characteristics and Function of a Secure Base," *Journal of Personality and Social Psychology* 98, no. 1 (January 2010): 57–76.

22. Kate Taylor, "Sex on Campus: She Can Play That Game, Too," *The New York Times*, July 12, 2013, https://www.nytimes.com/2013/07/14/fashion/sex-on-campus-she-can -play-that-game-too.html.

23. Ed Diener and Martin E. P. Seligman, "Very Happy People," *Psychological Science* 13, no. 1 (January 2002): 81–84.

24. Gillian M. Sandstrom and Elizabeth W. Dunn, "Is Efficiency Overrated? Minimal Social Interactions Lead to Belonging and Positive Affect," *Social Psychological and Personality Science* 5, no. 4 (May 2014): 437–42. See also Nicholas Epley and Juliana Schroeder, "Mistakenly Seeking Solitude," *Journal of Experimental Psychology: General* 143, no. 5 (2014): 1980–99.

25. Julie Hecht, "Is the Gaze from Those Big Puppy Eyes the Look of Your Doggie's Love?" *Scientific American*, April 16, 2015, https://www.scientificamerican.com/ar ticle/is-the-gaze-from-those-big-puppy-eyes-the-look-of-your-doggie-s-love/.

26. Sanderson, *The Positive Shift*.

27. Martin E. P. Seligman, *Learned Optimism: How to Change Your Mind and Your Life* (New York: Vintage, 2006). Seligman also wrote a research-based book on promoting optimistic thinking in children and teens, *The Optimistic Child: A Proven Program to Safeguard Children Against Depression and Build Lifelong Resilience* (New York: Houghton Mifflin Harcourt, 1995).

28. The world's expert on gratitude, Robert Emmons, has shown that gratitude improves mood, lowers stress and blood pressure, improves immune functions, and leads to strong social connections. See UC Davis Health, "Gratitude Is Good Medicine,"

November 25, 2015, https://health.ucdavis.edu/welcome/features/2015-2016/11/2015
1125_gratitude.html.

29. Sonja Lyubomirsky, Kennon M. Sheldon, and David Schkade, "Pursuing Happiness:
The Architecture of Sustainable Change," *Review of General Psychology* 9, no. 2
(June 2005): 111–31.

30. Martin E. P. Seligman, Tayyab Rashid, and Acacia C. Parks, "Positive Psychotherapy," *American Psychologist* 61, no. 8 (2006): 774–88.

31. The saying "F.A.I.L. stands for 'First Attempt in Learning'" is attributed to A. P. J.
Abdul Kalam, who also said, "End is not the end, as E.N.D. means Effort Never Dies."

32. As inspired by Princeton Professor Johannes Haushofer's viral CV of Failure, which
was itself based on Melanie Stefan's idea as published in *Nature*: Melanie Stefan, "A
CV of Failures," *Nature* 468 (November 2010): 467, https://www.nature.com/arti
cles/nj7322-467a.

33. University of Pennsylvania Penn Faces Resilience Project, http://pennfaces.upenn.edu/.

34. Abigail Lipson, "How to Have a Really Successful Failure," Harvard University Bureau
of Study Counsel publication (2009): 7–9, https://successfailureproject.bsc.harvard
.edu/files/success/files/bsc_pub_-_how_to_have_a_really_successful_failure.pdf.

35. James A. Blumenthal, Patrick J. Smith, and Benson M. Hoffman, "Is Exercise a Vi-
able Treatment for Depression?" *ACSM's Health and Fitness Journal* 16, no. 4 (July
2012): 14–21.

36. Laurie Santos talks about sleep deprivation and the importance of sleep in her lecture
"Psychology and the Good Life," Aspen Institute, 2018, https://www.aspenideas.org
/sessions/psychology-and-the-good-life.

37. Matthew A. Killingsworth and Daniel T. Gilbert, "A Wandering Mind Is an Unhappy Mind," *Science* 330, no. 6006 (November 12, 2010): 932.

38. Killingsworth and Gilbert, "A Wandering Mind Is an Unhappy Mind."

39. A very readable introduction to research on Transcendental Meditation is Dr. Norman E. Rosenthal's book, *Transcendence* (New York: Tarcher, 2011).

40. Numerous studies have documented significant reductions in anxiety and depressive
symptoms and improved academic performance in meditating middle school, high
school, and college students. Several have demonstrated the effects of meditation on
students in underserved middle schools and high schools, which include reductions in
anxiety, depression, aggression, and dropping out, along with increases in academic
performance, graduation rates, and happiness. See Staci Wendt et al., "Practicing Transcendental Meditation in High Schools: Relationship to Well-Being and Academic
Achievement Among Students," *Contemporary School Psychology* 19 (July 22, 2015):
312–19, https://doi.org/10.1007/s40688-015-0066-6. See also Laurent Valosek et al.,

"Effect of Meditation on Social-Emotional Learning in Middle School Students," *Education* 139, no. 3 (March 2019): 111–19. Very recently, a study examined the effects of students at a high-performing public school practicing Transcendental Meditation for fifteen minutes twice during the school day. Compared to students who engaged in silent reading for two fifteen-minute periods, the meditating students reported significantly reduced anxiety, anger, depression, and fatigue, as well as increased self-esteem. See Jane Bleasdale, Margaret C. Peterson, and Sanford Nidich, "Effect of Meditation on Social/Emotional Well-Being in a High-Performing High School," *Professional School Counseling*, January 2019, https://doi.org/10.1177/2156759X20940639.

41. Lutz Goldbeck et al., "Life Satisfaction Decreases During Adolescence," *Quality of Life Research* 16, no. 6 (August 2007): 969–79.

42. Ashley Whillans, Lucía Macchia, and Elizabeth Dunn, "Valuing Time Over Money Predicts Happiness After a Major Life Transition: A Preregistered Longitudinal Study of Graduating Students," *Science Advances* 5, no. 9 (September 2019), https://doi.org/10.1126/sciadv.aax2615.

43. https://brenebrown.com/podcast/brene-with-sonya-renee-taylor-on-the-body-is-not-an-apology/#close-popup.

Chapter 8: The Hard Ones: Talking with Kids about Sleep and Technology

1. In *The Self-Driven Child*, we wrote about the science of sleep primarily as it relates to a sense of control, and particularly to emotional regulation. We emphasized the dramatic degree to which children and teens (and adults) are more easily stressed when they are tired, the extent to which sleep restriction weakens the connections between the prefrontal cortex and the amygdala—resulting in poor emotional regulation, and the role that dream sleep plays in emotional healing. We also talked about the many benefits sleep confers for learning, memory, and optimal performance, including athletic performance. Much of this research is discussed in a recent book by the great sleep scientist Matthew Walker called *Why We Sleep: Unlocking the Power of Sleep and Dreams* (New York: Scribner, 2017). See also an article by Susan Worley called "The Extraordinary Importance of Sleep: The Detrimental Effects of Inadequate Sleep on Health and Public Safety Drive an Explosion of Sleep Research," *Pharmacy and Therapeutics* 43, no. 12 (December 2018): 758–63. Very recent research has also clarified mechanisms that help determine what we remember and what we (appropriately) forget. See Shuntaro Izawa et al., "REM Sleep–Active MCH Neurons Are Involved in Forgetting Hippocampus-Dependent Memories," *Science* 365, no. 6459 (September 20, 2019): 1308–13. Recent studies have additionally documented the links between irregular sleep patterns and metabolic disorders, the important role that microbes in the gut play in sleep, and the association of ADHD traits and insomnia. See Tianyi Huang and Susan Redline, "Cross-Sectional and

Prospective Associations of Actigraphy-Assessed Sleep Regularity with Metabolic Abnormalities: The Multi-Ethnic Study of Atherosclerosis," *Diabetes Care* 42, no. 8 (August 2019): 1422–29; Yukino Ogawa et al., "Gut Microbiota Depletion by Chronic Antibiotic Treatment Alters the Sleep/Wake Architecture and Sleep EEG Power Spectra in Mice," *Scientific Reports* 10, no. 1 (November 11, 2020): 19554; and Orestis Floros et al., "Vulnerability in Executive Functions to Sleep Deprivation Is Predicted by Subclinical Attention-Deficit/Hyperactivity Disorder Symptoms," *Biological Psychiatry: Cognitive Neuroscience and Neuroimaging* (October 28, 2020), https://doi.org/10.1016/j.bpsc.2020.09.019 (Epub ahead of print).

2. This formulation of what keeps kids awake comes from Dan Shapiro, M.D., a brilliant developmental pediatrician and the author of two excellent books for parents of complicated children, *Parent Child Journey* (North Charleston, SC: CreateSpace, 2016) and *Parent Child Excursions* (Los Angeles: Dagmar Miura, 2019).

3. Danny Lewin, PhD, a behavioral sleep specialist at Children's National Medical Center in Washington, D.C., suggests that parents (and professionals) dialogue with kids about sleep and sleep-related challenges. He recommends encouraging kids to try a sleep improvement plan for a week or ten days and see what they experience, noting that this is a model of experimentation they can use their whole lives. Lewin, personal communication.

4. A. M. Williamson and A. M. Feyer, "Moderate Sleep Deprivation Produces Impairments in Cognitive and Motor Performance Equivalent to Legally Prescribed Levels of Alcohol Intoxication," *Occupational and Environmental Medicine* 57, no. 10 (October 2000): 649–55.

5. Eli R. Lebowitz and Haim Omer, *Treating Childhood and Adolescent Anxiety: A Guide for Caregivers* (Hoboken, NJ: Wiley, 2013): 95–97.

6. Also, Wilson found the same patterns of brain activation (firing of exactly the same cells) when rats were learning to navigate a maze and during subsequent slow wave and REM sleep. See Daoyun Ji and Matthew A. Wilson, "Coordinated Memory Replay in the Visual Cortex and Hippocampus During Sleep," *Nature Neuroscience* 10 (2007): 100–107. Pierre Maquet similarly found on a PET scan study that brain areas activated where participants were learning a task were also activated during subsequent REM sleep. See Pierre Maquet et al., "Experience-Dependent Changes in Cerebral Activation During Human REM Sleep," *Nature Neuroscience* 3, no. 8 (August 2000): 831–36. Also, Robert Stickgold had college students play Tetris for seven hours over the course of three days. When awakened just after falling asleep, 75 percent reported experiencing visual images of the game, suggesting that the brain was continuing to work on the problem during sleep. See Robert Stickgold, "Replaying the Game: Hypnagogic Images in Normals and Amnesics," *Science* 290, no. 5490 (October 13, 2000): 350–53.

7. https://screentimenetwork.org/apa.

8. John Bingham, "Screen Addict Parents Accused of Hypocrisy by Their Children," *The Telegraph* (London), July 22, 2014, https://www.telegraph.co.uk/technology/news /10981242/Screen-addict-parents-accused-of-hypocrisy-by-their-children.html.

9. Emily Weinstein, of Harvard's Zero to Three program, asks parents to rethink three things we often say to our kids: "Can you just get off your phone?" "What are you even doing there?" and "Think before you post." She recommends "empathy over eye rolling." See Dr. Weinstein's presentation in the webinar Constantly Connected. Children and Screens, "Constantly Connected: The Social Media Lives of Teens," YouTube video, July 6, 2020, https://www.youtube.com/watch?v=BfX2TqD4rq8& feature=emb_logo.

10. Children and Screens, "Constantly Connected: The Social Media Lives of Teens," YouTube video, July 6, 2020, https://www.youtube.com/watch?v=BfX2TqD4rq8& feature=emb_logo.

11. Devorah Heitner, *Screenwise: Helping Kids Thrive (and Survive) in Their Digital World* (Abingdon, UK: Bibliomotion, 2016).

12. Ben Carter et al., "Association Between Portable Screen-Based Media Device Access or Use and Sleep Outcomes: A Systematic Review and Meta-Analysis," *JAMA Pediatrics* 170, no. 12 (December 1, 2016): 1202–8. See also Nicholas Bakalar, "What Keeps Kids Up at Night? Cellphones and Tablets," *The New York Times*, October 31, 2016, https://www.nytimes.com/2016/10/31/well/mind/what-keeps-kids-up-at-night -it-could-be-their-cellphone.html. Additionally, see Ann Johansson, Maria A. Patrisko, and Eileen R. Chassens, "Adolescent Sleep and the Impact of Technology Use Before Sleep on Daytime Function," *Journal of Pediatric Nursing* 31, no. 5 (September–October 2016): 498–504.

13. See Peter Gray's six conditions for self-directed learning as discussed in Chicago Ideas, "Mother Nature's Pedagogy: Insights from Evolutionary Psychology," video, retrieved January 28, 2021, https://www.chicagoideas.com/videos/mother-nature -s-pedagogy-insights-from-evolutionary-psychology. See also Gray's TED Talk: TEDx Talks, "The Decline of Play | Peter Gray | TEDxNavesink," YouTube video, June 13, 2014, and his 2013 article in *Salon*: "School Is a Prison and Damaging Our Kids," *Salon*, August 26, 2013, https://www.salon.com/2013/08/26/school_is_a_prison_and _damaging_our_kids/.

14. Douglas Gentile, "Pathological Video Game Use Among Youth 8–18: A National Study," *Psychological Science* 20, no. 5 (May 2009): 594–602.

15. Gentile, "Pathological Video Game Use Among Youth 8–18."

16. "Constantly Connected: The Social Media Lives of Teens," YouTube video, July 6, 2020, https://www.youtube.com/watch?v=BfX2TqD4rq8&feature=emb_logo.

17. Clive Thompson, "Don't Blame Social Media If Your Teen Is Unsocial. It's Your Fault," *Wired*, December 26, 2013, https://www.wired.com/2013/12/ap-thompson-2/.

18. The 81 percent figure is from a November 2018 PEW study. Monica Anderson and Jing Jing Jiang, "Teens' Social Media Habits and Experiences," PEW Research Center, November 28, 2018, https://www.pewresearch.org/internet/2018/11/28/teens -social-media-habits-and-experiences/), reported by Linda Chamaraman in Children and Screens, "Constantly Connected: The Social Media Lives of Teens," YouTube video, July 6, 2020, https://www.youtube.com/watch?v=BfX2TqD4rq8&feature= emb_logo.

19. Heitner, *Screenwise*, 36.

20. Jean Twenge, "More Time on Technology, Less Happiness?" *Current Directions in Psychological Science* 28, no. 4 (May 22, 2019): 372–79. Note there is no causal link between depression and social media, but there does seem to be a causal link with anxiety.

21. This is true! Check out research by Daphne Bavelier from the University of Rochester. Bavelier has studied how playing action video games enhances some aspects of attention, improves the ability to perceive salient detail, and speeds up perceptual processing. See Daphne Bavelier and C. Shawn Green, "Brain Tune-Up from Action Video Game Play," *Scientific American*, July 2016, https://www.scientificamerican.com/arti cle/brain-tune-up-from-action-video-game-play/. See also: TEDx Talks, "Your Brains on Action Games: Daphne Bavelier at TEDxCHUV," YouTube video, June 23, 2012, https://www.youtube.com/watch?v=e8hzowkUkR4&feature=emb_logo.

22. Taking a break is when you encode what you've learned. It's why professional athletes don't practice for hours at a time, or professional musicians don't practice all day. Time off-task is necessary for enabling your brain to integrate what it's learned (with sleep being the best example of how being *completely* off-task contributes to learning, memory, and skill development).

23. Twenge, "More Time on Technology, Less Happiness?"

24. Phyllis Fagell, *Middle School Matters* (New York: Da Capo Lifelong Books, 2019).

25. Clifford Sussman, "Healthy Digital Media Use," *Attention* (Winter 2017–18): 18–21, https://cliffordsussmanmd.com/wp-content/uploads/2020/09/Cover_plus_SUSS MAN_Attn_Winter2017_18-1.pdf. See also Dina Elboghdady, "The Battle," *Bethesda Magazine*, September 23, 2019, https://bethesdamagazine.com/bethesda-magazine /parenting/the-battle/.

Chapter 9: What about Consequences?

1. Alan Kazdin, "Can You Discipline Your Child Without Using Punishment?" Psychology Benefits Society, American Psychological Association, February 15, 2017, https://psychologybenefits.org/2017/02/15/can-you-discipline-your-child-without -using-punishment/.

2. Jane Nelsen, *Positive Discipline* (Ballantine, 2006), 13.

3. For excellent suggestions about conducting family meetings, see Nelsen, *Positive Discipline*, 208.

4. Alisha R. Pollastri et al., "The Collaborative Problem Solving Process Across Settings," *Harvard Review of Psychiatry* 21, no. 4 (July–August 2013): 188–99. See also Ross Greene's *Raising Human Beings* (New York: Scribner, 2016). Educators should see Greene's book about the application of collaborative problem-solving in schools called *Lost at School*, rev. ed. (New York: Scribner, 2014).

5. Katherine Reynolds Lewis, *The Good News about Bad Behavior* (New York: Public Affairs, 2019).

6. Additionally, Ross Greene's website, livesinthebalance.org, has several excellent videos of collaborative problem-solving.

7. See Nelsen, *Positive Discipline*.

8. The pediatrician and parenting author Ken Ginsburg recommends that teens and their parents have a code word for extrication. For example, if they are at a party that's going south, they can call and say, "I have to walk the dog? Seriously?!" as a way to dispatch Mom or Dad to come pick them up. Ken Ginsburg, "Blame Parents with a Code Word," Center for Parent and Teen Communication website, September 4, 2018, https://parentandteen.com/blame-parents-a-code-word-strategy/.

INDEX